Mastering Lean Product Development

A Practical, Event-Driven Process for
Maximizing Speed, Profits, and Quality

Ronald Mascitelli

Technology Perspectives

© Copyright 2011 by Technology Perspectives

All rights reserved
Editorial and Sales Offices: Technology Perspectives
P.O. Box 8539, Northridge, CA 91327
818-366-7488

Publisher's Cataloging-in-Publication
(Provided by Quality Books, Inc.)

Mascitelli, Ronald
   Mastering lean product development: a practical,
event-driven process for maximizing speed, profits, and
quality / by Ronald Mascitelli. – 1ˢᵗ ed.
   p. cm.
   Includes bibliographical references and index.
   LCCN 2010937943
   ISBN-13: 978-0-9662697-4-1
   ISBN-10: 0-9662697-4-8

   1. Manufacturing processes. 2. Production planning.
I. Title

TS183.M37 2011   658.5'752
                                  QBI10-600238

10 9 8
First Edition

ATTENTION CORPORATIONS, UNIVERSITIES, COLLEGES, AND PROFESSIONAL ORGANIZATIONS: Quantity discounts are available on bulk purchases of this book for educational, gift purposes, or as premiums for increasing magazine subscriptions or renewals. Special books or book excerpts can also be created to fit specific needs. For information, please contact Technology Perspectives, P.O. Box 8539, Northridge, CA 91327; phone 818-366-7488

Manufactured in the United States of America

Contents

Acknowledgments   vii

Introduction   ix

1   **Selecting and Prioritizing Development Projects**   1

2   **Managing Finite Development Capacity**   17

3   **An Event-Driven Development Process**   55

4   **Visual Workflow Management**   81

5   **The Market Requirements Event**   113

6   **The Project Planning / Risk-Mitigation Event**   147

7   **The Learning-Cycle Event(s)**   191

8   **The Lean 3P / Cost-Optimization Event(s)**   229

9   **The Design Review and Freeze Event(s)**   277

Conclusion: A Practical Approach to Implementation   305

Bibliography   313

Index   319

To my clients –
who have been my mentors,
my collaborators,
and more often than not...
my friends

Acknowledgments

The most pleasant part of writing a new book is the opportunity to acknowledge all those who have made this work possible. In the past, I have thanked the many great authors and researchers who have built the foundation upon which my thinking has been based. In this book, however, it is time to thank some unsung heroes – the clients and practitioners whose real-world insights and collaborative discussions have helped me see the world of new product development in an entirely new light. First, I'd like to thank some of my oldest friends and supporters. Sincere appreciation goes to the Association for Manufacturing Excellence (AME) and The Society of Manufacturing Engineers (SME) for their continuing commitment to practitioner-based knowledge sharing, and in particular to Doug Carlberg, whose friendship and support dates back to my first year of consulting. The Manufacturing Extension Partnership (MEP) system has been an advocate and collaborator in bringing the benefits of lean product development to small-to-medium-sized firms. Particular thanks go to Rick Korchak, Dan Pitkin, and Steve Thompson for their continuing support.

While I have learned from all of my clients, some have been instrumental in helping me create the vision of Event-Driven Lean Product Development described herein. These individuals include: Dan Chestnut and his team at Delta Faucet, Ralph Wilcox at Cobham Mission Systems, Michael Oberlander and Charlie Guild at WMS Gaming, Coleen Bentley and Susan Stone at Beckman Coulter, Tim Weyenberg, Jerry Dassler, Jerry Berg, Shawn Klinge, and Jerry Sevick at Foth Companies, Nicholas Phillips at Volvo Group, Paul Leech at Briggs & Stratton, and Kate Metz at Fres-co Systems USA. Finally, I'd like to extend a special acknowledgment to the Product Development Process team at Danfoss Corporation for creating one of the most fruitful and dynamic collaborative environments that I've experienced. Sincere thanks to Lars Ploug-Sørensen, Njal Pettit, Lee Schab, Claus Knudsen, Michael Holm, and Stine Pedersen.

This book could not have been published without the skill, effort, and patience of Shannon Bodie at Lightbourne. Last, and most important, my wife Renee has yet again taken my rough words and improved upon them immensely. To all of the above and to those I've failed to mention, my sincerest thanks.

Introduction

In the twenty-plus years since the first studies of the Toyota Production System were published, a revolution has taken place in the manufacturing world. Admittedly it has been a glacially slow revolution, but today the concepts of just-in-time inventory management, standard work, optimizing flow, pull systems, and so on, have become deeply embedded in the production strategies of many enlightened firms. The unquestionable success of lean manufacturing has led to the application of lean principles to other aspects of the enterprise as well, including lean office, lean accounting, and lean supply chain. Again, the results have been impressive: Processes and methods that enable organizational learning, eliminate waste, and enhance value-creation have rapidly spread to virtually every aspect of the business enterprise... except for one.

Not long after lean manufacturing began to take hold, it became obvious that the benefits gained from implementing a lean production process were heavily dependent on upstream product development activities. Unfortunately, if you fill a lean factory with fat products, you get fat products out the other end, making the need to design products specifically for a lean manufacturing environment a critical mandate. Moreover, if your development process is slow and inefficient, the time and effort invested in implementing a lean factory can never achieve its full potential. It should, therefore, be obvious that a lean product development process is essential to achieving long-term competitiveness for any manufacturing firm. Yet attempts to dogmatically impose the methods of lean manufacturing on the complex and nuanced world of new product development have failed miserably. The reason for this failure is clear: New product development is unique among business processes. For one thing, it is not a truly recurring process. Each new development project is at least in some respects distinct from all those that preceded it. These differences can be substantial: a minor product-line extension compared to a major new product platform, or a low-risk special order versus an innovative, breakthrough new product. Moreover, in new product development there is risk, uncertainty, problem-solving, discovery, experimentation, failures that we (hopefully) learn from, etc. Finally, new product development is the most intensely cross-functional and collaborative process in any business. Literally every function within a firm must contribute their knowledge to successfully launch a commercial product. In retrospect it seems obvious that ham-fisted attempts to impose lean manufacturing techniques on such an inherently variable, complex, and knowledge-based process are unlikely to succeed.

In this book, I will describe a practical approach to lean product development that is the culmination of thirty years of literature study and practical experience. This comprehensive framework has evolved through my work with over one-hundred firms, spanning twelve countries and virtually every industry sector. While the Toyota Development Process has been a significant inspiration, the approach presented herein is inclusive: There are a number of great firms out there that have solved intransigent product development problems in unique and powerful ways. The process that I will describe has benefited from collaboration with firms such as Danfoss Corporation, Beckman Coulter, Delta Faucet, Boston Scientific, WMS Gaming, Parker Hannifin, Briggs & Stratton, Foth Companies, and numerous others. In the world of new product development there are many Toyotas, each an icon of their industry sector, and each with a unique perspective on the creation, management, and commercialization of knowledge.

The target audience for this book is practitioners: designers and developers, team leaders, managers, improvement champions, and executives with new product development responsibilities. While I have made an effort to connect this pragmatic perspective to the popular literature, there are few words spent on philosophy and generalities. As with all of my writings, the objective is practical, real-world improvement. Those who have read my previous books will learn new and powerful tools and methods, and become reacquainted with familiar ones that have been enhanced and integrated into a powerful new framework.

That being said, there are no prerequisites: I have tried to provide enough background and detail to bring new initiates up to speed.

This book is about the *commercialization of knowledge*. To address this topic, we must go beyond problem-solving, knowledge creation, and organizational learning, although these skills represent vital enablers. The commercialization of knowledge encompasses both knowledge creation *and execution*. Execution of new product development, from its beginnings in initial project selection and portfolio management, through to production readiness and product launch. Execution to a business case, rather than a product specification. And finally, execution that balances all aspects of market success: customer value, profitability, time-to-market, and quality. This comprehensive perspective represents a rather large elephant to eat, and like the old Sufi saying, we will consume the beast a bite at a time. Each chapter addresses a specific aspect of new product development, with the chapters appearing in chronological order from initial project selection through to successful commercialization. Readers can move along this timeline at will: If you have a specific issue that is keeping you up at night, then you can jump to the appropriate chapter and gain immediate benefit. Naturally, it is my hope that you will eventually read all of these pages, but as a lean practitioner, I am more concerned with optimizing value-added for time spent. On the other hand, if your goal is to transform your development process from a traditional phase / gate approach to the powerful, Event-Driven Lean Product Development process described herein, you should read this book in the order it is written so that the "big picture" unfolds in a clear and logical manner.

Before we begin consuming our pachyderm, it is important to consider the criteria for successful implementation. As a consultant and educator, I wish that I could claim a 100-percent success rate. Realistically, however, my clients have fallen into three groups. The first group has held workshops and events, tried a few new tools and methods, and ultimately has fallen back into their wasteful status quo. The second group followed the same path, but through robust learning and active management support, they were able to sustain significant near-term gains. However, beyond this first wave of improvement, little further progress has been made. The final group has taken the ideas contained in this book and ran with them. They collaborated from the very beginning in adapting these generic concepts to fit their culture, products, and markets. They added value by integrating their own knowledge, experience, and internal best practices. They established a plan for implementation, and had the discipline to stick to their plan over a period of several years. The key to successful implementation of lean product development is persistence, not insistence. It takes continuous energy input over extended periods of time to transform an organization. If your firm ultimately falls within the first category, I regret your missed opportunity. If you fall into the second group, then I wish you well and hope that your one-time gains will sustain you. If you achieve membership in the final group, please write to me and share your experiences – I'd love to learn from you.

Ron Mascitelli
December, 2010

1

Selecting and Prioritizing Development Projects

Background and Overview

There are many sources of waste in new product development, but by far the greatest occurs at the very beginning. All the lean techniques in the world cannot turn a bad idea into a great product. It is all too common for firms to commit their organizations to the development of products that should never have left the starting gate. Rather than taking the time and effort up front to aggressively screen and validate product opportunities, they proceed based on gut feel, sales anecdotes, or a knee-jerk reaction to moves by their competition. In this chapter I will describe a straightforward method for filtering and prioritizing new product ideas that can dramatically improve your firm's "hit rate" without stifling creativity and innovation. You may have heard the expression "fail early, fail cheap." While I can't argue with this logic, it seems far better not to fail at all.

The most common approach to injecting discipline into the project selection process is two-dimensional "portfolio planning" (see, for example, Cooper, et al, (1998) and Gropelli, et al, (1995)). Product opportunities are mapped on a grid defined by two axes: the projected profitability of the new product (in the form of net present value or the like), and its strategic importance to the firm. The goal of this methodology

1

is to establish a balanced portfolio of products that will serve both the short-term cash-flow demands of the organization and also will provide for long-term growth. While this is certainly a step up from gut-feel project selection, it fails to meet the "lean test" in two ways: it doesn't adequately address risk, and it fails to consider the finite product development capacity of the firm. In the following sections, I will describe a significant enhancement to this traditional "MBA approach" to project selection and prioritization. This methodology will yield a far clearer picture of which products a firm should develop and how they rank in relation to each other.

Creating such a list is an interesting exercise, but for it to have any impact on your organization, it must translate directly into the tactical execution of development projects. Hence, I will suggest the creation of a "global priority list" for an entire business unit or firm. This list should be made available to all functional areas, and becomes a critical driver for resource allocation and the arbitration of resource conflicts. Alignment of priorities throughout an organization is key to achieving flow and maximizing development productivity. In the absence of clear and aligned priorities, mid-level managers will form their own opinions as to which projects should be given attention, and working-level team members may find themselves lacking clear direction as to what they should work on next. In this situation, the product strategy of the firm becomes muddied, and relatively unimportant projects interfere with the most vital ones.

Before addressing the above issues, it is worthwhile taking a moment to dispel some common myths about idea generation and project selection. The first myth is that the only valid source for new product ideas is in-depth market research. While I certainly advocate market research as a means to validate the business case for new product opportunities, great new product ideas can come from virtually any source within a firm. In fact, those employees who have direct contact with customers (e.g., customer service, installers, sales people, field technicians, etc.) have perhaps the greatest insight into the unarticulated needs of the market. Ideas from all sources should be given serious consideration, and funneled through the same vetting process as those derived from formal market studies.

There is also a pervasive myth in the current marketing world that new product opportunities must embody cutting-edge technology. It is easy to fall into this trap, given the proliferation of high technology products over the past few decades. In truth, however, great products simply solve problems in new and clever ways. Advanced technology is just one means to that end – it is not a substitute for a deep and empathetic understanding of your customers and their needs. Some of the most successful recent products have depended on nothing more than insight and creative design; they literally could have been designed and manufactured in the nineteenth century. Examples include an innovative nail that can hold a house together without damage through a Category 3 hurricane. A fleece blanket with holes for your arms that keeps you warm while allowing freedom of movement. An innovative pair of pliers that enables both instant adjustment to any size of bolt, and substantial gripping pressure, in a single movement. A colorful, egg-shaped computer enclosure that rocked the world of boring, beige boxes. Although decidedly technology-based, Apple's success with the original i-Mac was not due to the innards of the computer. It is a combination of appealing industrial design and intuitive ease of use that continues to make the i-Mac and all the other i-Things market winners. In short, there is simply no substitute for insight, intimacy, clever problem-solving, and artful creativity when it comes to generating new and powerful product ideas.

Creating a Rigorous Gauntlet for New Product Ideas

If new product ideas can indeed come from any source within (or outside of) a firm, how can these flashes of insight be efficiently harvested and tested? The trick here is to balance the time and effort required to document a product suggestion with the need to accurately assess the viability of the opportunity. The solution, not surprisingly, is a simple one-page template. I know that this may seem like a mundane answer to a vital business challenge, but if something simple works, why complicate things? If your organization has immersed itself in A3-formatted templates and knowledge briefs, then by all means adapt that format to this new purpose. For those readers who have not become obsessed with big, cumbersome sheets of paper, a standard letter-size template will suffice. To keep the barrier-to-use low, all that should be required is basic information:

- Person or source originating the idea.
- Name or identifier for the new product.
- Target customer group(s) or market segment(s).
- Specific problem(s) that the new product solves.
- Concept for how the solution(s) might be provided.
- Any associated market data or projections that support the viability of the new product. What are the reasons to believe in the idea?

It is vital that you do not put an unrealistic burden on people submitting ideas. If you want field technicians and sales people to contribute their insights, you can't expect them to perform a formal business-case analysis. (For some excellent suggestions on the harvesting of grassroots ideas, see Robinson, et al, 2004.) The ultimate goal is to cast a wide net, then rapidly filter out the weak from the strong. Hence, the next step in the process is to assign an individual the responsibility of "presorting" product ideas, and narrowing the field to those with reasonable market potential. This is one of those problematic tasks that combine hard, tedious work with high importance, mandating that an executive-level person roll up their sleeves and do some grunt work. Unfortunately, there is no substitute for the intuition and experience that a senior person can bring to this initial screening. That being said, some simple guidelines can be established that will make the job less painful. Once initial submittals have been screened, those that are deemed to be of acceptable merit are moved to the next stage of the "gauntlet," as shown in Figure 1.1. While the frequency of this screening process is dependent on the nature of your products and markets, performing a sweep of product idea submittals on a quarterly basis seems reasonable.

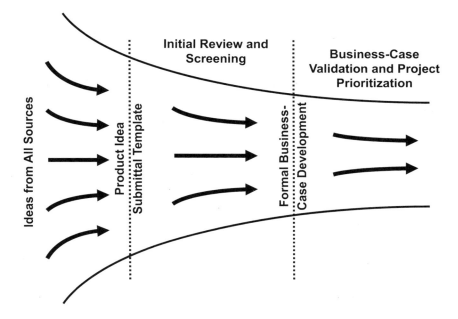

FIGURE 1.1: The first and best opportunity to eliminate waste in new product development is to aggressively challenge all new product ideas before precious resources are committed. All new product candidates should pass through the "prioritization funnel." Those that are deemed viable will be assigned resources based on their priority ranking.

Now comes the hard part. On a regular (e.g., quarterly) basis, a select group of senior managers should meet to review and update the product development strategy for the firm. This group must include representatives from all critical functions that impact new product development, including engineering / design, operations, marketing, finance, and potentially others. Many terms have been used for this type of committee: product-line steering committee, strategy board, project review panel…pick the name of your dreams. What is important is their role; to oversee the validation, selection, and prioritization of new product development projects. At the beginning of each product strategy meeting, the current status of ongoing projects is briefly reviewed (this is not a routine project review meeting, so don't waste time on details), and any recent changes to the current suite of projects are identified. Next comes the fun stuff. Any new product ideas that have passed through the initial screening process are presented and discussed. At this point, the goal is not to make a final determination on these ideas, but rather to determine a course of action for each. Some submittals can be rejected for obvious and practical reasons: failure to align with the current strategy of the firm, unrealistic assumptions, excessive investment required, and so on. Others will appear to warrant further investigation. These will be moved to the next step – the creation of a "business-case brief" that fleshes out the details of the new product concept, and embodies substantial market research (or what passes for it in your firm) and quantitative estimates of profitability. Each idea will be assigned to an appropriate member of the product steering committee who will be responsible for digging in more deeply and determining if there is merit to the concept. Typically, if the product steering committee meets quarterly, then a three-month window is given to conduct a detailed business-case analysis and report back to the group. For high-potential projects, however, a shorter timeframe may make sense, followed by an ad hoc meeting of the steering committee to address that specific opportunity.

A template for a business-case brief is provided in Figure 1.2. I have used the A3 format here since the amount of information required is substantial, and keeping it organized is essential. Naturally, as with all of the exhibits that I provide, you should plan to modify and tailor this generic suggestion to your firm's or business unit's specific needs. We will walk through the template one quadrant at a time, beginning with "Description of Opportunity." This first quadrant is intended to document the driving elements of the product concept, without any preconceptions about the ultimate product solution. In other words, this is the "what" without the "how." The description begins by stating the problem(s) that the new product will solve, along with an overview of the market segment or specific customers that will benefit from it. The next

FIGURE 1.2: An A3 formatted template for a business-case brief. The four quadrants capture the potential of a new product idea, and assess its priority for development. The first quadrant documents the basic concept, including key differentiating features. The second focuses on determining the risk-adjusted profitability of the future product. The third quadrant addresses the strategic importance of the product idea. Finally, the outputs of quadrants two and three are merged into the calculation of several priority "scores" that are presented in quadrant four.

Product Business-Case Brief	Date First Submitted:	Submitted By:
Product Designation:	Revision Number:	Prepared By:

Description of Opportunity

Financial / Risk Analysis

1 What specific customer problem(s) does the new product solve?

1 Market forecast:

Sales Volumes -	Minimum	"Most Likely"	Optimistic
Year 1			
Year 2			
Year 3			

Target Market Price =
Target Mfg. Cost =
Target Entry Date =

2 Description of target customers / market segments.

3 Key differentiating features / performance levels.
1
2
3

2 Risk Analysis:

Risk Impact (1-5) Description of Critical Risk(s)

Market Risk -

4 Critical physical characteristics (weight / dimensions / etc.).

Technical Risk -

Schedule Risk -

5 Critical performance requirements / features.

Cost / Quality Risk -

3 Investment: Total Non-Recurring Investment (Capital and Labor) =

6 Other critical requirements / mandates for competitive parity

4 Profitability Calculation:
Net Present Value (NPV) =
Risk-Adjusted NPV =   (Based on 3-Year "Most Likely" Sales)
(NPV / Max. Risk Impact)

Strategic Assessment

Opportunity Assessment

Description of Strategic Alignment:

Step 1 - Estimate the no. of design / development hours required to commercialize the new product.
Non-Recurring Engineering (NRE) =

Step 2 - Calculate the "Productivity Metric" for the proposed new product.
(Risk-Adjusted NPV / Est. NRE)
Project Productivity Metric =

Assessment of Strategic Impact (1 - 10 Scale):

Step 3 - Calculate Overall Project Rating .
(Productivity Metric x Total Strategic Score)
Overall Project Rating =

1	Supports Retention of Existing Customers -
2	Contributes to Growth of Market Share -
3	Encourages Pull-Through of Other Products -
4	Supports Development of New Markets -
5	Contributes to Product Line Cost Reduction -
6	Contributes to Image of Firm in Marketplace -
7	Increases "Mindshare" Among Customers -
8	Enables Implementation of New Technologies -
9	Supports Development of Core Competencies -
10	Supports Overall Strategic Roadmap -
	Total Strategic Score =

Notes and Comments:

item is crucial; "key differentiating features / performance levels" refers to those attributes of the proposed product that will position it in some profitable (and hopefully uncontested) space in the market. Certainly not every new product must have dramatic differentiating features; there is often a need to "fill the line" with minor enhancements to existing products, or to develop commodity-level products that pull in other, more profitable sales. That being said, you should never miss an opportunity to try for differentiation. Why? Because unique and valuable features give your firm *pricing power* in the marketplace, and hence greater margins and return on investment. The remainder of this first quadrant is self-explanatory, representing basic assumptions and constraints for the new product as they are currently understood.

The next section to be filled out is the "Financial / Risk Analysis" quadrant. Here is where we get serious about screening out the weak projects and highlighting the strong ones. I have heard many times that it is too difficult or time-consuming to perform a financial analysis on every new idea. Don't believe it! Every pocket calculator, and every copy of Microsoft Excel, has an automated formula for calculating net present value (NPV) and other business-case metrics. The hard part, of course, is putting valid data into the formula, but even here the process should not be onerous. The critical data that is needed is summarized in the template: a market forecast looking three years ahead, along with targets for market price, manufacturing cost, and market entry date. (Note that the NPV calculation also requires input of a "discount rate." This term is often used to adjust for project risk, but I suggest using a standard rate provided by your finance folks, and then correct for risk as I describe below.) This data provides all you'll need to calculate the "gross present value" of the new product. The "net" part comes from subtracting your best estimate of the non-recurring investment required to bring the new idea to market (e.g., dedicated capital equipment, development costs, etc.). In this section, I ask for three estimates of sales volume: a minimum, optimistic, and "most likely" forecast. This approach doesn't eliminate the huge error associated with market forecasts, but I've found that it forces whoever is doing the forecasting to confront reality, and not just puff up the numbers to get the new product into development. All of the numbers in this quadrant are best guesses based on data that can be gathered in a few weeks or months. While accuracy is a fine ideal, it is more important to get some rough estimates into this template, with further refinement to follow if the new product continues to look promising. Keep in mind that when it comes to rigorous screening of new product ideas, *something is better than nothing.*

Before we can leave the second quadrant, we are forced to face reality – not all projects are created equal from the standpoint of *risk*, as shown in Figure 1.3. Comparing new opportunities without taking into account their relative risks is like investing your money without first reading the fine print. Two projects may have identical NPVs, but can result in dramatically different real outcomes due to risk factors that have not been mitigated. I have learned to focus on four areas of risk: market risk, technical risk, schedule risk, and cost / quality risk. Each type of risk should be considered independently, and rated on a 1-to-5 scale, with a "1" implying negligible risk, and a "5" connoting a serious death threat to the project. Furthermore, we must recognize that, on average, high-risk projects will yield a lower percentage of their estimated NPV than low-risk ones. Hence, I use a sliding scale to derate the NPV of high-risk projects relative to lower-risk opportunities. For projects with negligible risk, the full NPV is used, whereas for projects with a serious death threat in one of the four risk categories, only 20 percent of the NPV is projected. This may sound harsh, and certainly you are free to use a different scale,

FIGURE 1.3: The spectrum of new product opportunities spans the range from minor product-line enhancements and special-order customization to aggressive, highly innovative new products. The relative risk of any new development opportunity should be seriously considered when making go / no-go decisions and setting relative project priorities.

but my experience has shown that most failed development projects had at least one known death threat at their inception, but were initiated anyway due to irrational optimism and / or executive-team denial.

The third quadrant addresses one of the most nebulous factors in selecting and prioritizing development projects: the strategic importance of the new product to the firm or business unit. The term "strategic importance" is often misused as an excuse to initiate development projects even when the financial numbers look like a black hole. While it is sometimes true that a new product is so important to a firm's future that its profitability is only a minor consideration, it is not necessary to equate the term "strategic product" with "money loser." The trick is to be as objective as possible about both the realistic future direction of the firm, and the alignment of new product ideas with that future vision. Does the new idea actually move that agenda forward, or is it just a pet project of some strong personality within the executive team? Does the firm really have to buy in (i.e., settle for little or no margin), or can the same strategic gains be achieved while maintaining a positive return on investment? The template provides a subjective scoring system for evaluating the strategic importance of a proposed new product. As always, you might need to tweak some of the factors listed to better suit your firm's markets and products, but the list is probably not far from the mark. Each factor should be discussed by the product-line steering committee, and ranked on a 1-to-10 scale by group consensus (again, accuracy is not critical). The total score will be used both on its own as a metric for project prioritization, and as an input to an overall project score that is calculated in the final quadrant.

The final step in completing our business-case brief is to assess the new product opportunity and create metrics that can be used for both go / no-go decisions and ongoing prioritization among active projects. The "risk-adjusted NPV" calculated in the financial / risk analysis quadrant is one of these metrics. However, as it stands, there is a critical factor missing; the impact of a new project on the finite product development capacity of the firm or business unit. I recognize that we took into account the *cost* of development (both capital investment and non-recurring labor) in the calculation of NPV. This calculation assumes, however, that your firm has infinite resources – all you have to do is pay the bills and you can develop all the products you wish. Obviously this is never the case. Hence, we must also take into account the demands of the proposed project on scarce design and development resources. If all other factors are equal, a project that utilizes the time of engineers and designers more efficiently than another is a better opportunity. In the subsection that follows, I will describe a critical metric for ranking development projects that takes the vital consideration of *design team productivity* into account.

Before we learn about this new and powerful metric, you should note that there is a final calculation performed in the business-case template. I've created an "overall project rating score" that attempts to integrate productivity (see next subsection), risk-adjusted NPV, and strategic importance into a single numeric score. Admittedly, trying to create such a metric is dangerous. Once a "goodness number" such as this is accepted, it is common for executives to lose touch with the factors that make it up and simply rank projects according to this single score. Not a great idea. First of all, any formula of this sort assumes that you can quantify the subtleties of company strategy and product opportunity, which is naïve at best. Moreover, to effectively execute a strategic vision it is often necessary to balance opportunities that have very different levels of risk and strategic importance. Without the availability of several contrasting metrics, this balancing act is virtually impossible. Therefore, I recommend using the overall project rating score as just one input toward a final decision about which projects live on and which ones are euthanized.

Capacity-based Project Prioritization

Sometimes all it takes is a new metric. The classical approach to selecting and prioritizing new product development projects involves two dimensions: projected profitability (in the form of net present value, internal rate-of-return, or the like), and strategic importance (typically based on a subjective scoring system). Ideally, the highest priority projects will have a high economic impact, and will strongly support the firm's strategic goals as well. There is a critical consideration that is missing from this two-dimensional world, however. Nowhere in this portfolio management scheme is the finite capacity of the organization to execute development projects considered. Instead, the matching of the project list to capacity is often done subjectively. Functional managers are asked if they can handle the projects that are on their docket, and in the absence of realistic capacity data, they tend to err on the optimistic side. Moreover, some of the "high-priority" projects in a two-dimensional approach to project prioritization may be capacity hogs when compared with other opportunities that might yield a far higher return from available resources. A third dimension (and a third metric) is needed to make truly informed decisions in a finite capacity environment.

Just such a metric is illustrated in Figure 1.4. Basically, this is a "project efficiency" metric, wherein the future profits generated per hour of development time for a proposed new product are estimated.

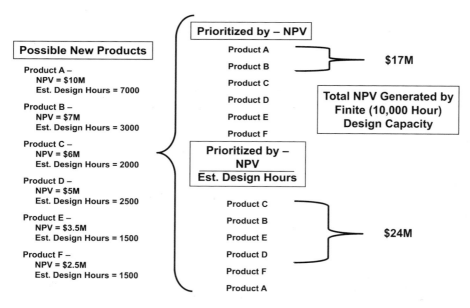

FIGURE 1.4: The impact of using "project efficiency" as a metric for project prioritization can be substantial. In the above example, the same development capacity yields nearly seven million more profit dollars simply by reprioritizing the project list based on this new metric: dividing the NPV of a development project by the estimated non-recurring design hours required to achieve commercialization.

To calculate this metric, the projected profitability of a proposed project (the risk-adjusted NPV) is divided by the estimated number of non-recurring hours required to execute that project. This ratio, in units of profit dollars per hour of design / development time, offers an important new perspective on the desirability of a proposed project. If used in concert with the other traditional metrics, portfolio management now becomes a three-dimensional trade-space, in which a truly excellent new opportunity will yield a high total return, have a positive strategic impact, and will make efficient use of scarce development resources. Including this new metric in your firm's strategic management methodology is the first step toward reconciling available capacity with the demands on that capacity, and will support the capacity management methods described in the next chapter.

The "Global" Priority List

At last we have reached the point where the product-line steering committee can establish a prioritized list of new product development projects. The business-case briefs for all new development opportunities provide inputs to a table such as the one shown in Figure 1.5. This summary table displays several alternative metrics for prioritization: raw NPV, risk-adjusted NPV, project efficiency, and finally my "overall project rating." Ultimately, our goal is to prioritize projects based on their financial impact on your firm. You will note that despite all of these calculated metrics, I still leave the actual priority-rating column on the far right with question marks. As I mentioned above, there is no metric, or combination of metrics, that can substitute for the collective insight of a firm's management team. One would hope that this suite of metrics would carry significant weight, but ultimately the prioritization of projects is best performed heuristically. That being said, objectivity is critical. If a project has poor metrics, there should be a compelling reason why it is given priority for development over its betters.

Once your firm has established a prioritized list of projects, what should you do with it? One of the most important factors in successful project execution is the alignment of the entire organization around a common set of priorities. Since virtually every function within a firm "touches" new product development at one time or another, it is critical that the entire firm be provided with a common (i.e., "global") priority list for all active projects. Note that it is not sufficient to prioritize just major projects, or even just development projects, but rather *all* projects that consume time and resources. Why is this so important? Because any misalignment of priorities among contributing functions (or among individual team members for that matter) can cause delays in your highest priority projects. Hence, a single, "official" published list of all projects, in priority order, should be made available to anyone in the firm who contributes to new product development. This is the first of many situations in which maintaining "one version of the truth" throughout a company or business unit is critical to successful new product development. There should be only one global priority list, rather than several, potentially different lists maintained by multiple entities within the firm.

The challenge, of course, in achieving this ideal is that tough choices will have to be made, particularly during initial implementation of this prioritization scheme. Executives will have to agree on priorities among a broad mix of projects, from short-term line extensions to major "tent poles" and everything in between. This is hard work, but consider the alternative: If your executive team doesn't make these tough calls, *then by default, priority decisions will be made by the team members themselves.* When resource conflicts occur, someone must make the priority decisions. It is far better that these decisions be made by the strategic visionaries of the company, rather than by working-level individuals on a day-to-day basis.

Generating a priority list of projects from one to one-hundred (or more) is quite difficult. Fortunately, it is not particularly important whether a given project is ranked number twelve or number thirteen on such a list. What *is* important is whether that project is number twelve or number thirty. A general ordering of projects will suffice for almost every situation involving resource conflicts. In fact, in the next chapter I will describe a practical approach to matching available resources to project priorities that will resolve most conflicts...as long as you follow a few simple "rules."

Project Designation	Net Present Value (NPV in $K)	Risk Adjustments			Risk-Adjusted NPV - (in $K)	Estimated Development Hours	P = Project Efficiency (Risk-Adjusted NPV / Est. Development Hrs.)	S = Strategic Importance (1 - 10)	Overall Project Rating (P x S)	Actual Priority
		Market Risk (0-100%)	Technical Risk (0-100%)	Schedule Risk (0-100%)						
Widget	1000	1.0	1.0	1.0	1000	1500	0.7	8	5	?
Thingamajig	500	0.8	0.4	0.8	128	2500	0.1	3	0	?
Whatchamacallit	700	1.0	0.8	1.0	560	500	1.1	7	8	?
Dohicky	2000	0.6	0.8	1.0	960	1000	1.0	10	10	?
Gadget	300	0.4	0.6	0.6	43	500	0.1	5	0	?

FIGURE 1.5: A multidimensional approach to ranking new product ideas ensures that the impact on the organization is well understood. This balanced prioritization approach takes into account profitability, risk, resource optimization, and strategic importance.

15

Chapter References

Betz, F., 1993, *Strategic Technology Management*, McGraw-Hill.

Cooper, R. G., Edgett, S. J., and E. J. Kleinschmidt, 1998, *Portfolio Management of New Products*, Perseus Books.

Groppelli, A. A., and E. Nikbakht, 1995, *Finance – 3rd Edition*, Barron's Business Review Series.

McGrath, M. E., 1995, *Product Strategy for High-Technology Companies*, Irwin Professional Publishing.

Robinson, A. G., and D. M. Schroeder, 2004, *Ideas are Free*, Berrett-Koehler Publishers.

2

Managing Finite Development Capacity

Background and Overview

I t is difficult to know when you've overloaded the cart, if you don't know how big the cart is. Generating a prioritized list of product development opportunities is a vital first step on your lean journey, but unless that list is matched to available resource capacity, it is likely that all projects will suffer from substantial and unpredictable delays. In my experience, by far the most common root cause of long development cycles and unacceptable time-to-market is poor management of resource capacity. Stated in simpler terms, this means too many projects and too few resources. In the world of fluid dynamics, the analogy is laminar and turbulent flow. The volume of fluid that is delivered through a pipe will steadily increase as the applied pressure is increased...up to a point. At some critical fluid velocity, the gains derived from further increases in pressure will decrease dramatically. This is the point at which flow through the pipe shifts from laminar to turbulent; the effective "carrying capacity" of the pipe has been exceeded, resulting in significant resistance to further gains. This effect is easily observable in the "flow" of new product development projects. If the number and scale of development projects is well-matched to the available design / development capacity of your firm, new products will flow smoothly from inception to commercialization. However adding even one more new project to the mix can cause turbulence – all projects begin to suffer from capacity constraints (i.e., resource conflicts). The result can be a dramatic increase in time-to-market for all the projects in your "pipeline."

Unfortunately, I have never seen a firm whose active project list doesn't exceed their available development capacity. Yes, I said *never*. Depending on the number and scale of projects, this may be a minor issue or a crippling disability. For example, if your firm develops large-scale, complex products with dedicated project teams of significant size, your resource conflicts will likely be a manageable annoyance. On the other hand, if your company has a broad mix of development projects, from small-scale line extensions and custom orders to major new platforms, and your teams range from single-engineer efforts to a few collaborators, you are likely suffering greatly from excessive multitasking of resources and constant conflicts. This problem is exacerbated by additional demands on the same designers and developers: sustaining support for the factory, proposal and quotation efforts, customer complaints, etc. In the extreme, the result is a virtual stagnation of new product introductions.

One of the first attempts at highlighting the dramatic impact that capacity management can have on productivity has come to be known as "Theory of Constraints." The concept is quite simple: The productive capacity of an entire system (e.g., a factory, a project team, etc.) is limited by its constraining resource. Whether this resource is a machine in the factory, an operator with unique skills, or a developer that is shared among five different project teams, the result is the same. A bottleneck, a weak link in the chain – pick the metaphor that works for you (see, for example, Goldratt and Cox (1992)). The good news is that by increasing the capacity of the constraining resource, you can increase the capacity of the entire system. Unfortunately, unlike the relatively predictable and recurring environment of a factory, product development is highly dynamic. If a machine on the factory floor is determined to be a capacity bottleneck, adding additional capacity will yield immediate and sustainable benefits. In new product development however, capacity constraints shift constantly depending on the immediate needs of multiple, unsynchronized, and relatively unpredictable projects. In a given month, a single designer or engineer might be working on one or two major new products, have responsibility for several minor line-extension projects, and be called upon to fix problems on the factory floor as well. This might be manageable if that individual's workload was stable, but of course it isn't. The demands on this same engineer could be significantly different in the following month.

It has been proposed that the powerful ideas of Theory of Constraints can be adapted to address this more challenging capacity management situation. The idea is to look forward several months and estimate the types and numbers of resources that will be required to service the current list of development projects, along with the estimated risk associated with both task duration and resource availability. Armed with this information, various schemes have been suggested for managing these future demands, including resource buffers, capacity pools, and risk buffers (see, for example, Goldratt (1990), (1997)). The effectiveness of these techniques, however, depends on the future being relatively stable. In firms where project durations are long and the cadence of development is predictable, this assumption is reasonable. Indeed, if future resource needs and project risks can be accurately estimated, then a development pipeline can be established that has many similarities to a production system, and flow can be achieved in much the same way. In the majority of companies, however, the predictable future is measured in days rather than months or years. A combination of high project mix, invasive changes to product requirements (i.e., scope-creep), special orders, firefights, and constantly shifting priorities can render attempts at resource buffers and the like virtually ineffective.

The approach described in this chapter has benefited greatly from the work described above, but incorporates a more flexible and dynamically adaptable perspective, based on insights derived from queuing theory. (For a truly mind-expanding experience, see Smith and Reinertsen (1997), and Reinertsen (1997) and (2009).) Unfortunately, the concepts of queuing theory can be quite arcane, and any effective capacity management system must balance sophistication with the ability of an organization to understand, accept, and maintain that system. Hence, my pragmatic nature will intercede on the reader's behalf. The approach that I propose aims for the 80/20 win; achieve much of the potential benefit of a rigorous application of queuing theory but in a practical and easily implementable form.

Our first step will be to analyze the current state: What are the root-cause issues that limit a firm's ability to balance capacity with workload? Based on this groundwork, some straightforward techniques will be proposed that will enable your firm to gain substantial benefits in the short term. Finally, a comprehensive, *hoshin*-like approach will be described that links all levels of the organization, from strategic planning to day-to-day workflow, into an integrated feedback system for resource optimization. As always, the reader is encouraged to pick and choose elements of this approach that address acute pain-points within your organization. Remember that there is no dogma here; just proven ideas that can help you craft your own customized approach. If product development in your firm takes the form of large projects with dedicated teams, you will find opportunities to smooth-out flow and improve time-to-market and schedule fidelity. On the other hand, if you live in a high-mix, rapidly changing environment, the methods described in this chapter can enable your firm to transform its new product pipeline from a squirt gun into a fire hose.

Understanding the Current State

For us to begin defining countermeasures to reduce resource conflicts and optimize finite capacity utilization, we must first understand the nature of the problem. To accomplish this, I will create a mythical firm, tellingly named Overload Inc., that is experiencing typical issues with respect to capacity management. Overload Inc. is a moderate-sized company (or a business unit of a larger firm, if that better fits your situation) with a finite pool of development resources. These resources represent a number of specialized functions: engineering disciplines such as electrical, mechanical, software, quality, and manufacturing, along with industrial designers, marketers, and critical support functions. Although these resources are organized into functional departments, they are certainly not "interchangeable parts." Each developer has unique skills, knowledge, and experience. In some cases, these individuals are subject-matter experts that cannot be replaced by any combination of alternative resources.

The challenges facing this pool of resources are illustrated in Figure 2.1. The same developers must handle a diverse mix of responsibilities: long-term major platform initiatives, moderate-duration product-line enhancements, quick-turn special orders, and a pantheon of "emergencies," including line support, customer inquiries, quotations, and more. The moderate and long-term projects typically go through an initial planning process, wherein a master schedule and resource plan are created. However, these plans are often not worth the paper they're printed on after the first few weeks of a project. Project replanning is frowned upon at Overload, so project schedules are rarely useful to the developers as more than a rough outline of required tasks. Short-duration projects and all other walk-in interruptions and emergencies are not planned; they are addressed on a reactive basis through the best efforts of the department / functional managers. Unfortunately, despite these best efforts, developers are often contacted directly to provide support, circumventing managers in the process. In summary, developers are overbooked, overworked, and, well...overloaded.

After missing their revenue projections for several successive quarters, the executive team at Overload was motivated into action. Fortunately, the executives were well-versed in lean thinking, so they began their quest for a solution by asking "why" several times. The following is a simplified version of their root-cause analysis:

- Why did Overload miss their quarterly revenue targets?

  —Because several major new products failed to meet their planned launch dates.

- Why did these critical projects significantly slip their schedules?

  —Because the initial plans for these projects were inaccurate.

- Why were the project plans / schedules inaccurate?

  —Because the durations of critical-path tasks were underestimated.

- Why did developers underestimate their task durations?

  —Because they failed to account for their total workload, resulting in optimistic estimates.

- Why didn't they consider their total workload when estimating their tasks?

  —Because they were expected to handle an unrealistic and rapidly changing workload without clearly communicated priorities – they literally had no control over their time, rendering their task-duration estimates essentially meaningless.

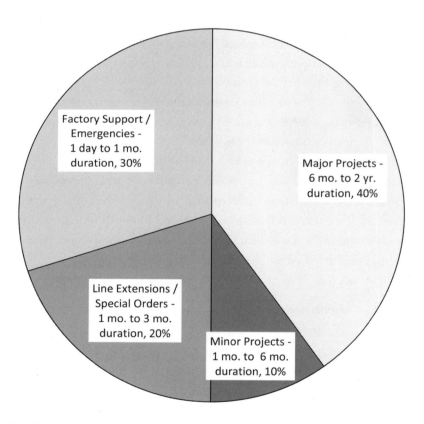

FIGURE 2.1: The demands on product development resources at Overload, Inc. are divided into several categories, ranging from long-duration platform projects to emergencies and firefights.

Being the good lean practitioners that they are, the executives at Overload needed data to support their root-cause analysis. Based on their suspicion that working-level developers were being pulled in too many directions, they asked their entire development staff to participate in a month-long time study. Employees from every function involved in new product development were given a simple log sheet to fill out each day that tracked the time they spent on various activities. Note that if you wish to perform such a survey, it must be *anonymous* to ensure that your data is valid. After all surveys were gathered and analyzed, the results were plotted Pareto-style, as shown in Figure 2.2.

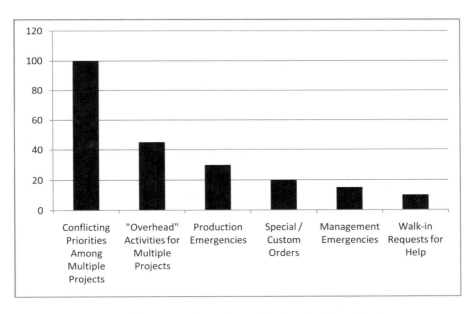

FIGURE 2.2: Results of a time study performed by Overload Inc. Development resources from all functions were asked to track their activities for a period of one month. The results shown above reflect the frequency of occurrence of activities that were determined to have a negative impact on the ability of team members to meet schedule milestones on major / minor product development projects.

It was not surprising that conflicts among multiple projects for shared resources were the highest-ranking cause for project schedule slips. What was unexpected was the magnitude of the problem. After digging somewhat deeper, the Overload executive team discovered that in some cases individual developers were assigned to five or six projects at any one time, with the average being greater than three. Resource conflicts were occurring literally on a daily basis, with the only means of resolution being arbitration among team leaders. Unfortunately, this arbitration most often took the form of strong personalities winning out over weaker ones, with the poor shared resources being caught in the middle of this tug-of-war. Moreover, when the developers' commitments to each of their project assignments were totaled, they often exceeded 100 percent of their workweek, and this did not take into account non-development-related activities.

As if this situation were not enough to motivate Overload toward a more sane approach to resource management, the second ranked issue made the problem even more compelling. As their data demonstrated, being assigned to a project demands more time than just performing the value-creating work. There is inherent "overhead" associated with just being part of an active project. Each project assignment carries with it all of the status meetings, e-mail correspondence, schedule updates, and hallway discussions required to be a credible team member. In my experience, this project-assignment overhead can amount to five hours per week or more. This tax is not unreasonable if a developer is working on a single project (although I will describe tools to reduce even this productivity drain in later chapters). However, if a resource is assigned to three projects, nearly half their standard workweek is consumed by enabling activities rather than value creation. In the extreme case of having five or six project assignments, a shared resource can do little more than keep the wolves at bay, with virtually no progress being made on any of their assignments. (In the real world, a dedicated professional will begin consuming their own personal time on nights and weekends to do the real work, while accepting that their normal workday is essentially lost to them. This is an unacceptable and unsustainable situation, and represents a failure of management if accepted as the norm.)

Beyond the top-two root causes for slipping project schedules, there is a mix of unexpected demands that are not directly related to product development work. I refer to these short-term interruptions as "unplanned work" since they are not captured in any formal project plan or schedule. There is no question that activities such as factory sustaining support or customer special orders must be serviced. The damage that such unplanned, high-priority interruptions cause to schedule fidelity on longer-term projects, however, can be catastrophic. Hence, any strategy that Overload considers (or that you should consider, if this example is hitting close to home) must embrace these issues and deal with them. Traditional remedies for dysfunctional product development, such as phase / gate processes or even value streams, assume that resources can be predictably applied. When this is not the case, this root cause must be addressed before any improvement to the process itself can be successful. Indeed, that is why we are discussing this issue prior to Chapter 3, where the product development process is discussed.

Some Practical First Steps toward Effective Capacity Management

Hopefully I've made a compelling argument for improving your firm's resource management methods. At Overload, Inc. the executive team was energized…but uncertain. Although they recognized that something must be done, the problem seemed overwhelming. Should they seek out a workload-management software application to help alleviate their resource conflicts? Would the formation of dedicated teams be a better first step? Having been burned by false starts and poor execution during previous improvement initiatives, the executives were wary. Ultimately, they decided to start with some fundamental concepts, and then build a comprehensive system for capacity management on that solid foundation.

The eight basic "rules" for capacity / flow optimization presented in Figure 2.3 represent just such a foundation. Each rule is derived from practical experience, but is anchored by a powerful conceptual basis. Although there is substantial synergy among the rules, they can work independently: You can choose to implement just one rule and your firm will still derive a significant benefit. Collectively, these basic guidelines represent an excellent starting point for a comprehensive approach to finite-capacity management. I will discuss each rule, from both a conceptual and practical standpoint, but first a few words about work rules in general. A work rule is a simple, typically one-sentence statement about how your organization will function. It is intentionally brief to avoid ambiguity and to facilitate rapid diffusion within the organization. Although there is always the risk of oversimplifying a nuanced and complex situation, my experience has proven time and again that work rules can change both behavior and culture faster and more effectively than any other change management approach. Moreover, a work rule represents a form of standard work that enables continuous improvement over time. If a work rule is not achieving the desired result within a firm, a simple wording change can correct this shortfall. It is imperative, however, that work rules remain brief and clear; you don't want to clutter your "high concept" with lots of caveats and clauses. The fewer the words, the less chance that a work rule will be misunderstood or misapplied. One final thought: Although work rules provide a general guideline, the old adage that "rules are made to be broken" applies. A work rule defines a desired behavior, but should never override common sense. There will always be exceptions to any work rule, and although it is important to consider these exceptions carefully, you should not fear stepping out of bounds when a unique situation demands it.

Rule 1 – Sane teams, not dedicated teams

Back at our fictional firm, some clarity was beginning to emerge. The Overload executive team decided to begin by addressing the project workload of their designers and developers. On the one extreme, they could form dedicated project teams. Literally one project assignment per developer. While this solution is tempting from the standpoint of resource conflict avoidance, it has a major drawback. Suppose an engineer on a dedicated project team is designing a circuit board that is critical to meeting her project schedule. She works merrily along the critical path of her project until the board design is complete. Then she must wait several weeks for a prototype sample to be fabricated and available for testing and validation. If the project she is working on is large and complex, this engineer might have other vital work that she

26

Basic "Rules" for Capacity / Flow Optimization

Rule 1 – No more than two major (i.e., "tent-pole") projects or three minor projects per developer.

Rule 2 – Among those projects, priorities must be clear and stable over an extended period.

Rule 3 – No development resource is committed to project work beyond 100 percent of their realistically available time. (Available time *excludes* time typically spent on non-product-development related activities.)

Rule 4 – Whenever possible, a shared resource should allocate time to assigned projects in "time-slices" of four hours or more, and when possible, those time-slices should be communicated to and synchronized with teammates and team leaders.

Rule 5 – All resources involved in new product development should be provided with a common time-slice each day for dedicated project work. This so-called project time should be at least two hours in duration.

Rule 6 – Critical-path (i.e., schedule-driving) activities should always receive higher priority than non-critical-path activities. If two critical-path activities are in conflict for the same resource(s), then the project that has the greatest sensitivity to a schedule slip (i.e., will suffer the greatest economic impact) wins.

Rule 7 – All short-duration, walk-in demands on development resources must pass through a "filter" that sets priorities and assigns individual responsibilities.

Rule 8 – Workflow should be dynamically, flexibly, and visually managed in small time increments – in other words, time batches should be minimized.

FIGURE 2.3: The eight rules outlined above represent an effective starting point for optimizing resource capacity and achieving flow in a multi-project environment. These rules are fundamental, and will form the basis for a more sophisticated *hoshin*-like system described later in this chapter.

could perform. On a more typical project, however, she would just sit on her hands until the prototype arrives. This is an unacceptable waste of productivity, and represents a fundamental weakness in the dedicated-team concept. Work on product development projects inherently comes in fits and starts; there is a great deal of *variability* in the duration, dependencies, and sequencing of tasks. This variability leads to unpredictable workloads, and in most cases leaves gaps that must be filled to optimize resource productivity. In other words, for all but the most complex projects, dedicated teams lead to waste.

On the other end of the spectrum, the Overload executives could just let project assignments fall as they may, and perform some type of triage when resource conflicts occur. Unfortunately, even if this dynamic conflict resolution were possible, it wouldn't solve the problem of excessive project overhead. Every active project assignment drains away some of a developer's time performing non-value-added activities (status meetings, schedule updates, etc.). As the number of active project assignments increases, the percentage of a developer's time that is available for value-creating work diminishes rapidly. Although resource conflicts might be dynamically managed, the overall productivity of development resources is severely diminished as the number of project assignments expands. What emerged from Overload's analysis of this situation is the curve shown in Figure 2.4. Although the precise scale of the curve depends on the magnitude of overhead associated with each project assignment, the conclusion is the same: There is a happy medium between dedicated teams and an unconstrained, multi-project environment.

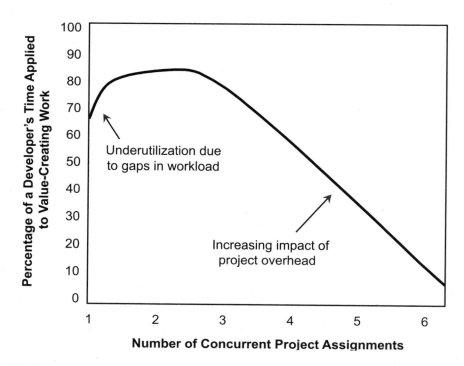

FIGURE 2.4: There is a region of optimal resource productivity that balances the underutilization of resources that can result from dedicated teams, and the waste caused by project-assignment overhead. Depending on the size and complexity of the projects involved, that optimal point is either two or three concurrent project assignments per developer.

In my experience with many different firms, the point of productivity maximization occurs somewhere between two and three project assignments per developer. The optimal number of assignments depends on several factors, but the most important is the relative size of the projects involved. If project durations are long (e.g., one or more years), and the scope is substantial (e.g., system-level products versus component-level products), then two assignments is most appropriate. If your development projects tend to be shorter and less complex, then the inherent variability in these smaller activities will mitigate toward three assignments per developer. In other words, large and complex projects allow for some degree of "internal" level-loading of resources, while smaller projects must be "externally" level-loaded.

At Overload, this first rule appeared to address a critical and fundamental issue, and certainly represented a step forward from the five or six projects per developer situation. Almost immediately, however, a flaw was identified by the executive team. Although the waste due to project-assignment overhead would be significantly reduced by applying this rule, resource conflicts were still inevitable. The conflicts would occur less frequently, but they would still create unpredictable schedule delays and interruptions to flow. In particular, certain critical resources (i.e., subject-matter experts) would still be in high demand, potentially resulting in long wait-times for their attention. It appeared that a second rule, one that could alleviate this queuing effect, was required.

Rule 2 – Always prioritize the work through any queue

If you go to the cubical of a valuable development resource and find that a line has formed outside their office, then you have a queue. Of course I am being overly literal here, although on occasion a physical line might actually exist. In reality, the "line" will most likely be temporal rather than physical. Whenever there is a wait-time associated with the availability of any developer, there is a queue. If this is a persistent problem, there may be cause to do some hiring or cross-training. In the more common scenario, however, queues shift sporadically among developers, depending on peaks and valleys in the demand for their services. These queues can dramatically increase the variability in project schedules, and if the tasks in the queue are schedule-critical, they will result in slipped launch dates for new products. Queues are almost inevitable in any firm, and their management is a mandatory next step in achieving optimal flow for all projects (for valuable insight into the principles of queuing theory, see Reinertsen (2009), pgs. 53-83).

Consider the case of one of Overload's most valuable development resources – I'll call him Dan Downtrodden. Dan is a subject-matter expert who is often on the critical path of product development projects. (The critical path is the longest sequence of serially dependant tasks in a project schedule that has no slack-time. If you slip a day along the critical path, then the project's end-date slips at least one day. A practical method for identifying critical-path tasks will be discussed in Chapter 6.) Well, poor Dan finds himself in a terrible situation. He is assigned to three moderate-sized projects, and just by bad luck (or bad planning), he has a critical-path task to perform on all three at the same time. The team leaders for these projects are chasing him down the hallways reminding him that their project schedules depend on his immediate attention. Without clear prioritization by his management, Dan has no way of deciding among these team leaders' demands, which causes him to switch back and forth among the projects so that he can keep everyone happy. This seems like the only fair way to handle this situation.

Now suppose that Dan has a week of work to perform on each project to remove himself from the critical path. Without prioritization, he multitasks among his three assignments on a daily basis, driven largely by which team leader screams the loudest. How long would it take Dan to complete all three tasks? I hope that you answered "more than three weeks." Certainly it would take at least three weeks, but why more? Because there is inefficiency associated with moving back and forth among several projects, similar in many ways to the setup and change-over waste in a factory. Even assuming that Dan is perfectly efficient at shifting from one project task to another, all three projects will still suffer two weeks of delay, as shown in Figure 2.5.

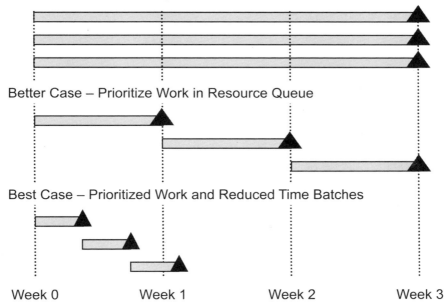

FIGURE 2.5: There are three ways to handle a queue of three, one-week tasks. The first and worst is for a resource to multitask among their project assignments without completing any one task in a timely manner. A better approach would be to prioritize the work in their queue, and complete each task in priority order. The best approach is to determine the minimum work required to satisfy each project's critical path, then deliver that minimal time batch to each project in priority order.

Fortunately for Dan, the Overload executive team has just released a prioritized list of all product development projects (see Chapter 1). He refers to this list and realizes that Project A is the highest priority among his three assignments, followed by Project B and then Project C. He is now able to focus on the highest-priority task first, and continues to work on it until completion and handoff. He then moves on to the next highest priority and so on. Project A recieves the output it needs after one week and stays on schedule. Project B must slip one week, but this is still better than a two-week slip. Surprisingly, Project C is no worse off by being the lowest priority! It suffers a two-week slip as before, but since setup and changeover time has been virtually eliminated, it is probably better off than without prioritization.

This is an unambiguous result, and represents a fundamental conclusion of queuing theory: *You must always prioritize the work through any queue.* In fact, any prioritization is better than no prioritization. Even if the priorities among Dan's projects were switched, no project would suffer a greater slip than the worst-case scenario of multitasking among several critical-path tasks without completing any one of them. Provided that priorities remain stable during that three-week period, Dan has clear direction and all projects are better off. Ah, but you say, "Great, but two of the three projects will still experience delays." This is true, and in fact Dan could do better. Suppose that Dan carefully considers the critical-path work he must perform on each project and realizes that he can parse his work into smaller increments that would still enable each project to move forward. Two days of work on Project A would be sufficient to allow the rest of the team to take the next few steps, and let Dan move on to Project B, and so on. He would need to return to Project A rather quickly to complete the rest of his one-week task, but as long as he is temporarily off of the critical path, that project won't suffer. If the same two-day commitment could service the critical paths of both Projects B and C, then Dan has managed to turn a catastrophic situation into a non-issue. Project A is actually able to move forward three days *ahead* of schedule, Project B is essentially on time, while Project C suffers only one day of delay. Please note that the reason why this works is that Dan is able to deliver a two-day package of work that enables each project to move forward. Without a handoff that removes him from the critical path, this parsing of work is no better than his previous multitasking approach.

So we now have two rules that can deliver dramatic gains in productivity and schedule fidelity: an optimized number of project assignments per developer, and clear priorities that allow arbitration of conflicts. At the highest level, these rules represent a major step forward in capacity management. There is, however, much more that we can do. In fact, the first two rules are actually an oversimplification. While they will certainly help, they do not take into account a number of more subtle issues that impact productivity and resource conflicts. The remaining six rules in Figure 2.3 describe a more sophisticated and effective system for maximizing productivity and minimizing schedule delays.

Rule 3 – Even with prioritization, overbooking leads to delays

The good news about the prioritization of queues is that if it is·done effectively, the most important projects in your firm will not suffer from resource conflicts or shortfalls. But what about those projects with lower priority? Well, if only Rules 1 and 2 are applied, then lower-priority projects just fall off the table (they will suffer unpredictable delays). The problem is that we haven't actually matched product development workload to available resource capacity; we have simply provided a default mechanism that ensures the success of the lucky few at the top of the priority list. Rule 3 addresses this issue by placing restrictions on the total time-commitments of resources down to the individual developer. This individual-level resource allocation is critical in new product development: Each person brings a unique set of skills to a project team, and achieving the right mix is vital to project success. (It should be noted that, for this very reason, cross-training of devel-opers in adjacent skill-sets can enable flexible management of emerging queues.) In practice, this personalized form of resource-loading can be accomplished though the use of a simple spreadsheet, such as the template shown in Figure 2.6.

You might have noticed in the wording of Rule 3 that I have suggested, "No resource should be loaded to more than 100 percent of their realistically available time for project work." Isn't this a statement of the obvious? In my experience, it is quite common for developers to be loaded to considerably more than 100 percent for extended periods. This occurs because the resource demands of concurrent projects are not rationalized, and loading assumptions are not consolidated among team leaders to ensure that developers are not double and triple booked. Moreover, the other demands that the developers must service (e.g., sustaining support, special orders, etc.) are almost never captured formally, and can represent a significant drain on their available time. Hence the need for a straightforward planning tool to capture and make visible all project-loading assumptions, thereby avoiding the overbooking of any resource.

At the top of my suggested template are the names of individuals within a resource pool who contribute to product development work.

This spreadsheet is typically maintained by a functional manager, but could also be the responsibility of a project team leader or project manager for cases of large, multifaceted projects. The template represents a one-month snapshot of project assignments for each individual resource pool. At the beginning of each month, the functional manager polls team leaders for their projected resource needs over the next monthly period. Based on their project plans (assuming that such plans exist), the team leaders request blocks of time from specific individuals. Obviously these requests should be developed in collaboration with the resources involved, so that they represent a realistic allocation of their time to meet upcoming schedule milestones. Now here is where the existence of a global priority list is critical. The team leaders' requests are loaded into available resources in priority order, following the mandate from Rule 1 that no resource is allocated to more than two major projects (or three minor ones, as the case may be). This process continues until all resources are fully loaded to 100 percent of their available time. The following month, team leaders will provide feedback on their project schedules, and determine what their needs will be for the upcoming month. Eventually, both the team leaders and the functional manager will gain insight into the accuracy of their time estimates (both project and non-project related) and the amount of actual time available for each individual resource.

If this loading process is followed, then resource capacity will be automatically matched to project priorities. In the template, I've categorized projects as A, B or C. By definition, the "A" projects have received all of the requested resources for the upcoming month. As soon as a team leader's request for resources cannot be fully met, that project becomes a "B" project. Those development efforts designated as "C" projects have not received any resources for the upcoming period. Based on this scheme, the "A" projects should have little or no schedule

---

FIGURE 2.6: A simple spreadsheet tool can help a manager visualize resource-loading and support the straightforward implementation of Rules 1 through 3. This is typically a monthly snapshot of resource requirements, and is updated regularly based on the projected needs of project team leaders. Note that the highlighted projects (i.e., the "A" projects) have received all of their requested resources, and hence should have a low risk of resource conflicts.

Managing Finite Development Capacity

Priority	Prioritized Active Project List	Tom	Dick	Harry	Fred	Cathy	Nada	Renee	Naresh	Thor	Dave	Sara
	Hours Available for Project Work (for upcoming month)	120	160	140	80	100	120	160	140	160	100	120
A	Widget 1.3	80	100	0	0	80	0	80	0	0	0	0
A	Thingamajig B3	40	0	100	0	0	0	0	40	0	0	20
A	Dohicky Update	0	60	0	0	0	20	0	0	80	0	100
A	Whatchamacallit	0	0	0	0	20	0	80	0	0	60	0
B	Widget 1.4	0	0	0	80	0	0	0	0	80	0	0
B	Thingamajig B6	0	0	40	0	0	0	0	100	0	0	0
B	Mini-Dohicky	0	0	0	0	0	100	0	0	0	40	0
C	Bluesky 6.0	0	0	0	0	0	0	0	0	0	0	0
C	Dream 1.0	0	0	0	0	0	0	0	0	0	0	0
C	Wish 1.0	0	0	0	0	0	0	0	0	0	0	0
C	Prayer 1.0	0	0	0	0	0	0	0	0	0	0	0
	Sustaining Support	20	0	0	20	20	0	0	0	0	20	0
	Special Orders	20	0	20	0	40	20	0	20	0	0	40
	Customer Support	0	0	0	40	0	20	0	0	0	20	0
	Other ???	0	0	0	20	0	0	0	0	0	20	0

35

risk with respect to resource availability. The "B" projects will be able to move forward, but will have some level of schedule risk, depending on how well their resource demands were met. Finally, the "C" projects *should be put on hold for the upcoming period.* The definitions of these three categories are summarized in Figure 2.7. If "C" projects are kept active, they will impose an overhead burden on resources and can become a distraction to the flow of projects that have received reasonable levels of staffing. In this way, your firm can begin to size the number of active projects to available capacity. Over time, some projects will be completed, and others will move up the priority list from C to B to A. If this process is maintained over an extended period, more projects will be completed with higher efficiency and greater schedule predictability than would be the case without priority-based capacity management.

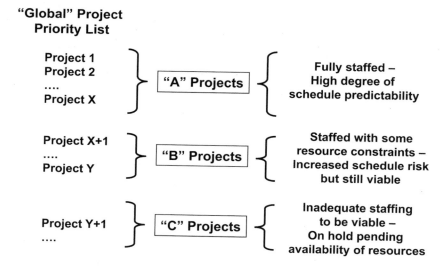

FIGURE 2.7: Three categories of project are defined above, based on their level of resource staffing for an upcoming month. An "A" project has received all of the resources requested by its team leader, a "B" project has received most of the required resources, but with some constraints or shortfalls, while the "C" projects have received inadequate staffing and should be put on hold.

As a final note, you might be questioning why I've allocated 100 percent of each resource's available time. There has been a great deal of discussion in the literature and around the water cooler about what is the appropriate level of resource-loading. On the one hand, some thinkers have stated that to avoid resource conflicts and unacceptable variability, you should only load resources to 80 or 90 percent. Alternatively, some real-world managers feel that if you don't load resources to at least 120 percent, there will be gaps in workload resulting in underutilization of resources. From my experience, there is so much "noise" (i.e., variability) in the estimates of resource needs and in the unanticipated demands on developers that this entire argument is irrelevant. This is the reason why, in my template, I allocate the time of developers in twenty-hour blocks; any finer granularity would be well within the noise level of the system. In my opinion, the only way to determine the proper level of resource-loading for your firm's developers is through actuals-based measurement and feedback. Theory is great, but practical experience, captured visually and updated frequently, will yield a much more reliable result.

Rule 4 – Time-slices enable focus and synchronization

The first three rules listed in Figure 2.3 are almost universally beneficial. Implementation of any one of them will yield positive results in the vast majority of situations. Rule 4, however, will likely require some adaptation to fit within your firm's product development environment and company culture. That being said, the underlying principle is powerful, and when appropriately applied can help maximize your product development speed and capacity. The motivation for this rule becomes apparent by asking a simple question: If a given individual is allocated 50/50 between two projects, what exactly does that mean? Do they work two solid weeks out of the month on Project A and the remainder of the month on Project B? Or do they alternate every other week between the two? Perhaps it should be every other day, or hour, or...you get the idea. Allocating monthly blocks of time among project assignments ensures that an individual resource is not overbooked, but does nothing to determine how that resource will divvy up their time.

If project team members were microprocessors, the answer would be easy. As we saw in the last section, when Dan Downtrodden parsed his work into smaller deliverable chunks, all three of his projects were better off. A microprocessor takes this logic to an extreme, multiplexing among several tasks at such a speed that it appears to be doing many things at once. In fact, one of the conclusions of queuing theory is that faster processing speeds yield lower wait times and reduced schedule variability. Unfortunately, people are not microchips. Project team members suffer from two human limitations. The first I've described above as setup and changeover time. Whenever a person must shift gears between project assignments, there is some period required to get their heads out of the first project and into the second. This may be brief when the work is relatively routine, but for more complex tasks, the required time and effort can be substantial. In fact, if we neglect this effect, then we may find that the number of errors in project work will increase – confusion among multiple tasks can cause mistakes to be made. This leads to the second human limitation; the need for *focus*. Studies have shown that people's ability to concentrate, solve problems, and innovate is directly related to how focused they are on a single problem. Interruptions cause us to lose focus, and reduce our ability to produce our best quality work. Microprocessors don't suffer from these constraints, but developers certainly do.

Hence, we have (yet again) a tradeoff to manage. If a time-shared resource allocates the first half of the month to one project and the second half to their other assignment, there is virtually no setup and changeover waste, and they can certainly focus. However their project teams must wait unacceptable periods for collaboration, delivery of work outputs, and even answers to their questions. On the other hand, if the same resource bounces among projects in short bursts, then focus is lost and changeover-waste expands. Back at Overload, Inc., one of the members of the executive team had a possible answer. This individual had spent a number of years optimizing high-mix production lines, and proposed a solution that has worked extremely well on the factory floor: *time-slicing* (see Suri (1998), pgs. 142-144). In a low-volume, high-mix environment, it is common for expensive capital equipment to be shared among multiple production lines. To manage this suboptimal situation, the shared equipment can be time-sliced in synchronization with the various lines, such that each line receives a predictable allocation of capacity. The time-slices are determined based on a balance between changeover time and the need to minimize batch size on all involved lines. Although "one-piece flow" cannot typically be achieved, time-slicing enables smaller batches and shorter cycle-times than would be achievable in any other way.

A similar result is often possible with shared resources on project teams. If the tasks required from an individual for an upcoming month are relatively well-understood, it may be possible for them to negotiate blocks of time that would be allocated to each of their project assignments. These blocks would be synchronized to the work being performed by their teammates to maximize team productivity, while still allowing the shared resource to focus when high levels of concentration are required. At Overload, team members were asked to plan their activities several weeks in advance and then communicate those plans to their teams on a regular basis. In general, time-slices of several days seemed to achieve a good balance, with the occasional need for longer or shorter slices when the work demanded it. By negotiating these planned slices with their project teammates, each resource could synchronize their availability to the teams' needs. In practice, these time-slices were guidelines only; if a serious need arose on any of their projects, the resource would make themselves available. Still, this approach increased focus and reduced much of the turbulence associated with a multi-project environment.

From a practical standpoint, I recognize that projecting out slices of time for forthcoming months is challenging, and in many cases, just not realistic. As it turns out, by implementing the Visual Workflow Management system that I will describe in Chapter 4, many of the benefits of time-slicing can be achieved in a straightforward and practical way. Before we leave the concept of time-slicing, however, there is one more opportunity to consider. This one is big, easy, and has worked in many firms under a wide variety of conditions. In fact, it deserves its own rule...Rule 5.

Rule 5 – Part the waters of waste through "project time"

Several months after implementing the four capacity / resource management rules described above, the executive team at Overload, Inc. was feeling pretty good about themselves. Employee morale was up, resource conflicts were down, and project schedules were beginning to accelerate. But like the good problem-solvers that they were, they decided that some direct follow-up investigation was needed. They created a brief survey that they distributed to all employees with product development responsibilities. The results of the survey were both gratifying and challenging. While the feedback was generally positive on the effectiveness of the new rules, some missed opportunities were also highlighted. These challenges are summarized as follows:

1. Employees were still finding it hard to focus on high-concentration work, due to frequent meetings, walk-in interruptions, phone calls, e-mails, etc. They found themselves trying to fit value-creating work in the cracks between interruptions, resulting in suboptimal productivity.

2. While the prioritization that was provided by following Rule 2 was helpful, it seemed to be too broad and general. Was it always the case that a higher-priority project on the global priority list should receive immediate attention? Or were there circumstances that might mitigate in favor of a lower-priority project?

3. Managing resource capacity from a product development perspective was a great first step, but other drains on the capacity of this same resource pool (e.g., sustaining support, special orders, etc.) were still causing unexpected delays.

4. Finally, there was a general lack of flexibility and responsiveness among project teams, caused in part by rigid schedules for major projects, and long "time-batches" between team coordination meetings.

It appeared that some additional rules were needed to deal with the above concerns. The final four rules in our suite of eight are designed to deal with these challenges in the order presented, beginning with the constant interruptions associated with virtually every office environment. The problem is a significant one: In my experience, the number-one cause of waste in new product development is a chaotic work environment. Frequent and unexpected interruptions can cripple a team's ability to meet schedule estimates, and represent a huge drain on their focus and productivity. The solution is derived from the time-slicing concept presented in Rule 4.

Suppose that your firm announced tomorrow that the first two hours of every workday would be allocated exclusively to value-creating work. No meetings are to be scheduled during that period. Employees should send incoming work-related calls to voice mail (except, of course, for those employees whose value creation depends on their being available, such as sales people, technical support, etc.). E-mail communication should be delayed until after this two-hour period. Finally, walk-in interruptions are discouraged, unless a legitimate emergency exists. You could think of this time-slice as "personal work time," "study time," or my preferred title, "project time." Whatever you choose to call it, this two-hour block represents a predictable, synchronized portion of the workday allocated for individual work, or small-group, informal collaboration.

Assuming that this concept could be implemented successfully, is there any employee that wouldn't see the benefit? At last, the normal workday would allow for the same kind of productivity typically reserved for early mornings, late nights, and weekends. Although the rest of the day might be consumed with sporadic meetings and other interruptions, at least some focus time could be counted on. The scheduling of this two-hour block could vary; the first two hours of the morning are typically the most productive, but you could also consider the last two hours of the day. Why two hours? This has proven to be a good compromise between allowing sufficient time to be beneficial, while not completely disrupting the status quo. Over time, you may decide to increase the duration of this time-slice, assuming that the organization is receptive.

From a practical standpoint, there are several tips that I can offer to ensure a successful implementation. First, the time-slice allocated to project time should be synchronized throughout a business unit or company. If people are allowed to choose their own time-slices, then it will become nearly impossible to schedule a meeting at any time during the day. This will result in almost immediate abandonment of the concept. Second, while developers may have the most to gain from project time, all functions that can benefit should be offered the same opportunity. This will avoid fostering resentment toward those lucky few who are being treated differently from the rest. Finally, a communication memo should be distributed throughout the organization that explains what project time is, why it is being implemented, and how it will work. I've provided a sample memo in Figure 2.8 that you can use as a starting point. It is important that this memo provide detail with respect to which functions are impacted, and in particular, what constitutes a legitimate "emergency" that would permit violation of project time.

Even the most straightforward and intuitively beneficial improvements can experience significant obstacles to successful implementation. Project time is no exception. There are two issues, in particular, that deserve attention. The first can be a real showstopper. If your firm has frequent interactions with customers, suppliers, or business units in remote geographic locations, then finding an appropriate period for project time may be quite challenging. For example, if you work with suppliers in Europe or Asia, the morning time-slice that I've recommended may be the only common time during which conference calls can be scheduled. Your first recourse would be to look for a time-slice that would not be interrupted by overseas calls. A second alternative would be to select the best time-slice for the majority of developers, and just live with the occasional interruptions that teleconferences would create. Remember that this is not an "all-or-nothing" tool. Even if project time is interrupted four out of five days in the week, it is still better than no project time at all. Also keep in mind that typically not every developer will be involved in every overseas call, so on average, the benefits should still be substantial.

The second challenge to project-time implementation is more insidious. Any strategy of this type requires a level of organizational discipline

Objective:
To provide employees with a dedicated block of time that will allow them to focus on value-creating work without interruption.

Impacted Functions:
All functions within the organization, except sales and technical support.

When:
Monday – Friday from 8:00 a.m. to 10:00 a.m.

Guidelines:
- Project time will be blocked out on Microsoft Outlook calendars.
- No regularly scheduled meetings will be held during this period.
- Participants will not be required to attend staff or functional-level meetings during this time.
- Time is not intended to catch up on e-mails – e-mail / text messaging should be minimized.
- Minimal phone interruptions – set phone to voice mail.
- No walk-in interruptions, unless it is an emergency (see below).
- You may use a visual indicator of project time such as a flag at your functional manager's discretion.

Emergencies:
- Critical documents requiring signature.
- Questions relating to time-critical production-support issues.
- Issues relating to customer service / support that are highly time-sensitive.

FIGURE 2.8: An example of a communication memo outlining the purpose, rules, and exceptions to project time. A tailored version of this memo should be distributed to all impacted employees, and may need to be reissued every several months to avoid backsliding into constant interruptions and a chaotic work environment.

that is not common in most companies. At first, project time will be embraced and used effectively. Over time, however, an entropy effect will undoubtedly occur (entropy is the natural tendency of any system to degrade into its lowest and most random energy state). Walk-in interruptions will start to increase, since everyone thinks that their needs are an emergency. Managers will take advantage of their employees' synchronized availability to hold ad hoc meetings "just this one time." And so it will go until project time is nothing but a distant memory. Make no mistake about it; *this will happen.* Your countermeasure is to persistently renew the tool. Every few months you may need to send out a reminder memo reinforcing the rules, and letting everyone know that project time will not be abandoned. In some cases, you might need to gently admonish an employee (or more likely, a manager) who frequently disrupts project time. Most important, you need to set a good example yourself. Whatever your position, lead by your own behavior. There is nothing that undermines organizational change faster than a "do as I say, not as I do" attitude. This tool is worth fighting for; I've seen dramatic gains in productivity from effective implementation of project time, and the barriers to implementation are lower than with almost any other improvement to your product development process.

Rule 6 – Economic impact should drive real-time priority decisions

Is it always true that the highest-priority project on a "global" priority list should win out over a lower-priority project when it comes to resource conflicts? While this approach to conflict resolution will work much of the time, there are circumstances in which such a simplistic rule will result in suboptimal outcomes. Let's return to our valuable subject-matter expert, Dan Downtrodden, for another example. Suppose that Dan is assigned to two projects: an "A" priority project that is critical to his firm, and a "B" project with somewhat lower priority. On the "B" project, Dan needs to deliver a technical package to a tooling supplier so they can begin fabrication of a production molding tool. This tool is vital to meeting the scheduled production launch date (i.e., it is on the critical path of the "B" project). Simultaneously, Dan is scheduled to perform some documenta-tion tasks on his "A" project assignment. Although this latter assignment is on a higher-priority project, it has "slack-time:" There are no critical-path dependencies on this documentation. In fact, the task could slip several weeks of schedule with no impact on the "A" project whatsoever.

What should Dan do? In this situation, blindly following the global priority list would lead to an unnecessary slip in the completion of the "B" project. While a global priority list is an excellent first step toward optimizing productivity, a more nuanced approach will result in greater economic output from your finite development resources. Hence, I propose the more sophisticated "arbitration rules" outlined in Figure 2.9. Rather than just considering the overall priority of a project as the basis for conflict arbitration, these rules take into account the *economic impact of a delay* on the involved projects. In Dan's situation, the "A" project would suffer no economic impact if he were to delay his task by a few weeks, whereas the "B" project would suffer a substantial negative impact. His choice in this situation would be clear; work on the "B" project until handoff of the required technical package, and then complete the less critical documentation task on the "A" project.

When a resource conflict between two projects occurs –

Rule 6.1 – If one task is on the critical path of its project and the other task is non-schedule-critical, then the critical-path task wins.

Rule 6.2 – If both tasks are on the critical path of their respective projects, then the project that would suffer the greatest economic impact from a schedule delay should win.

Rule 6.3 – If neither task is on the critical path of their respective projects, then use the global priority of the two projects to determine the winner.

Rule 6.4 – If both tasks have similar global priority (e.g., they are both tasks on "A" projects), and the economic impact is nearly equivalent, then the shortest-duration task should always be performed first.

FIGURE 2.9: The "arbitration rules" described above represent a more sophisticated approach to resource conflict resolution than simply deferring to the project that ranks highest on a global priority list.

Assuming that the critical paths of your projects have been identified (see Chapter 6 for more on how this can be realistically achieved), then Rule 6.1 in the above figure is just common sense. If all projects involved in a resource conflict can retain their scheduled launch dates, that would be the obvious choice. Things become a bit more complicated when the conflicting tasks are both on the critical path of their respective projects. In this case, as Rule 6.2 states, we must consider which project would suffer the greatest economic impact if a slip in the launch date were to occur. Unfortunately, economic impact is a nebulous concept. From a practical standpoint, we are concerned with which project has the greatest *schedule sensitivity*. If a new product must appear at a specific trade show to support its business case, and a schedule slip would cause that show to be missed, then that project has very high schedule sensitivity. Likewise, products that are seasonal in nature (e.g., apparel, sporting goods, weather-related tools and equipment, etc.) have relatively higher schedule sensitivity than those without seasonal constraints. In general, we are concerned with the relative loss of unit sales and / or market share resulting from a slipped launch date. If there is an obvious distinction among conflicting projects, the most sensitive critical-path task should be performed first. If this distinction is not evident, then fall back to the global priority list to arbitrate the resource conflict. Likewise, as stated in Rule 6.3, if neither task involved in a resource conflict is schedule-critical, then the global priority list can be used for arbitration.

Finally, what if several competing tasks are, for all intents and purposes, the same priority (they are just "too close to call")? With all else being equal, you should give priority to the task within the queue with the shortest duration, as stated in Rule 6.4. By moving the shortest-duration tasks to the front, you minimize the negative impact on the other involved projects. This is only true when the relative economic impacts are quite similar. However this last arbitration rule is a great fallback if consensus cannot be reached quickly on the priorities of conflicting tasks. Not surprisingly, even the more nuanced rules outlined in Figure 2.9 are somewhat oversimplified. If we had all the time and discipline in the world, we could calculate the estimated economic impact of every resource conflict situation, but from a pragmatic standpoint, we have to draw the line somewhere. Remember that achieving successful improvement within a firm is always a balance between the effectiveness of the proposed improvement and the ability of an organization to understand, absorb, and maintain that improvement. I'd rather see you implement a pared-down version of my rules, then have you attempt an overaggressive system that will die of its own weight.

Rule 7 – All work must flow though a common funnel

Suppose that you and your spouse share a common checking account. You each have your own checkbooks, and merrily write checks against that account without reconciling your balances with each other.

Before long, you will be receiving a notification from your bank that you are overdrawn. The same logic holds true when managing a pool of development resources. Until now, we have only considered how to manage resource capacity among product development projects. If this were the only "checkbook" that could draw from this account, there would be no problem. Unfortunately, in almost every company, the same pool of developers is expected to service myriad short-term, high-urgency tasks that are not captured on any project list. Whether it be requests for factory support, quick-turn customization efforts, quotations, or customer requests, these activities drain capacity, and create a disproportionate amount of turbulence to product development flow. This problem is aggravated by the fact that, in many cases, this type of work is not managed; the requests for work go directly to individual developers without filtering or prioritization. In the absence of active management, resources try to fit these short-term tasks into their daily work, often resulting in high levels of multitasking waste and unanticipated slips to project schedules.

This issue can be resolved in two ways. The first, and most important, is to ensure that all requests for development resource capacity pass through a management filter. Ideally, a given pool of resources would have a single manager who is responsible for performing "triage": How urgent is the request for work? Who is best suited to perform the task? Which projects might be negatively impacted by a new task assignment? Based on this triage assessment, the manager would divvy out tasks to the resource pool so as to maximize responsiveness and minimize turbulence to flow among development projects. Such a scheme is shown in Figure 2.10. Even though the amount of work to be performed (i.e., the drain on capacity) is the same as before, the productivity of development resources will be greatly improved. Consider the analogy of a metered onramp to a freeway (if you don't know what this is, you are a very lucky individual). The metered onramp creates a short delay between cars that enter a freeway. If traffic is heavy, the delay can be several seconds, but in most cases, the delay is minimal. In fact, you might think that the meter is doing nothing at all. You would be wrong. Studies have shown that even a brief interval between merging cars can reduce or eliminate turbulence in the flow of traffic. The management filter that I described above is just such a "metered onramp" for unanticipated, short-duration tasks. Moreover, by passing all work through a common filter, there is increased visibility into the type and frequency of disruptions; a vital input to long-term capacity planning.

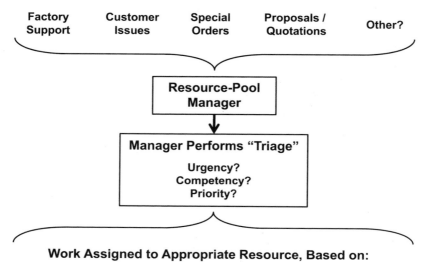

FIGURE 2.10: It is vital that all work that must be performed by a pool of development resources pass through a common management filter. In the graphic above, the manager performs "triage" on incoming requests for capacity, and based on that assessment, allocates tasks so as to maximize responsiveness and minimize the negative impact on development projects.

I mentioned above that there are two possible solutions to this challenging resource capacity issue. The first is instituting a management filter. The second is to carve out a segregated pool of resources whose primary responsibility is to service quick-turn tasks, such as those listed at the top of Figure 2.10. To implement this solution, your firm must have a fairly large pool of development resources to draw from, and there must be some redundancy among the functional disciplines involved. By forming such a "quick-response team" you accomplish several things.

First, you significantly reduce the number of disruptions to longer-term product development projects. Although there may still be times when a specific resource must be pulled from project work to handle a unique situation, these interruptions will be minimized. Second, by grouping short-duration tasks together within a common resource pool, you enable far better level-loading of these tasks; random variability will tend to cancel when small batch-size, uncorrelated tasks arrive at frequent intervals. In simpler terms, the quick-response team can dynamically manage a collection of small tasks far better than a team that must handle both short and long duration tasks. Finally, by rotating developers into and out of the quick-response team, you accelerate organizational learning; there is no better education for new product developers than to spend several months dealing with factory emergencies and customer issues. When they return to long-term project work, they will have gained tremendous insight into the ramifications of their design decisions once those products go into production.

Rule 8 – Just-in-time communication is critical to achieving flow

Toyota has taught us that inventorying large batches of raw production material leads to waste. Instead, materials should arrive at a factory "just in time" to be consumed by the production process. In new product development, the batching of materials is not a problem, but batching of time and information can represent an intolerable source of waste. The ubiquitous weekly coordination meeting for development teams represents a time batch; developers will often delay the sharing of information, requests for help, and reporting of progress (or the lack thereof) until this regularly scheduled meeting takes place. If a problem occurs on Monday, for example, it will likely remain unresolved until the Friday team meeting. In the interim, progress slows and a few precious days of schedule may be lost. Over time, these few days add up to a "death by a thousand cuts" situation; many projects fail to meet planned delivery dates due to numerous small schedule slips accrued over the entire duration of the project.

The batching of information and communication can be alleviated by a simple but extremely powerful technique; frequent, short-duration stand-up coordination meetings. If a project team meets several times per week for a fifteen-minute huddle, the weekly time batch described above is eliminated, and just-in-time communication and decision-making are enabled. As tempting as it is for me to elaborate further at this point, I will defer the reader to Chapter 4 for a detailed discussion of this critical component of Visual Workflow Management. Suffice to say that the benefits of frequent stand-up meetings are both significant and well-documented. From a capacity management perspective, combining these meetings with a visual task planning tool can allow flexible, real-time optimization of your development teams' productivity. Stay tuned for much more on this topic.

■ ■ ■

The product development environment at Overload, Inc. has changed dramatically over the past few years. Time-to-market for new products has been reduced by almost half, through a combination of increased focus and reduced turbulence. As a result, revenue and profits are being realized far earlier, and the morale of both the executive team and the firm's developers is at an all-time high. It has taken several years of persistence, but the payback has been well worth the investment. In fact, the latest meeting of Overload's executive team has a new agenda topic. The company's leaders are considering changing the name of their firm to EasyFlow, Inc. ... somehow it just seems more appropriate.

Advanced Topic: A *"Hoshin*-like" System for Capacity / Resource Optimization

New product development should be thought of as a vital *system* within your firm. To perform like a system, there must be multiple elements (various development projects) working together toward a common goal (maximizing revenue and profits). However, a system without feedback can never reach its full potential. We should, therefore, take a final step toward a truly optimized capacity management methodology by seeking a feedback mechanism that will allow our system to self-optimize over time. To accomplish this, I will steal a page from the Total Quality Management (TQM) movement.

In the 1980's, a systematic architecture for strategy and policy deployment was proposed that provided just the type of feedback we are seeking. It was called *hoshin* planning (see Akao, (1991)), and over the past few decades it has become the gold standard for applying systems thinking to organizational governance. This approach involves creating a cascaded and interconnected set of goals for each level of an organization. At the executive level, a general set of objectives and targets is established. Each of these goals is then flowed down to the functional groups within the firm as a set of more specific objectives, along with key performance indicators (KPIs). A third tier is often included in larger organizations that directly links working-level teams and functional units to the goals and strategies of the firm. Again, a set of even more detailed objectives and KPIs is created, such that every level of the organization is aligned and interconnected. The feedback loop is closed by the reporting of KPIs, and can be dynamically managed through iterative replanning and refocusing of the organization.

A similar approach can be implemented for the management of product development capacity, as shown in Figure 2.11. Let's take if from the top (of the figure, that is). The process begins with a global priority list of projects from all sources within a firm, divided into the A / B / C categories defined previously. As each "A" or "B" project is kicked off, the project team leader (with facilitation help, if necessary) conducts a Project Planning / Risk-Mitigation Event (see Chapter 6 for details). The output of this event, among other things, is a calendarized plan for resource requirements, by month and function. Although this initial plan may be crude, it forms the starting point for a continuously updated monthly planning activity.

This information is fed in two directions: it is provided to the strategic executive committee for future capacity planning purposes, and it is provided to the manager of each functional area to allow real-time capacity management. Note that the three-month update period shown in Figure 2.11 is a recommendation, but a quarterly update of the company-wide capacity plan seems reasonable. The functional areas, however, should be reassessing (and potentially reassigning) resource capacity on a monthly basis. The functional managers use a simple spreadsheet tool, such as the one shown in Figure 2.6, as a means to allocate their individual resources for the forthcoming monthly period. It is important that the functional managers include in their plans any non-project-related drains on resource availability, and only allocate resource hours based on realistic availability for development projects. Initially, the unplanned capacity demands may be rough guesses, but over time these estimates will become more accurate as feedback is gained from visual project boards (described in Chapter 4).

Every month, the project team leaders will provide updated estimates of their resource needs to the functional managers. Each project then becomes one row on the spreadsheet shown in Figure 2.6. If there is ever a resource shortfall, then the "A" projects always get their needed resources first. If all "A" projects cannot be satisfied, this should immediately raise a red flag, and if serious enough, should trigger action by upper management to resolve the conflict. Based on the monthly assignments of individuals by functional managers, project teams will meet on a frequent basis to hold stand-up meetings in front of visual project boards. This working-level communication strategy is described in detail later in this book. The output of these workflow management meetings is a continuously updated picture of project status, progress, and future resource needs. Hence the loop can now close. As projects proceed, team leaders will determine if their staffing levels are adequate, and will use that understanding to update their monthly resource requests as their projects move forward. Functional managers will update their understanding of resource availability as better data on unplanned work becomes available. Ultimately, the executive team will update their high-level capacity model to incorporate this feedback, and so it goes. New project proposals will now be prioritized based on a realistic, fact-driven assessment of development capacity.

If this process seems complex, then recognize that this represents the culmination of several years of rule implementation and refinement. Hopefully, this vision will provide you with a target to shoot for.

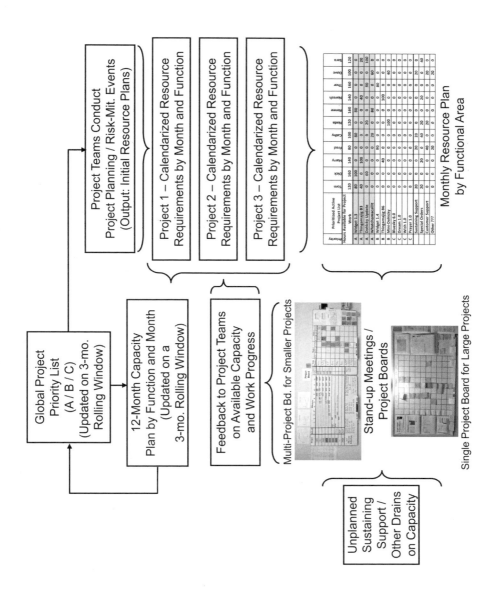

FIGURE 2.11: Applying systems thinking to the management of development capacity can enable steady improvement over time. The *hoshin*-like process shown above represents a vision of what can be achieved after implementation of the eight rules for capacity optimization described previously in this chapter.

Depending on where your organization is on the capacity management maturity curve, pick the rule from our list of eight that best suits your needs and get started. Remember that even the longest journey begins with a single step.

Chapter References

Akao, Y. (Editor), 1991, *Hoshin Kanri: Policy Deployment for Successful TQM*, Productivity Press.

Allen, D., 2001, *Getting Things Done*, Penguin Books.

Cowley, M., and E. Domb, 1997, *Beyond Strategic Vision: Effective Corporate Action with Hoshin Planning*, Butterworth-Heinemann.

Goldratt, E. M., 1990, *Theory of Constraints*, The North River Press.

Goldratt, E. M., 1997, *Critical Chain*, The North River Press.

Goldratt, E. M., and J. Cox, 1992, *The Goal: Second Revised Edition*, The North River Press.

Leach, L. P., 2000, *Critical Chain Project Management*, Argent House.

Reinertsen, D. G., 1997, *Managing the Design Factory: A Product Developer's Toolkit*, The Free Press.

Reinertsen, D. G., 2009, *The Principles of Product Development Flow: Second Generation Lean Product Development*, Celeritas Publishing.

Smith, P. G., 2007, *Flexible Product Development: Building Agility for Changing Markets*, John Wiley & Sons.

Smith, P. G., and D. G. Reinertsen, 1998, *Developing Products in Half the Time: New Rules, New Tools, Second Edition*, John Wiley & Sons.

Suri, R., 1998, *Quick Response Manufacturing*, Productivity Press.

3 An Event-Driven Development Process

Background and Overview

This chapter begins with a question: Is new product development a *process*, or is it a series of *projects*? The answer will determine how we will proceed in implementing a lean product development process, so it is worth careful consideration. Those of you with a background in lean manufacturing (or any other process improvement methodology) no doubt answered quickly and firmly; product development is a process. Not so fast. A process is defined as a "recurring activity that transforms inputs into outputs," and indeed there is a substantial transformation that goes on in the development of new products. However, is this activity actually recurring? Although there are certainly aspects of each new development effort that are similar, there are also elements that are unique to each new product your firm creates. In fact, if you were to truly standardize your product development process (i.e., eliminate all of the variability), *you would hinder its ability to create value*. The value of a new design is determined by its differentiation from other currently available products. If each new product your firm develops is identical to the one before it, you won't be in business very long.

Then perhaps new product development is actually a series of projects. A project is defined as a "non-recurring activity that transforms inputs into outputs." In principle, each new development effort could be planned from scratch, and executed using well-established project management tools and methods. Moreover, it is entirely possible that this effort would be successful, provided that the right skills were applied in the appropriate way. The problem is that this start-from-square-one approach would be exceedingly time-consuming and fraught with risk. Without some form of standard work to capture knowledge, we cannot directly leverage the learning and experiences of the past, resulting in both wasted time and a high potential for errors and missteps.

Hence, the answer to our initial question is that new product development must have attributes of both a process *and* a series of projects. Depending on the nature of the products involved, the optimal ratio of process to project could be very different. In the shoe industry, for example, every new design follows a virtually identical path to commercialization. While the designs themselves are unique, the steps required to transform a conceptual rendering into a pair of shoes are very similar. In this situation, new product development can be formalized into a fairly rigid process, with highly detailed process maps and an almost metronomic cadence. At the other extreme, consider a firm that develops automated production equipment for high-volume manufacturers. To be successful, this firm must tailor each new product to the unique requirements of a specific customer. In this case, only a very high-level project execution process can be standardized, thereby retaining the latitude required to meet the needs of diverse customers. In general, to optimize new product development, we must capture in the form of standard work the process aspects of development (i.e., those that are common and recurring), while preserving a sufficient project perspective to enable flexibility and differentiation. A balance of standard work and creative freedom is the essence of a truly lean product development methodology.

If your firm has a formal new product development process, it is very likely that it involves phases and gates. Although the terminology may differ (e.g., stage / gate, tollgate, etc.) the concept is the same; a time-based template that defines major phases of work, followed by gates that provide feedback and control to the process (see, for example,

Clark, et al (1993), Cooper, et al (1993), and McGrath (1996) and (2004)). My opinion of the phase / gate methodology has been well-documented in earlier books (see Mascitelli (2002) and (2007)), so I won't repeat my earlier rantings. Suffice to say that phase / gate, as it is often implemented, can represent a great starting point for structuring new product development, but has fundamental limitations that must be overcome to maximize flow, creativity, speed, and flexibility. The primary drawback of a phase / gate process is that it really isn't a development process at all. In most cases, it constitutes little more than a series of gate-review checklists paired with business-case criteria at each gate to mitigate financial risks to the firm. This is a governance process, with little or no guidance for development teams as to the methods they should use for collaboration, decision-making, problem-solving, workflow management, schedule optimization, cost reduction, or any other execution-related activity. As a result, many firms with a formal phase / gate process also employ project management tools and methods to mitigate this shortfall (a tacit acknowledgement of the process / project duality of new product development). On the other hand, project management offers a means to guide execution (see, for example, Project Management Institute (2008)), but by its very nature is typically too generic to be an ideal fit for a given firm's design efforts.

In this chapter, I will propose a unique approach to balancing standard work with flexible execution in design and development. Before I describe this new paradigm, let's consider the attributes that a lean product development process should embody:

- Optimizes flow by minimizing time batches and eliminating arbitrary barriers.

- Enables organizational learning and knowledge-based development.

- Provides sufficient risk-monitoring to protect the business from financial losses.

- Allows adequate flexibility to encourage creativity and innovation.

- Can be scaled to fit the full spectrum of development activities, from minor line extensions and special orders, to major new platform initiatives.

- Captures and communicates standard work in both governance and execution.

- Drives cross-functional teams toward effective collaboration.

- Enables speed and agility in response to market needs.

- Can be easily understood, used, and maintained by a typical development organization.

This seems like a tall order, and indeed the above attributes represent an ideal future state rather than an immediately obtainable goal. That being said, I wouldn't have created such a daunting list if I didn't believe that the process I propose can meet the challenge. At the heart of this new approach are transformative, standard-work "events" that encourage cross-functional collaboration at critical junctures in the flow of new product development. The very good news for firms that have an established phase / gate process is that you can keep your checklists and gate criteria; the standard-work events that I will describe can be embedded into an existing governance process without asking for either permission or forgiveness. If, on the other hand, you have avoided the phase / gate bandwagon (or are tired of the rigidity and waste), then you can refer to the final section of this chapter for a full-blown, continuous-flow lean product development process that integrates both governance and execution. In either case, the benefits will be creativity, speed, and flexibility, along with an ever-growing knowledge base upon which your next product breakthroughs can be launched.

A Formal Definition of Value

Many attempts have been made to characterize the transformation that takes place in new product development. It has been variously defined as a problem-solving process, a method for converting soft-form ideas into tangible goods, a knowledge-creating process, and so on. My preference is to think of new product development as a *process for transforming knowledge and information into customer value* (for variations on this perspective, see Kennedy (2003), Nonaka, et al (2005), Ward (2007), and Schab (2008)). Whichever viewpoint you prefer, it is important that we agree on what "value-added" means in the context of product design and development. I propose the following definition:

"A design / development activity is value-added if it transforms a new product design (or the essential deliverables needed to commercialize it) such that the product's profit margin and / or market share are positively impacted."

The above statement reflects an inclusive view of design and development: All functions within a firm that contribute to the ultimate commercialization of a new product can create value, provided that their contribution enables a successful business case to be achieved. The term transforms in my definition means "to bring closer to commercialization." The term deliverables refers to the myriad elements that must be in place for a firm to make money from a new design: drawings, tooling, supplier relationships, advertising materials, distribution logistics, and so on. Finally, I require that to be value-added, an activity must have a positive impact on hard-nosed business metrics, such as market price, recurring cost, or market share. This is admittedly a tactical definition. It excludes, for example, the building of a foundational knowledge base for the creation of future products, or the training of employees in new and better professional skills. Aren't these endeavors valuable? Of course they are. In fact, they are vital to the long-term success of your firm, as later chapters in this book will attest. However, we must recognize that there is a difference between strategic activities which support a firm's competitiveness over time, and the specific tasks required to develop a commercial product. The latter can be thought of as the "core process" of new product development. There are a number of strategic processes that feed and support this core, but for now our focus is on getting new products from idea to profit in the most efficient and effective manner possible.

Based on the above definition of value, we can consider three categories of new product development activities:

- Value — Meets the above definition by transforming the new product design or its supporting deliverables into commercial form.

- Enablers — Not directly value-added, but provide essential support to the process that yields a positive return on the time invested.

- Waste — Everything else, at least from the perspective of commercializing a new product.

These three categories provide us with a target to shoot for, as shown in Figure 3.1. In time studies that I've performed over the past several years (see Mascitelli (2007)), the amount of time spent by developers on value creation has averaged about two hours per standard workday (not counting nights and weekends). The rest of developers' time tends to be divided roughly equally between enablers and waste. What is perhaps the most interesting aspect of these studies is that most of the waste appears to be a direct result of *not performing enabling activities effectively*. In lean manufacturing, enablers are often referred to as "type 1 waste" and are considered to be necessary evils to be minimized and potentially eliminated over time. The situation is quite different in new product development. Because of the high degree of uncertainty, complexity, and risk associated with the design of new products, enablers are elevated to a pivotal role. For example, effective capacity management is clearly an enabler, but can dramatically improve the productivity of development teams. Identifying and proactively mitigating project risks is another great example of a critical enabler, as is the coordination and communication of project status and plans within a development team. In fact, I would argue that performing enabling activities better and faster should be a key objective of any lean product development process. More efficient and effective enablers result in a double savings – less time spent on these vital activities, combined with far less waste. The outcome resembles the lean future state shown at the bottom of the figure. As you will soon learn, one of the primary objectives of the event-driven process that I propose is to establish standard work for critical enabling activities, resulting in far more time available for value-creating design and development work.

Current State –

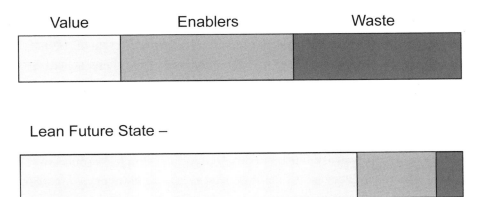

FIGURE 3.1: In time studies performed by the author spanning ten firms and multiple industries, the amount of time spent by developers on value creation during the standard workday is surprisingly low. By performing both value-creating and vital enabling activities in a lean manner, a future state can be achieved that allows far more time for productive product development work.

What are "Events"?

One of the most unambiguous success stories to come from the lean manufacturing movement has been the use of highly focused *kaizen* events. These intensive multi-day sessions involve a cross-functional team of empowered individuals who collaboratively define an improvement opportunity, identify and test possible solutions, and implement the best alternative in real time. On the factory floor and in the front office, these events have yielded amazing results, due in no small part to the nature and structure of the events themselves. By bringing together a cross-functional team for an uninterrupted period of time, the level of efficiency and cooperation is dramatically increased. Moreover, using a standardized agenda and tools for the event provides assurance that the activity will achieve high value for the time spent. Although in recent years some firms have overdone it a bit with respect to the number and duration of *kaizen* events, there is something fundamental going on here that can inform our approach to lean product development.

In my experience, the most difficult aspect of creating a successful new product development methodology is finding ways to ensure that true cross-functional collaboration occurs at every stage of the process, from inception through to rate production. The most notable of these opportunities occurs whenever the transformation of knowledge shifts from one key development function to another. This typically first takes place during the transition from marketing (those who presumably are responsible for the "vision" of the new product) to design / engineering (those who must create a product solution that matches the vision). The other significant transition is from design / engineering to production (those who must live with the solution that design / engineering creates). Beyond these two critical transitions, there are myriad other minor handoffs and collaborative opportunities that must occur throughout development to ensure that the best possible product reaches its intended customers.

What if we harnessed the power of standard-work events, such as the *kaizen* events described above, to structure and guide the knowledge transformation process in new product development? These events are not a substitute for day-to-day collaboration and individual design / development work, but rather are used at critical junctures in the process to improve collaboration, time efficiency, and quality, while reducing overall development risk. Furthermore, events can become a repository for organizational learning by capturing and sustaining proven methods for innovation, execution, and decision-making. An example of what a generic lean product development event might look like is shown in Figure 3.2. The standard work begins by defining the pre-work required to prepare for the event. This would normally include a list of desired attendees, a set of expectations for each function that will be represented, and a detailed list of the prerequisite inputs (e.g., market research, design documentation, test data, etc.). Once the inputs to the event are available, a dedicated timeslot is scheduled that will allow the attendees to collaborate without interruption. A standardized agenda defines the tools and methods that will guide the team through a specific knowledge transformation, resulting in standardized outputs that enable the development project to move forward. The event closes with the assignment of action items to finalize the event outputs and resolve any open issues. The process of closing out the event is standardized as well.

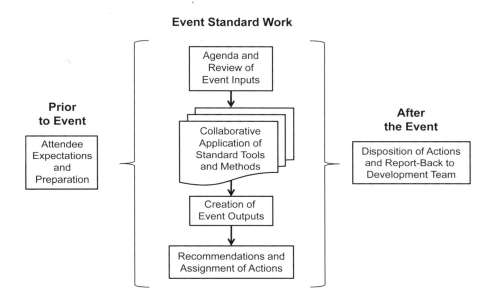

FIGURE 3.2: A block diagram for a generic product development event. Each event embodies a critical knowledge transformation that demands a high level of cross-functional collaboration. Standard work is defined for each event that covers the preparation, execution, required outputs, and closure.

Over the past five years, I have worked with a number of leading companies to define the structure and nature of product development events, and to refine the standard work involved. The results of this collaboration are summarized in Figure 3.3. Although the listed events represent a proven starting point, there is no reason why you cannot create your own event and add it to the list. Once you have learned the methodology, and experienced some of the benefits of using this execution approach, you will be well-prepared to morph my generic list into one that best suits your firm's specific needs. For now, let's identify the common attributes of the events listed in the figure.

A Preview of Coming Events

Market Requirements Event – Identifies key differentiators for a proposed new product based on market research and voice-of-the-customer. Establishes a prioritized list of product requirements / features that ensure a successful business case.

Project Planning / Risk-Mitigation Event – Collaborative development of an optimized project plan, including master schedule, resource plan, and budget. Identifies and prioritizes project risks and assigns mitigation actions.

Learning-Cycle Event(s) – Collaborative identification of "knowledge gaps" and development and review of A3-formatted knowledge briefs. Event is repeated as necessary to establish a solid foundation for development.

Design Review and Freeze Event(s) – Rigorous review of product design occurring several times within the development cycle. Focuses on issues / errors / improvements. Final event is a "production-readiness review."

Design 3P Event – First step in achieving product / process co-development. Identifies critical-to-quality and critical-to-cost issues with new design, and uses value engineering and other tools to improve cost, quality, and manufacturability.

Process 3P Event – Second step focuses on optimizing internal (factory) and external (supply-chain) value streams, application of design-for- manufacturability and design-for-six-sigma tools, and optimization of product-specific capital equipment.

Production 3P Event – Final step addresses line design, equipment readiness, fixturing, poke-yoke, flow, *takt* times, and capacity constraints. Establishes production readiness – a "line-*kaizen*" event.

FIGURE 3.3: An overview of the product development events that will be described in later chapters of this book. Each event performs a critical knowledge transformation that requires a high level of cross-functional collaboration.

First and foremost, each of the events described in Figure 3.3 performs a critical knowledge transformation that demands a high level of cross-functional collaboration. In theory, this collaboration should occur through ad hoc communication and teamwork. However, the reality is that few cross-functional teams naturally achieve this level of collaboration, particularly across functional boundaries. Events act as a forcing function to ensure that the right people work together at the right times within the development process to achieve a truly collaborative product design. A second common attribute is that each of the proposed events mitigates a significant risk to product development success. For example, if market requirements are not well-understood and carefully vetted at the inception of a product development project, there is a high likelihood that misunderstandings will occur, or that scope-creep will cause delays and turbulence later in the process. A final common attribute is that these events provide structure and discipline to an otherwise ill-defined activity. It is well known, for example, that manufacturability considerations should be injected into the earliest stages of the development process, but how exactly is this accomplished? In some cases, to be sure, a proactive manufacturing engineer will engage at the appropriate times with the necessary tools and skills, but why leave this critical success factor to chance? A standard-work event levels the playing field for all development projects, and ensures that the best tools will be used in the proper way at the optimal time.

A last point must be made with respect to events: They are designed to be *scalable*. As previously noted, product development projects span a broad range of scope and complexity. A major new platform project might benefit from several days being spent on each event, whereas a minor product enhancement may only require a few hours per event. Without scalability, an event-driven process would undoubtedly create waste, particularly for smaller projects. In the chapters that follow, each of the events listed in Figure 3.3 will be described in detail. For each event, I will also provide examples of how the standard work can be adapted to the full range of projects. Indeed, even a project team consisting of one designer (wearing a multitude of hats) can benefit from a scaled-down version of an Event-Driven Lean Product Development process.

Step 1 – Imbed Critical Events into an Existing Development Process

One of the biggest obstacles to implementing any new product development tool or method is its impact on the status quo. Many firms have gone through a gut-wrenching effort to put in place a formal development process, often including considerable time spent with highly paid consultants. Once in place, such a process is tough to change in any significant way; with management finally in alignment and teams well-trained, opening the door to improvement can be daunting. This is where an event-driven approach delivers an unexpected benefit; it can be implemented in stages over time, causing little or no conflict with existing processes. Hence, I will describe a typical step-by-step deployment of Event-Driven Lean Product Development, beginning with the highest-leverage opportunities and ending with a comprehensive future vision.

For this discussion, I will assume that your firm has some form of phase / gate process in place. This is obviously not a prerequisite, since my preference would be to start with a blank sheet of paper, but one must accept reality. However, if you are starting from scratch, the same steps will work for you. The first phase of implementation includes three of the most vital events in my lineup: the Market Requirements Event, the Project Planning / Risk-Mitigation Event, and the Design Review and Freeze Event, as shown in Figure 3.4. The Market Requirements Event (see Chapter 5) has the greatest leverage of any event in the process by establishing a cross-functional consensus on the critical attributes of a new product that will ensure a successful business case. This event should be held as a kick-off meeting for each development project, so it is literally the first thing that a cross-functional team does on the road to commercialization. The output of this event is a prioritized list of high-level product requirements, and an implicit validation of the proposed product's business case. Once completed, the team will likely have open issues to address, such as verification of market research, initial technical investigations, sanity checks on critical cost and quality factors, etc. That being said, only a short period (e.g., roughly two weeks) should be allowed to close these actions before the team reconvenes for their next event: the Project Planning / Risk-Mitigation Event (see Chapter 6).

The second event in our basic process is intended to establish a roadmap for success, determine schedule and resource demands, and identify major risks that the team will face going forward. If there are only a few open issues from the Market Requirements Event, then the Project Planning / Risk-Mitigation Event could be held virtually back-to-back with this first meeting. Once completed, the team will have a viable plan, the firm will have a collaboratively agreed-upon launch date and non-recurring budget, and project execution can begin. From this point forward, I strongly recommend implementing a Visual Workflow Management system to help facilitate team communication, and allow rapid and flexible response to new information and changing conditions

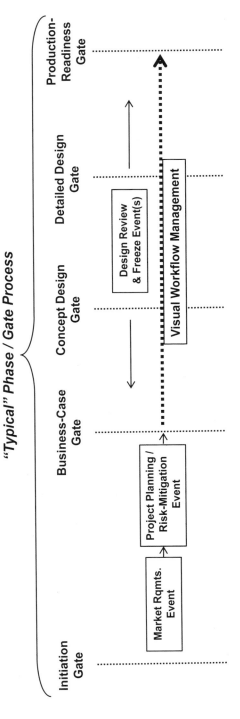

FIGURE 3.4: The first step toward implementation of Event-Driven Lean Product Development includes three vital events, plus the use of Visual Workflow Management. A typical phase / gate structure is included in the figure to illustrate the approximate timing of the three Events relative to common gate-review milestones.

(see Chapter 4). This system will carry the team through the entire development process, up to and including launch to production.

I suggest that one final standard-work event be included in your first wave of implementation: the Design Review and Freeze Event (see Chapter 9). This meeting provides a rigorous structure for validating a design concept proposed by the development team, and should be held at least twice; once after a concept has been identified and rough prototypes have been tested, and again upon completion of the detailed design but prior to major capital investment (if possible). The precise timing of each design review will be discussed in Chapter 9, but the most important scheduling consideration is proactivity. It is wasteful to hold design reviews too late in the development process to make the necessary changes. I recommend holding design reviews a bit on the early side to allow time for fixes and improvements to be incorporated into the design without a negative impact on schedule.

These first three events, combined with Visual Workflow Management, represent a substantial step toward achieving an Event-Driven Lean Product Development process. Now it is time to catch your breath. Some suggestions for implementation are covered in the last chapter of this book, but one point is clear: Organizations take time to absorb change. It might require a year or more to institutionalize these first steps and gather feedback from teams on how well they work and what should be improved. Take your time! I once read an interview with a famous art collector who, over fifty years, had amassed one of the world's most valuable art collections. He was asked whether he had been born with a unique gift for identifying art that would someday become highly valuable. His response has stuck with me ever since: "At first, I was a complete idiot, and made terrible choices...but I got a little smarter every day." A patient and measured approach to organizational change will bring success faster and more reliably than an unrealistic push for dramatic change. Only after the above foundation is working well for you, should you consider moving on to the next major step in deploying Event-Driven Lean Product Development.

Step 2 – Close "Knowledge Gaps" Early in Development

In Step 2, we add only one more event to our process – but it is a game-changer. As discussed in the opening section of this chapter, much has been written about "knowledge-based development," wherein project teams focus their initial activities on mitigating technical risks and closing knowledge gaps prior to beginning any formal design effort. I recognize that this philosophy seems counterintuitive: How can spending more time at the front end of the development process lead to faster time-to-market? I've had highly respected clients balk at this concept, saying that they "just don't have time to build a foundation of knowledge and still stay ahead of the competition." In truth, it really doesn't make practical sense to stop everything and go into knowledge-building mode for a year or two. As with most idealistic philosophies, there is a purist's vision, and then there is a pragmatic reality. The Learning-Cycle Event shown in Figure 3.5 is designed to provide project teams with immediately useful knowledge that directly mitigates project risks, while enabling future projects to benefit from this captured knowledge. In this way, a firm can steadily evolve toward knowledge-based development, without sacrificing speed and competitiveness.

This still leaves the question of whether, on any given project, the use of the Learning-Cycle Event can actually accelerate the commercialization of a new product (for the Toyota perspective, see Ward (1995), and for a software point of view, see Poppendieck (2003), Schwaber, et al (2002), and Pichler (2010)). The answer depends on understanding risk. When a firm initiates a product development project, it is like a gambler at a blackjack table. It recognizes that there is the possibility of failure, but it weighs the risks and places its bet. If everything (and I mean *everything*) goes well, the project is completed on schedule, the cost of the new product is acceptable, and the sales volumes are all that the firm could hope for. Similarly, it is possible that you could have a streak of winning hands at the blackjack table, resulting in an early retirement. Neither situation is realistic, however. In most cases, risks will catch up with you and things will not go according to your optimistic plans. In new product development, a more likely scenario is that the first proto-type of a new product fails to meet requirements and must be iterated (perhaps several times), the production cost grows unexpectedly, and the sales volume falls short of forecasts. Although the probabilistic nature of product development cannot be avoided, many risks can be averted by front-end loading a serious risk-mitigation effort. This is exactly the purpose of the Learning-Cycle Event.

What if our gambler could take a peek at the blackjack dealer's hole card? It wouldn't guarantee that he would win every hand, but he would find himself with much better odds, and over time would no doubt walk away a winner. In the Learning-Cycle Event (see Chapter 7), a cross-functional project team proactively identifies knowledge gaps; critical technical, market, or process knowledge that is needed to design and commercialize the desired new product. This is facilitated by the output of the previous event, the Project Planning / Risk-Mitigation Event, wherein a prioritized list of project risks in each of these categories is generated. Based on this "learning plan," the team begins a series of short-duration learning cycles in which systematic problem-solving tools are employed, including A3-formatted knowledge briefs. Every few weeks, the team reconvenes to report on their progress and establish a plan for the next learning cycle. Once the team agrees that the most critical project risks have been mitigated and the associated learning has been well-documented, the project can proceed with a very high probability of success. As with every event, the needs of each individual project will dictate the number and duration of Learning-Cycle Events. For a low-risk project, this event might not be necessary at all. For a high-risk, complex project with multiple "death threats," several iterations of the event spanning one or more months might be appropriate.

Taking this next step in the implementation of Event-Driven Lean Product Development requires a leap of faith. It is difficult to get teams to hold back on the design of a product until knowledge gaps have been closed. Truisms such as "never enough time to do it right, but always enough time to do it over" may seem trite, but few of us can argue with their validity. Read Chapter 7 with an open mind and consider whether you can muster the discipline and patience within your organization to pilot this powerful event. It will change the nature of your development work, and ultimately lead to a solid foundation upon which your firm can build a sustainable competitive advantage.

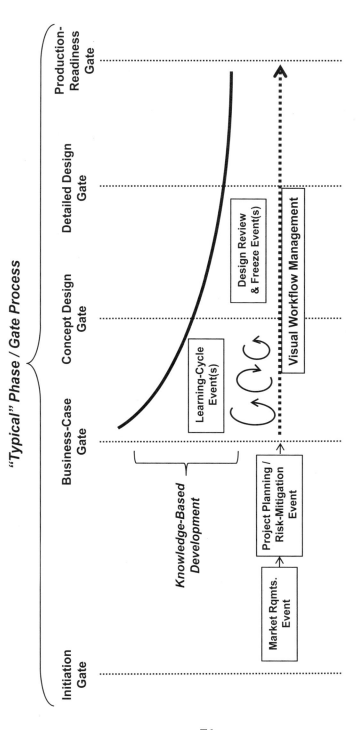

FIGURE 3.5: The next step in implementing an Event-Driven Lean Product Development process involves the inclusion of one or more Learning-Cycle Events. These problem-solving events are designed to mitigate technical (and other) risks, close knowledge gaps, and ultimately accelerate time-to-market.

Step 3 – Achieve Product and Process Co-development

The last step in the implementation of Event-Driven Lean Product Development addresses a painfully familiar problem; the timely consideration of the cost, quality, and manufacturability of a new product design. Clearly the right time to begin discussing these critical factors is during the very earliest stages of the development process. In fact, the production process for a new product should evolve in parallel with the design itself, with continuous communication and collaboration between the process and product design efforts. The ultimate goal should be true product and process co-development, as exemplified by Toyota's so-called Production Process Preparation (more familiarly known as "3P," see Morgan, et al (2006) and May (2007)). At Toyota, a dedicated team of process designers works in constant collaboration with the product design team, with neither group making any significant decisions without validation by the other. The result is a virtually seamless transition of a new product to rate production, without all the fits and starts that are common to traditional over-the-wall product launches.

All of this sounds great...if you have vast resources to draw from and only a few huge projects underway at any one time. If your firm develops commercial aircraft, for example, then the Toyota 3P model would work for you. However, most firms could not possibly dedicate a full-time team to production process development, and in fact may find it difficult to spring free a single manufacturing engineer to collaborate on each new development project. For this far more typical scenario, we must adapt the 3P ideal to work with scarce resources and multiple parallel design efforts. Over the past five years, I've worked with some great companies, both in the U.S. and in the E.U., to refine a three-event approach to 3P implementation that has been highly successful. These three events are timed to provide critical collaborative inputs throughout the development process, as shown in Figure 3.6. The first event, referred to as the Design 3P Event, focuses on innovative cost reduction and

FIGURE 3.6: The addition of three new events completes the picture of Event-Driven Lean Product Development. These so-called 3P events provide collaborative inputs on cost, quality, and manufacturability at critical points in the design process.

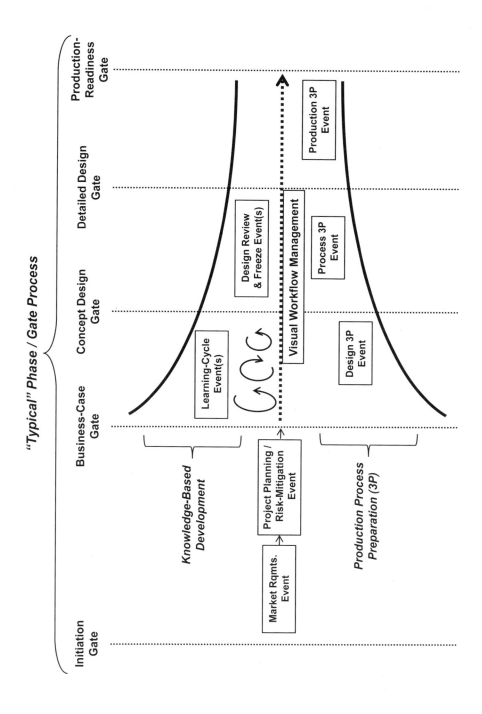

73

quality enhancement for the proposed new product, and is scheduled prior to finalization of a conceptual design. The emphasis here is on fundamental design architecture, functional analysis, simplification, and value engineering. Although a preliminary manufacturing plan is discussed at this event, detailed process design considerations are delayed until the next 3P event.

Once a conceptual design is finalized and detailed design is under-way, the Process 3P Event is held to begin serious production planning. Design opportunities are still addressed, through the use of Design for Manufacture and Assembly (DFMA) and Design for Six Sigma (DFSS). In this second event, however, the emphasis shifts to more of a 50 / 50 balance between product and process design. Value-stream maps are developed for the external supply chain and the internal manufacturing process. Initial capacity plans, *takt*-time estimates, and line / cell layouts are discussed. Finally, multiple alternatives are considered for critical assembly steps and those process steps that require significant capital investment.

The third opportunity for collaborative process development occurs near the end of the development cycle. The Production 3P Event is intended to finalize the layout of the factory, address any remaining incompatibilities between the product and process designs, and perform a "line *kaizen*" to validate and refine production flow. The outputs of the Production 3P Event is an assurance of production readiness, and approval to initiate pilot production. In combination, these three discrete 3P events provide much of the benefit of a Toyota-like 3P methodology, but with far less demand on scarce resources. With these final events in place, your firm will have achieved a full implementation of Event-Driven Lean Product Development. You can choose to rest on your laurels, or you can consider a last dramatic enhancement – the elimination of your now redundant phase / gate process, in favor of true continuous flow.

Advanced Topic: Transitioning from Gate-Controlled Governance to Continuous Flow

It is amazing to me how long it takes for great ideas to move from one arena of business to another. Diffusion of lean product development tools and methods, for example, is lagging behind lean manufacturing by at least a decade. Ten years may seem like a long delay, but how about fifty years? The concept of *exception management* dates from Deming's heyday in the 1960's, in the better-known form of Statistical Process Control (SPC). Just to refresh your memory, SPC was a breakthrough in production quality control that allowed significant reductions in testing and inspection, while achieving unprecedented quality. The basic concept is quite simple: Rather than performing in-line testing and inspection at each manufacturing process step, SPC requires that specific metrics of the process itself be continuously monitored. If these control variables stay within acceptable boundaries, the resulting products will be of acceptable quality. However, if any control variable drifts outside of its tolerance band, an exception is noted and immediate action is taken to bring the process back under control. In this methodology, no action is needed unless there is a well-defined exception. This simple concept has obvious ramifications for new product development, and after fifty years, it's about time that it takes center stage.

Imagine that at the initiation of a new product development project, a set of control variables was established that allowed continuous monitoring of the proposed product's business case. For example, based on the schedule sensitivity of the proposed product, a metric for acceptable schedule variance would be defined. As the project moves forward, the team leader would monitor this control variable by displaying schedule status on the team's visual project board (see Chapter 4). As long as the project stays within its tolerance band (e.g., within plus or minus two weeks of the planned project schedule), there would be no need for management involvement. If, however, an exception occurs (in this case, a slip in schedule of more than two weeks), then an ad hoc "gate meeting" would be called by management to review the situation and take remedial action. This same approach can also be used to continuously monitor cost and customer value, as shown in Figure 3.7. On the cost side, it might make sense to monitor deviations from the product's target unit production cost and / or the project team's non-recurring budget. To control for customer value, a list of "must-have" performance requirements and features could be defined that are essential for the new product's business case to remain valid (see Chapter 5). In each instance, if the project is within its predefined boundaries, no management intervention is warranted. Exceptions would trigger immediate action to bring the project back under control, or in the worst case, to suspend or cancel the project.

This concept is not as exotic as it sounds. Exception management has been successfully used for years in the realm of contract-based project management. In the aerospace and construction sectors, for example, schedule, budget, and deliverables are often tracked based on agreed-upon control limits, in some cases with penalty clauses in place to enforce these boundaries. What this system does require, however, is a change in behavior on the part of both team leaders and management. The project leader must keep a finger on the pulse of the project and report its health on a frequently updated basis (something that they should be doing anyway). Rather than being an onerous task, this reporting can be accomplished with surprising ease through the use of visual management techniques, as will be demonstrated in the next chapter. Management's role requires a more significant modification. In a typical phase / gate governance process, management sits back and waits until a gate review is held to make critical decisions about funding, resource allocation, and project direction. In the interim between gates, project status is still reported, but it is often treated as informational rather than action-inducing. This time-batching effect is wasteful, and places the burden on the team to "prove the worth"

FIGURE 3.7: New product development can benefit from an exception-based approach to process governance, similar to that used on the factory floor to monitor quality. Instead of time-batched gate reviews, several control variables are continuously tracked by the project team leader and compared to predetermined control limits. If the project stays within these limits, there is no need for a gate review. An exception, however, would trigger immediate management intervention.

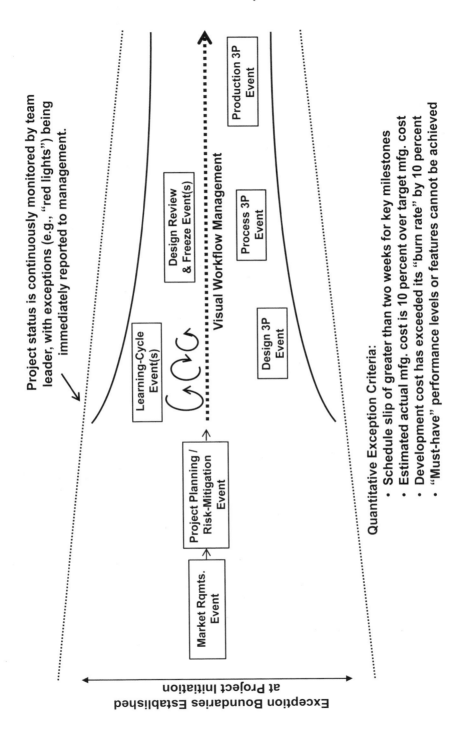

Project status is continuously monitored by team leader, with exceptions (e.g., "red lights") being immediately reported to management.

Learning-Cycle Event(s)

Design Review & Freeze Event(s)

Production 3P Event

Process 3P Event

Design 3P Event

Visual Workflow Management

Project Planning / Risk-Mitigation Event

Market Rqmts. Event

Exception Boundaries Established at Project Initiation

Quantitative Exception Criteria:

• Schedule slip of greater than two weeks for key milestones
• Estimated actual mfg. cost is 10 percent over target mfg. cost
• Development cost has exceeded its "burn rate" by 10 percent
• "Must-have" performance levels or features cannot be achieved

of their project at each gate. With exception-based process control, management must keep an eye on the competitive landscape (those business-case variables outside of the team's control), while trusting their project leaders to accurately assess and report on the health of their projects.

Indeed, this is a new mindset; one that requires higher levels of discipline and empowerment than a rigid and heavy-handed phase / gate process. The benefits, however, can make the effort worthwhile. Instead of following gate-review checklists, the team's focus is on meeting the input requirements of each successive event. The events themselves represent "knowledge gates," in that project teams are held accountable for achieving a successful outcome before being allowed to proceed to the next event. Without the distraction of gate reviews, project teams will benefit from a continuous flow of information and ideas, and optimize their schedules based on project-specific factors rather than on an arbitrary governance structure. Finally, the firm benefits from a more timely response to business-case threats than can be achieved with a time-batched gate process. If you find this concept tempting, you can implement a zero-risk form of this continuous-flow process: Retain your existing gate-control process while "test driving" exception management on the same project. Is the team leader maintaining her project board? Is the information sufficient to monitor the health of the project? Can management respond to an exception in a timely manner? Would decisions have been better, worse, or the same as with the current phase / gate structure? Using this piloting approach, the details of an exception-based methodology can be worked out without placing a project in jeopardy. With the risk of experimenting with this approach mitigated, what is stopping you from giving it a try? It is time for new product development to adopt the same level of discipline and efficiency as was accomplished on the factory floor half a century ago.

Chapter References

Beck, K., 2000, *Extreme Programming Explained*, Addison-Wesley.

Brown, T., 2009, *Change by Design*, HarperCollins.

Clark, K. B., and S. C. Wheelwright, 1993, *Managing New Product and Process Development*, The Free Press.

Cooper, R. G., 1993, *Winning at New Products – 2nd Edition*, Addison-Wesley.

Esslinger, H., 2009, *A Fine Line: How Design Strategies are Shaping the Future of Business*, John Wiley & Sons.

Fiore, C., 2005, *Accelerated Product Development*, Productivity Press.

Kennedy, M. N., 2003, *Product Development for the Lean Enterprise*, Oaklea Press.

Jackson, T. L., 1996, *Implementing a Lean Management System*, Productivity Press.

Mascitelli, R., 2002, *Building a Project-Driven Enterprise*, Technology Perspectives.

Mascitelli, R., 2007, *The Lean Product Development Guidebook*, Technology Perspectives.

May, M. E., 2007, *The Elegant Solution: Toyota's Formula for Mastering Innovation*, The Free Press.

McGrath, M. E., 1996, *Setting the PACE in Product Development*, Butterworth-Heinemann.

McGrath, M. E., 2004, *Next Generation Product Development*, McGraw-Hill.

Morgan, J. M., and J. K. Liker, 2006, *The Toyota Product Development System*, Productivity Press.

Nonaka, I., and H. Takeuchi, 1995, *The Knowledge Creating Company*, Oxford Press.

Pichler, R., 2010, *Agile Product Management With Scrum*, Addison-Wesley.

Poppendieck, M., and T. Poppendieck, 2003, *Lean Software Development: An Agile Toolkit*, Addison-Wesley.

Project Management Institute, 2008, *A Guide to the Project Management Body of Knowledge*.

Schab, L., 2008, *Faster, Better & Cheaper: Linking Practice to Successful Product Development Project Execution*, Doctorial Dissertation, Jesus College, Cambridge.

Schipper, T., and M. Swets, 2010, *Innovative Lean Development*, CRC Press.

Schwaber, K., and M. Beedle, 2002, *Agile Software Development With Scrum*, Prentice Hall.

Smith, P., 2007, *Flexible Product Development*, Jossey-Bass.

Ward, A. C., 2007, *Lean Product and Process Development*, The Lean Enterprise Institute.

Ward, A., et al, 1995, "The second toyota paradox: how delaying decisions can make better cars faster," *Sloan Management Review*, Vol. 36, No. 3.

Womack, J. P., and D. T. Jones, 2005, *Lean Solutions*, The Free Press.

4

Visual Workflow Management

Background and Overview

One of the questions that I am asked most frequently by clients who are interested in implementing lean product development is "where should we start?" Given the manifold forms of waste associated with new product development, deciding on a starting point for your lean journey can be difficult. In principle, your firm should begin as this book begins, with a highly effective project selection and prioritization process. From there, you would move through the chapters in the order they are presented. That is not, however, the way that I answer the above question. Instead, I tell my clients with absolute confidence: "Start by implementing Visual Workflow Management." There is no tool or method in my repertoire that has had greater success, both from the standpoint of impact on team performance and from the perspective of ease of implementation. Organizational change is a beast that feeds on success: Quick and highly visible wins are critical to building momentum and gaining credibility for any improvement initiative. Visual Workflow Management is quite simply the best place to begin your lean product development transformation.

The background for this methodology begins with the straightforward concept of stand-up meetings. In the early days of my career as a development team leader, I was assigned a high-risk technical project and provided with a team of brilliant scientists. Unfortunately, after several weeks of virtually no progress on my new project, I discovered that these clever folks had no idea how to be productive. Each Friday I held my obligatory team coordination meeting, statused my schedule, cajoled the team to get their act together, and was consistently disappointed. Then early one morning I took a walk through our factory and everything changed. As I was wandering the production line, I noticed a group of about twenty people clustered around a large whiteboard. Curious, I inserted myself into the group and observed what I later learned was a shift-change meeting. Ten minutes of intensive interaction, coupled with a detailed list of actions, issues, status, and progress, all updated and captured in real time on the whiteboard. After the meeting, I spoke with the shop foreman who had led the meeting and learned that this took place every single morning. Somewhat in desperation, I instituted a similar meeting with my team of unproductive scientists and the results were immediate and dramatic. Frequent, short-duration stand-up meetings created a sense of urgency, instilled positive peer pressure to be productive, enabled synchronization of work, allowed the rapid resolution of conflicts and issues, and much more. In the twenty-five years since those first meetings, my techniques have evolved and improved (see Mascitelli (2002) and (2007)), but the basic concept remains the same: Just-in-time management of a team's workflow is critical to maximizing productivity.

Actually, the use of frequent stand-up meetings is more common than you might think. Many restaurants and retail establishments hold brief staff meetings just prior to opening their doors each day. In law enforcement, a similar meeting is held to prepare patrol officers for their shift. The obvious sports analogy is the football huddle, which in rugby is called a "scrum." Interestingly, the term scrum has been adopted by agile programmers to describe their version of the stand-up meeting (see Pichler, et al (2010), Poppendieck (2003), and Schwaber (2002)), which is an integral part of this very successful methodology. In every case, the benefits are the same: In a rapidly changing environment, it is vital that team members frequently resynchronize their efforts, coordinate, communicate, and flexibly adapt to current conditions.

The stand-up meeting is actually only half of what I refer to as Visual Workflow Management, as shown in Figure 4.1. The other half is equally important; the use of a visual management tool to capture the current state of a team's activities and enable real-time planning of future actions. The concept of visual communication dates back to the dawn of history. Roman legions used color-coded banners to communicate orders across a vast and noisy battlefield. For centuries, ships at sea have employed signal flags to communicate under similarly challenging conditions. Much more recently, the idea of visual management became a core tool of the Toyota Production System, in the form of *andon* boards and visual *kanbans* (see Bicheno (2004) and (2009), Galsworth (1997), and Grief (1991)). Toyota and other Japanese firms subsequently adapted visual tools to the office workspace through the use of *obeya* rooms and boards (which are closely analogous to the "war rooms" used by major project teams for many decades, see Shinbum (1995)). In each instance, the use of colors, graphics, and symbology provides clear and unambiguous information that can be understood in a heartbeat.

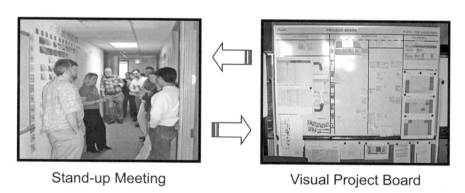

Stand-up Meeting   Visual Project Board

FIGURE 4.1: Visual Workflow Management consists of two techniques used synergistically. Stand-up meetings provide a forum for intensive exchange of information among team members, and encourage rapid resolution of issues and conflicts. When combined with a visual project board to capture status and facilitate near-term planning, a significant increase in team effectiveness and productivity can result.

In the sections that follow, I will describe an extensively tested and proven approach for implementing Visual Workflow Management.

As always, your own creativity must carry you beyond my generic methodology. However, I strongly recommend that you consider using my templates and guidelines as a low-risk starting point. Although my initial discussion will focus on the visual management of individual project teams, I will later extend this technique for use in a multi-project environment, and even into support groups and other value-creating resource pools. Visual Workflow Management is not just a product development tool; it will benefit any group of individuals who must work together as a team toward a common goal.

The Basics of Stand-up Meetings

The most important attribute of a successful stand-up coordination meeting is brevity. The purpose of this meeting is not to deep-dive into technical details. It is intended to answer three specific questions: what has the team accomplished since the last meeting, what actions must be completed by the next meeting, and what issues or obstacles might prevent the team from achieving those goals. I've found that fifteen minutes is an optimal duration. Keeping your stand-up meetings brief is vital to imparting a sense of urgency to your development team, and given the fact that participants are actually standing, fifteen minutes is about the limit of people's comfort. Maintaining this discipline can be a challenge, given the tendency of engineers and designers to go off on tangents. You must stand your ground: If you allow these meetings to be open-ended, you risk alienating the attendees and poisoning the waters for this highly beneficial tool. As trite as it may sound, I recommend that teams use a kitchen timer at first to condition team members to this short duration. Once the team has a sense of the pace required, the timer will become unnecessary, but someone should still keep an eye on their watch to make sure that your stand-up meeting doesn't turn into an endless dirge.

The timing of your meetings is also important, although there is more flexibility here. Getting the team together first thing in the morning is ideal, provided that the arrival times of attendees are not too far out of sync. If your firm has instituted "flex-time," for example, you may have to schedule your meetings just before lunch. Try to avoid holding stand-up meetings near the end of the day: There is little point in creating a sense of urgency as people are walking out the door. Location is arbitrary, and certainly not restricted to a conference room. As long as others in the vicinity will not be disturbed by the team's conversation, a hallway, large cubical, laboratory space, or even a break room will work perfectly well (note that once the visual project board is integrated into this methodology, some wall space will be required). Several firms that I've worked with have established dedicated rooms for their stand-up meetings, with multiple project teams sharing a common dedicated space (at different times, of course). A few have even installed chest-high conference tables to allow attendees to take notes without the need to sit down.

The most unusual attribute of stand-up coordination meetings is not their brevity, but rather their frequency. The primary goal of this communication tool is to break up the time batches caused by the typical weekly (or even twice monthly) team coordination meeting. If we think of coordination meetings as points of synchronization and alignment, then every day that passes before the next meeting increases the likelihood of team members drifting from the optimal path. Depending on the pace of the project and the criticality of team communication and collaboration, the rate of drift can vary considerably. However the probability of misunderstandings, missed opportunities to interact, delayed handoffs, indecision, and incorrect assumptions will steadily grow as the gap between coordination meetings increases, as shown in Figure 4.2.

The appropriate frequency for your team's stand-up meetings should be determined by answering a simple question: How rapidly do things change on this project? Information theory tells us that for communication to have value, it must contain something new, different, or unexpected. If your team members have little new information to share at their stand-up meetings, then they are being held too frequently. If a lot happens between meetings, and it is evident that communication and alignment opportunities have been missed, then the frequency should be increased. Even within the life of a single project, the frequency can (and should) change, depending on the pace of activity. During periods of intensive collaboration, such as prior to critical milestones, gate

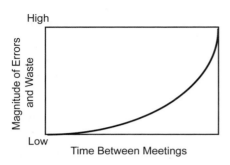
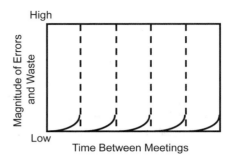

FIGURE 4.2: In any collaborative team activity, the greater the gap between coordination meetings, the higher the potential for errors and waste to occur. More frequent communication of status, progress, issues, and priorities will ensure team alignment, avoid schedule delays, and encourage a truly collaborative environment.

reviews, prototype tests, integration points, etc., the frequency of meetings should increase. Conversely, in lull periods where work is slowed by supplier delays, waiting for regulatory approvals, and so on, the frequency should be reduced. That being said, I've found that for most projects, holding stand-up meetings three times per week is about right, as shown in Figure 4.3. This allows enough time for significant work to be completed between meetings, but avoids the time-batching effects described above. Remember that stand-up meetings are a replacement for the usual weekly team get-together, so in principle, team members will spend less time attending three fifteen-minute stand-ups than they would spend in longer (and more boring) formal meetings.

The stand-up meeting represents a feedback and control system for your product development projects. In this context, the frequency of meetings determines the degree of control. Some real-world examples will make this abundantly clear. Returning to the analogy of a football huddle, imagine what would happen if the team coach decided on the plays for the entire game before the coin toss, and then just sat back and watched the game unfold. Of course this would result in a catastrophic loss. Instead, huddles occur after every play, enabling the team and coach to adjust their strategy based on their current situation. Likewise, imagine a car with a steering wheel that has a substantial delay between your steering action and the response of the front wheels. If you are

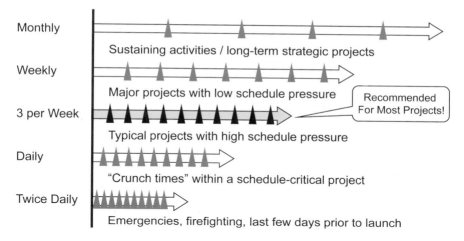

FIGURE 4.3: The frequency of stand-up meetings should be based on the pace of activity of a project. For a typical project, three times per week is sufficient to avoid time-batching effects, while still allowing enough work time between meetings for progress to be made.

driving on a straight and open highway, this might not be an immediate problem. However, on a winding road or in traffic, even a one-second delay would be potentially deadly. As the pace and urgency of a project increases, the need for rapid feedback becomes compelling, and the frequency of stand-up meetings should increase accordingly.

The specifics of what transpires during a stand-up meeting will be discussed in a later section, but one point must be made upfront: *this forum is owned by the team, not the team leader.* Initially, the team leader will have to provide the impetus. Getting people to show up on time, holding to the fifteen-minute duration, imparting a sense of urgency, and so on, will require leadership. However, once these meetings reach a steady state (typically after just a few weeks), the team leader should retire to a passive role, and only intercede when decisions are required, or to provide guidance as to priorities and direction. In fact, I strongly recommend that the facilitation of the meeting rotate among the team members, so that everyone has a chance to play this role. If stand-up meetings become little more than frequent flogging sessions by the team leader, you will have entirely missed the point. This tool is intended to encourage collaboration, overcome obstacles, and ultimately build the emotional commitment that is vital to a team behaving like a team. If properly instituted, the stand-up meeting will take on a life of its own. However, if team members do not recognize the benefits of their participation, it will never achieve its full potential.

A Proven Format for Visual Workflow Management

My first "visual project board" was nothing more than a flip-chart easel and a handwritten list of short-term tasks. From those humble beginnings, I've been evolving this tool for two decades, always mindful of the tradeoffs. If the visual board does not facilitate real-time statusing and planning of a project, then it fails to achieve its goals. On the other hand, if the board becomes so complex that it requires excessive time to maintain it, then we have created waste rather than reducing it. The format presented in this section is my current recommended approach, and can be adapted to virtually any development project. Again, the focus in this section will be on applying the tool to a single project: This technique will then be adapted to managing multiple small projects in a subsequent section.

The primary goal of a visual project board is to provide a "snapshot" of the status and progress of a project that is intuitively understandable to both the team members and upper management. For this tool to be useful as more than a wall-mounted status report, however, *interactivity* is essential. I want more from a project board than just information; I want engagement, commitment, and real-time issue resolution. The format illustrated in Figure 4.4 meets this broader goal successfully, and requires virtually no time to maintain. Before I discuss the details, however, it is worthwhile covering some of the logistics. First, I typically recommend that a four-foot-by-six-foot whiteboard be used for this display; plenty of room to cover all the bases, but still a manageable size. Smaller dimensions can certainly work, but avoid turning your visual board into an eye chart. Remember that the whole idea is to engage both the team and management in the flow of your project, so a board the size of a microfiche is not ideal. Location is arbitrary, but sufficient space must be available

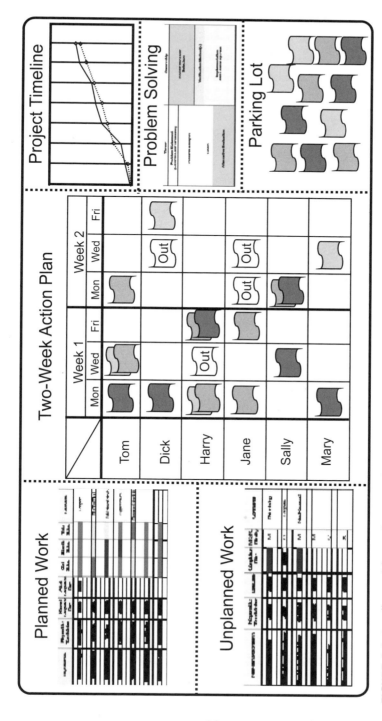

FIGURE 4.4: A well-tested format for a visual project board that captures the status, progress, and plans for a single development project. A multi-project version of this board will be discussed in a later section of this chapter.

for the team to hold their stand-up meetings. In the best of worlds, the board would be situated in close proximity to the team's cubicles, and in convenient view of management. Don't let the lack of physical space hold you back from implementing this tool. There are a number of innovative solutions to limited wall space, including sandwiched multi-boards (three overlapping boards that slide relative to each other), freestanding multi-boards, and even pull-down boards. Several virtual solutions are also possible (these options will be discussed in the final section of this chapter), but heed a word of warning. Visual Workflow Management is a *human engineering tool*: It depends on the physical interaction of the team with the board to achieve its maximum benefit. Use physical project boards whenever possible, and only resort to virtual solutions when logistics or other issues cannot be resolved in any other way.

Now for the details. The left-hand side of the visual board format shown in Figure 4.4 displays the upcoming work commitments of the project team. These commitments are divided into two categories: planned work and unplanned work. The planned-work template lists task milestones that are derived from the project master schedule (the creation of a suitable project schedule will be discussed in Chapter 6). In a perfect world, this planned-work section would be all that is necessary to guide the team toward success, but often this is not the case. The unplanned-work template shown at lower left is designed to capture unexpected tasks or action items that arise during the execution of the project. If unplanned work is of substantial scope, it should be folded into a replan of the project. Smaller activities that can be dispositioned in just a few days or weeks, however, would not warrant a replan, but must nonetheless be captured and integrated into the team's daily workflow. When combined, the two templates shown at left should represent the entire workload of a given project team. Note that if team members are committed to other projects as well, those demands would be captured on other visual boards, in such a way that there is no duplication or overlap among the boards. If sustaining factory support or other non-project resource demands are draining time from team members, a variation of this format will be described later that can make those conflicts visible.

Examples of a planned-work and unplanned-work template are shown in Figures 4.5 and 4.6. The planned-work template displays a

Progress Milestone	Responsible Team Member	Planned Completion Date	Actual Completion Date	Cost Status	Schedule Status	Tech. Status	Comments
Fabricate Prototype	David Copperfield	2/7/11	2/7/11	G	G	G	Complete
Prototype Testing	Oliver Twist	3/5/11		G	Y	Y	First Test Failed
Prototype Validated	Tiny Tim	4/14/11		R	R	Y	May Require Rework
Production Tooling	Charles Darney	4/24/11		G	R	G	Supplier Issues
Test Plan Complete	Sydney Carton	5/20/11		Y	Y	G	Resources Unavailable
Final Drawing Release	Lucy Mannette	6/17/11		G	G	G	
Fabricate Qual Units	Charles Dickens	7/14/11		G	G	G	

FIGURE 4.5: The upper left-hand section of the visual project board format shown in Figure 4.4 contains a template for planned project work. This template displays a two-month "magnified" view of the project's master schedule. I suggest using a spreadsheet rather than a Gantt chart to improve readability, and allow inclusion of red / yellow / green exception-statusing of individual tasks.

Unplanned Task or Action	Responsible Team Member	Due Date	Completion Date	Priority (H / M / L)	Comments
Diagnose Quality Problem	Jane M.	4/27/11	▓▓▓▓	H	Parts missing
Find New Supplier for Widget	Joe P.	5/1/11	5/8/11	L	Complete
Correct Circuit Simulation	Cedrick M.	5/1/11	▓▓▓▓	M	Need Resources!!
Refurbish Injection-Mold Tooling	Joline Q.	5/5/11		M	
Meet with Key Supplier	Harry P.	5/10/11		H	
Prepare for Customer Meeting	Dave N.	5/10/11		L	

FIGURE 4.6: Minor deviations from the project plan would not warrant a formal change to the project master schedule, but must nonetheless be visually captured and managed. The template shown above is just a typical action-item tracking sheet which can be used to monitor short-duration activities such as risk-mitigation tasks, minor changes to the product design, responses to management or customer requests, and so on. A red indicator is used to signal when a task on this list has missed its agreed-upon completion date. A priority column is provided to help the team focus their time.

two-month, rolling-window view of the project's milestones. The two-month window provides sufficient forward visibility for the team to plan their efforts, yet helps keep them focused on the actionable near term. I use a basic spreadsheet format with appropriate columns to capture the nature and ownership of each milestone, along with red / yellow / green visual status indicators. A Gantt chart would work here as well, but I've found that the task-list format is easier for team members to read, and allows more information to be presented (e.g., status, owner-ship, comments) than a typical bar-chart schedule. The granularity of tasks listed in the planned-work template depends to some degree on the duration of the project. Relatively short-duration projects, of say six months or less, should have a task milestone every week or so, on average. Longer-duration projects should have milestones every two to three weeks on average. As time moves forward on the project, the rolling window moves forward as well, acting essentially as a magnifying glass for the project's high-level master schedule. This level of granularity is important: For the project board to enable real-time planning, there must be a seamless connection among the high-level master schedule, the two-month rolling-window plan, and the center portion of the board, which will be described in the next section.

Since one of our lean goals for new product development is to institute exception management, the use of red / yellow / green status indicators is ideal. In this familiar scheme, a green color indicates that a specific task is meeting its goals, whether they are cost (typically referring to unit manufacturing cost), schedule, or technical performance. A yellow color represents a warning that the given task is entering dangerous waters. Finally, a red color signifies that the task has exceeded its exception boundaries, and deserves attention and possible intervention by management. For exception management to be effective, your color indicators should be defined as quantitatively as possible. For example, a red for cost could be defined as exceeding the product's target manufacturing cost by greater than 10 percent. A red for schedule might imply a critical-path schedule slip of more than two weeks, while a red for technical status would highlight a shortfall in some mandatory design requirement or feature. Your goal should be for this template to represent a self-contained management status report, and over time you should collaborate with upper management on its contents to avoid the need for any other statusing of the project.

The lower left-hand section of the project board contains a template for capturing unplanned work, as shown in Figure 4.6. This is critical to the success of Visual Workflow Management, since all work performed by the team on the development project must be managed through this board. Any stray tasks or minor distractions will create turbulence to the flow of a project, and must be visually managed to minimize disruptions to planned work. The suggested template is just a typical action-item list, with ownership, due date, etc., explicitly shown for each task. The type of activities that might populate this template include minor task modifications (e.g., running a retest of a prototype, making a small change to a design element, deviations from normal procedures, and so on), along with actions required to reduce risk, or accommodate management or customer requests. Rather than dignify these quick-hit activities with full statusing, I simply use a red indicator for tasks that have missed their agreed-upon completion date. When combined with the planned-work template, all project work should now be clearly documented for both the team and upper management, and will be dispositioned using an interactive short-term planning tool as shown in Figure 4.7.

The heart of the visual project board is the center section – an interactive extravaganza of colored sticky notes. Before we delve into this powerful, but somewhat unusual tool, let's consider what should be included on the right-hand side of the board. This area is much more flexible than the left and center sections, and is a great place for you to inject your own preferences, or integrate the requests and feedback from your project team. I'll provide you with some suggestions, but feel free to improvise. The first element that I recommend is a visual representation of the overall project schedule, with a focus on the critical path. The format that I've found to be most successful is the "snake diagram" shown in Figure 4.8. The two curves that make up the snake diagram represent the planned and the actual completion dates for critical-path project milestones. Note that every milestone on the project schedule should not be included here; just major progress points that are unambiguous indictors of schedule fidelity. Since the y-axis of the graph represents time, the vertical separation between the two curves at any milestone is an indicator of how far the project is ahead of or behind schedule. Ideally, the two curves would lie on top of each other, but of course this is rarely the case. Hence, when the vertical separation (i.e., the schedule variance) becomes significant, this should raise a big red flag that remedial action must be taken immediately. There are two advantages of this graphical format. The first is its understandability. I've personally created hundreds of Gantt charts, and I still find them cumbersome to interpret. Of course software helps, but that requires an understanding of project management tools that a typical team member will likely not possess. The snake diagram can be understood by everyone from management to a machine-shop foreman with little or no explanation. The second advantage is unique to this graphical format: You can easily determine the approximate slope of the two curves at any point throughout the project. If the slopes are substantially different (most often in a bad way), this tells the team leader that there is something fundamentally wrong. For this to be the case, either the resource-loading on the project is inadequate, the

Two-Week Action Plan

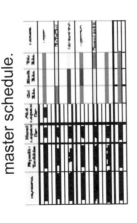

	Week 1				Week 2		
	Mon	Wed	Fri		Mon	Wed	Fri
Tom							
Dick						Out	
Harry	Out						
Jane							
Sally					Out	Out	
Mary							

Planned Work: Scheduled key milestones based on project master schedule.

Unplanned Work: Unscheduled tasks, including sustaining support, problem-solving, fire-fighting, etc.

FIGURE 4.7: The left-hand side of the visual project board provides a feed of both planned and unplanned tasks to the center section, referred to as a "wall-Gantt." This powerful workflow management technique will be described in the next section.

95

scope of work is greater than originally assumed, or some other system-atic problem exists. If this situation occurs, either a significant correction should be made to project staffing, or a replan should be initiated to adjust the end-date of the project.

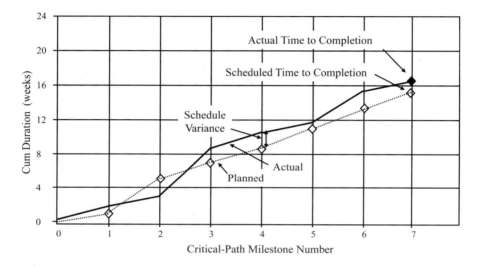

FIGURE 4.8: This so-called snake diagram is an excellent way to visually display high-level schedule status. The two curves represent the planned and actual progress toward project completion. The vertical separation between the two curves indi-cates the schedule variance of the project at any given milestone. If the curves are consistently different in slope, this should be taken as a warning that something is fundamentally wrong with the current project plan, and additional resources or other remedies should be immediately implemented.

I generally include two additional sections on the right-hand side of my visual project boards. The first is a place to display A3-formatted "knowledge briefs" that have been created by the team throughout the duration of the project. These problem-solving briefs capture solutions to critical technical (and other) issues, and form a knowledge base for future projects as well. The creation of these knowledge briefs will be described in detail in Chapter 7. The final section that I recommend is simply a parking lot for open issues. This can be nothing more than a blank space on the project board, where open issues written on sticky notes are placed as they arise. This parking lot is available 24 / 7 to project team members, so that if an issue arises between stand-up meetings, it can be captured for disposition at the next meeting. Beyond these recommended sections, anything is possible. You can add any information to your project board that you feel will benefit the team, provided that clutter doesn't obscure the vital information needed to effectively manage workflow. Keep in mind one of my favorite quotes from Cicero: "The purpose of communication is not to be understood, it is to make it impossible to be misunderstood."

Interactive Management of Daily Workflow Using the Wall-Gantt

At last we have arrived at the most interesting and powerful element of the visual project board; the so-called wall-Gantt shown in Figure 4.9. This tool is designed to engage the team in the real-time planning of near-term activities, and encourage ownership and accountability by team members. Again I use a rolling-window view of project activities, but this time the magnification is increased such that only a two-week interval is displayed at any given time. A horizontal row is provided for each project team member who is actively involved in value creation. The number of vertical columns is determined by the frequency of the team's stand-up meetings; one column for each meeting day spanning a two-week period. Finally, a column is provided on the far right for "Week 3+" to allow for overflow tasks that extend past the two-week window, but are integral to the current plan. At the intersection between each row and column is a box that is slightly larger than a standard sticky note.

The wall-Gantt is populated with sticky notes, written and placed by the team members themselves. Each note describes a near-term task or achievement that must be accomplished by a given team member during the two-week period, as shown in Figure 4.10. These are not intended to be formal milestones, but rather informal progress points necessary for the completion of the significant tasks listed on either the planned- or

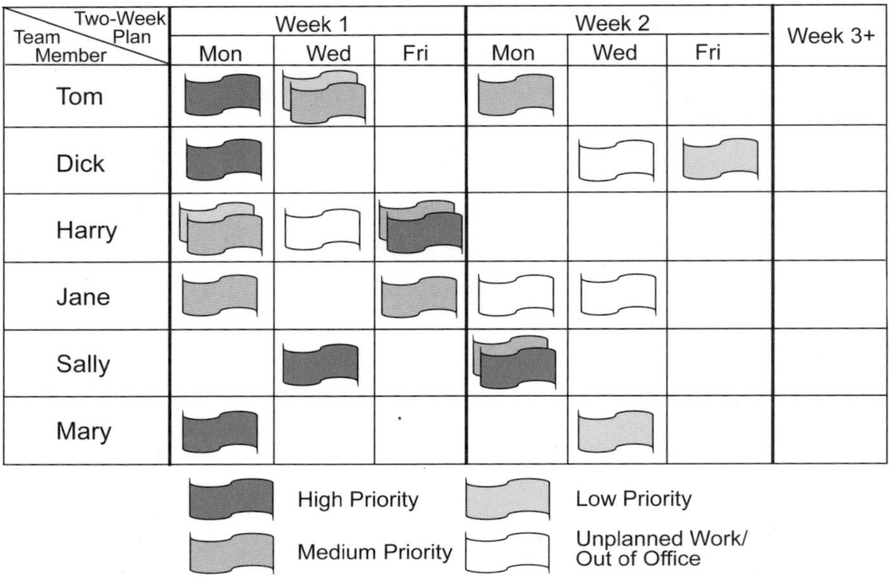

Team Member / Two-Week Plan	Week 1			Week 2			Week 3+
	Mon	Wed	Fri	Mon	Wed	Fri	
Tom	High Priority	Low Priority		High Priority			
Dick	High Priority				Unplanned Work/Out of Office	Low Priority	
Harry	Low Priority	Unplanned Work/Out of Office	High Priority				
Jane	Low Priority		High Priority	Unplanned Work/Out of Office	Unplanned Work/Out of Office		
Sally		High Priority		High Priority			
Mary	High Priority				Low Priority		

Legend:
- High Priority (dark)
- Medium Priority (dark)
- Low Priority (light gray)
- Unplanned Work/Out of Office (outline)

FIGURE 4.9: The wall-Gantt represents a two-week snapshot of a project team's planned activities. Each sticky note captures a near-term progress point toward achieving a major project milestone. For this tool to be effective, the sticky notes must be written and placed by the team members themselves, thereby representing a commitment to accomplish a given task by a specific date.

unplanned-work templates. The granularity is somewhat arbitrary, but I like to see at least one sticky note per week for each team member, with two or three being more typical. In every case, the completion date of the task described on a note must be in alignment with higher-level milestones. In this way, the wall-Gantt captures commitments by the team over a two-week period which will ensure that the project remains on schedule. Basically, the wall-Gantt is a tool that is owned by the team, and represents its response to the challenges presented in the planned- and unplanned-work templates. The only time that the team leader (or management) needs to become involved is if it is clear that the team's two-week plan does not lead to major project milestones being completed on schedule.

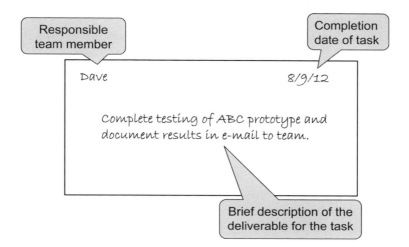

FIGURE 4.10: The sticky notes that populate a wall-Gantt should include the name of the person responsible for the task, the date that the task will be completed, and a brief description of the deliverable for the task involved.

One of the advantages of using sticky notes is the huge range of available colors. For the single-project version of the wall-Gantt shown in Figure 4.9, we can use color to denote the priority of a given task or activity. A red sticky note can be used for the highest-priority activities, and in particular for work along the project's critical path. Yellow sticky notes indicate a moderate level of priority; important, but not yet schedule-critical. Finally, those tasks that have significant slack-time, and hence can slip somewhat without risk to the project, are indicated by green notes. I've found that other colors can be useful as well, such as defining a blue sticky note to indicate either "out of office" or that a task represents unplanned versus planned work. Use your imagination; there are a lot of colors available and each can be used to communicate a different category or type of work.

To bring Visual Workflow Management to life, we must understand how a project team interacts with the project board. I will use the team members listed in Figure 4.9 to illustrate the flow of a typical stand-up meeting, and show how the board is updated in real time. Let's assume that Mary is the team leader for a mythical project (note that the team leader should always have a row on the wall-Gantt). It's 8:00 a.m. on a Monday morning, and the team has gathered around their visual project board. Mary calls the meeting to order, and begins by asking Tom (the first team member listed on the wall-Gantt) to provide his input. Tom comes up to the board and briefly describes the work he has accomplished since the last meeting. If he has completed the task posted in the Monday column corresponding to his name, then he removes the sticky note and hands it to Mary (what the team leader does with removed sticky notes will be explained in the final section of this chapter). If, however, the task is not complete, he must move it to a later date in his row. If the task moves, Tom lines through the original completion date and writes the new completion date below it. Once he describes his current status, Tom will then share with the team his plans for the next few days. If a new task is involved (one that is not already posted in Tom's row), he creates a sticky note for that activity and places it on the date that the task will be completed. Note that the priority level of the sticky note is Tom's decision, but feedback from the team and team leader will influence this choice. Finally, Tom will share with the team any issues or problems that might prevent him from meeting his commitments. At this point, the team and leader will briefly discuss these issues, and determine if they can help. After about a minute or two with Tom having the floor, Mary will call on the next person listed on the wall-Gantt and they will approach the board for their time in the spotlight. So it goes until all team members, including Mary as last on the list, have had their turn. Once all have spoken, Mary may share some final comments, and the meeting adjourns.

A few procedural notes should be considered. First, it is important that once the stand-up meeting is completed, the entire column for that day has been cleared. Each team member has three options: they can pull the note because that task has been completed, they can move the note to a later date in their row, or they can ask for help from the team and possibly move the note to someone else's row. In the latter case, the original name on the note would be lined through, and the new responsible team member's name would be added. Second, although there is no hard rule regarding how many people can attend a stand-up meeting, from a practical standpoint the group should be restricted to no more than ten to twelve people. Any larger and the time allowed per person will not be adequate, and the duration of the meeting will inevitably grow beyond the fifteen-minute limit. Third, it is very likely that issues will arise during someone's turn that will cause discussion and debate to occur. While this ad hoc collaboration can be very valuable (indeed it is one of the advantages of frequent meetings), it should be "parked" until everyone on the team has given their status update. Once everyone has had their turn, the team leader can allow detailed discussions to continue for those interested in the topics, while everyone else can get back to work. Ad hoc discussions are not subject to the fifteen-minute time limit, and can continue indefinitely, provided that all uninvolved parties are allowed to leave. Finally, it is critical that the wall-Gantt not be modified between stand-up meetings. It might be tempting for a team member to pull their sticky note as soon as their task is complete (or possibly move a sticky note because they know they will be late). This must be avoided; if the team is not aware of changes to the wall-Gantt, the vital synchronization of team workflow may be jeopardized. Although Tom, for example, may be perfectly comfortable with moving his task note to a later date, others on the team may be counting on his output to allow their own work to proceed. If they are not aware of the move, their own work schedules may be negatively impacted.

Beyond these basic rules, your own experience will be the best guide. Ask the team for feedback after a week or two of stand-up meetings, and be a good listener. A few minor tweaks to format or procedures can make all the difference in the successful implementation of this methodology. Although the format I recommend is only a starting point, it has proven to be successful under many different work conditions. A fine example of a single-project visual board is shown in Figure 4.11 as a guide to the creation of your own masterpiece.

FIGURE 4.11: A well-crafted example of a single-project visual board. Note that the recommended format is closely followed in this example, with all elements described in this section represented.

Variation on a Theme: The Multi-Project Visual Board

If your firm's product development projects are of a substantial scale, then each new effort might warrant its own dedicated visual board. On the other hand, if either the number (too many) or scale (too small) of the projects you deal with renders single-project boards impractical, there is a straightforward alternative. With just two easy modifications, you can convert the single-project-board format discussed in the previous section into a multi-project board capable of tracking a dozen or more separate development activities in one concise location. I'll first describe these changes, and then discuss how a multi-project board functions in practice.

For a visual project board to represent a multi-project environment, the left side of the board (i.e., the side that feeds work into the central wall-Gantt) must capture status and upcoming milestones for several distinct projects. In principle, you could just stack up a number of single-project status sheets (representing both planned and unplanned work), with one sheet for each of the projects included on your board. This might make sense if you only need to manage a few activities, but would become unwieldy as the number grows. Instead (or in addition), you can use a "project cadence tool" to illustrate multi-project status, such as the one shown in Figure 4.12. In this template, several distinct projects are listed along the left-hand column. For each project, a kickoff date and planned completion date are displayed, along with a single "progress bar." The progress bar is intended to communicate the high-level schedule status of each project, relative to a standard set of milestones that all projects must complete. The exact nature of these standard milestones will vary depending on the types of projects represented, but a generic list is provided at the bottom of the figure for your reference. The bar extends to the most recently achieved milestone, thereby indicating status relative to project completion. Along each bar, I typically show the planned date (above the bar), and add the actual completion date (below the bar) as the milestones are completed. Finally, I use a single color-coded circle to the right of the bar in each row to show the general status of the project relative to cost, schedule, or performance. If you want to get fancy, you can use symbols of different shapes to indicate each of these three metrics separately, or just lump them together as I have done by displaying a single red / yellow / green status symbol.

The best thing about this tool is the time scale along the top… there isn't one. More precisely, time is represented by the milestones achieved, not by weeks or months on the calendar. This normalization trick allows projects of varying durations, start dates, and end-dates to all be illustrated on a single graph. You can effectively represent a two-month-duration project and a two-year-duration project on the same cadence chart with no loss of clarity. Another advantage is that there is no limit to the number of projects you can simultaneously track using this tool. In the past, I worked with a major apparel manufacturer that used a cadence tool such as this to manage dozens of running-shoe designs at one time. The only rule is that the projects represented must all align with a common set of predetermined milestones (or at least most of them, since you can waive a milestone or two without much confusion). This is actually quite easy; just think generically about your development process and identify a set (ten or twelve is a nice number) of serial milestones that occur on virtually every project. Although the cadence tool doesn't allow for the same level of detail as a single-project status template, it still provides a feed of planned work to the wall-Gantt. If more detail is required, you can include a supplemental status / action template for each project, and use the cadence tool to view the big picture. Incidentally, for unplanned work (i.e., the lower-left section of my standard project-board format), I use a combined action-tracking sheet for all projects, with an added column to indicate which project is associated with each action.

The other modification required to transition from a single-project to a multi-project visual board is the structure of the wall-Gantt itself, as shown in Figure 4.13. This is surprisingly easy. By defining a different sticky-note color for each project, you can display the tasks for up to a dozen simultaneous projects on your wall-Gantt. Although this might seem like visual overload, in practice it is quite simple to follow the thread of any one project by just focusing on the appropriate color. The only thing that is lost in this technicolor scheme is the ability to indicate the priority of each task. This can be achieved by using red sticky dots to indicate high-priority activities (yellow and green dots can be used as well, if your esthetic sensibilities allow). In fact, you can transform a single-project wall-Gantt into a multi-project one with no effort at all; just change the convention you use for sticky-note colors, and you are off and running. A particularly well-crafted multi-project visual board is illustrated in Figure 4.14. In this case, the cadence tool is shown as a separate board on the left, and provides a color key for the sticky notes on the multi-project wall-Gantt on the right.

FIGURE 4.12: The project cadence tool allows the display of multiple projects of varying durations and schedules on a single template. By using a time scale that is normalized to a standard set of project milestones, the status of all projects can be illustrated in a concise manner. Note that planned completion dates for each project's milestones are shown above the bar, and actual completion dates are shown below. To avoid clutter in this figure, only the last set of dates for each bar is shown.

Project Designation	Kickoff Date	Milestone Number								Completion Date	
		1	2	3	4	5	6	7	8	Planned	Est. Actual
Project 1	1/2/11			Y	■ 10/1/11	R				1/2/12	6/5/12
					11/20/11						
Project 2	3/5/10		■ 9/24/10							3/5/12	3/5/12
			10/5/10								
Project 3	2/5/10						■ 7/1/10	R		10/5/11	5/13/12
							9/20/10				
Project 4	5/2/10	■ 11/1/10	G							8/19/11	8/19/11
		11/1/10									
Other?	10/3/10							■ 10/1/11	Y	5/13/12	5/13/12
								11/20/11			

Planned

Actual

Key Milestone Definitions:

1. Engineering Spec Complete
2. Conceptual Design Review / Approval
3. Prototype Performance Validated
4. Drawing Pkg. Rev. 0 Released
5. Critical Design Review / Approval
6. Long-Lead Items Ordered
7. Qualification Testing Complete / Approval
8. Release to Production

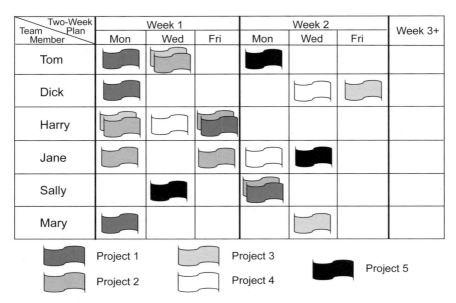

FIGURE 4.13: A multi-project version of the wall-Gantt is almost identical to the single-project format, except for the colors of the sticky notes. In this case, multiple colors are used to indicate the various projects included on the board. The priority of each task can be communicated by using a red sticky dot to indicate high priority, yellow for moderate, and so on.

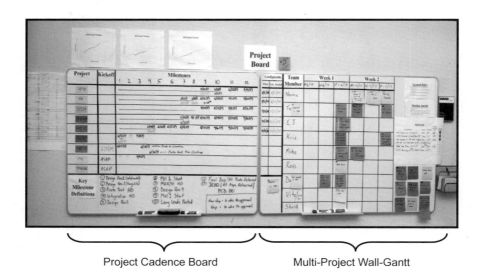

FIGURE 4.14: A fine example of a multi-project visual board. At left, the cadence tool is presented as a separate board, with each project color-coded to serve as a legend for the multi-project wall-Gantt shown at right.

106

There are two general modes in which the multi-project board can be used to visually manage workflow. In the first scenario, several separate project teams use the board at different times to conduct their stand-up meetings, with each team focusing on their associated color. This would be the preferred mode when the membership of the various project teams has very little overlap. In a sense, each team uses the tool as a single-project board, and ignores the other projects represented. More commonly, there is significant overlap in the membership of the project teams represented on the board. This is often the situation in smaller firms or business units that have a single pool of developers that must handle all new product development work. When this occurs, the resource pool would hold a single, multi-project stand-up meeting, and discuss all projects at once. Actually, this is not as overwhelming as it sounds, since each team member still updates his or her two-week planned activities at the same level of detail as they would for a single-project meeting. The only difference is that their work will be dispersed among a number of separate efforts, instead of being directed toward a single, larger project. This latter case is where the multi-project board can represent the difference between sanity and chaos. Just making the workload of a multi-project resource pool visible will be a major step forward. Add to that the ability to allocate these shared resources dynamically and flexibly to meet the disparate needs of multiple projects, and you have converted a nightmare situation into a manageable plan for success.

Advanced Topic: Team Metrics and the Virtual Project Board

You might have been wondering, "What do I do with all the sticky notes that come off of my wall-Gantt?" Naturally, recycling is always an option, but with just a small effort by the team leader, some powerful team performance metrics can be generated using those notes. All that is needed is a three-ring binder filled with blank sheets of paper. At the beginning of each stand-up meeting, the team leader writes the date at the top of a blank sheet, and draws a line running down the center of the page. As the meeting progresses, whenever a sticky note is pulled from the board, the team leader pastes it onto that page. If the associated task was completed on schedule, it is placed to the left of the center line, whereas if the task slipped one or more times, it is placed on the right-hand side. Thus, with little more than a few minutes of time invested on a weekly basis, the team leader can gain some valuable insight into his team's on-time performance. Depending on how the team defines the colors of their notes, either one or both of the graphs shown in Figure 4.15 can be generated. With just the basic red / yellow / green priority indicators, and a record of how many times a task has slipped (i.e., the lined-through dates on the upper-right corner of a note), you can create the chart shown at left. This histogram displays the frequency of occurrence of slipped tasks, allowing both the team and leader to determine the percentage of on-time task completions, and the number and severity of slipped tasks. By updating this histogram weekly, the team will have a metric that will help them focus on completing their tasks on schedule.

By defining some additional colors (beyond red / yellow / green) for your sticky notes, even more can be learned. Suppose that the team leader defines a separate color for each type of non-project-related activity that is consuming the team's time and capacity. When team members are pulled away from project work to do sustaining support, proposals, special orders, etc., they place an appropriately colored sticky note for those activities on the wall-Gantt. Upon completion, the notes go into the loose-leaf notebook. Periodically, the team leader can count the number and type of occurrences, and plot the results as shown on the right of Figure 4.15. This chart can be invaluable in identifying the magnitude of resource conflicts between project and non-project work, and can help the team identify remedial actions to reduce or eliminate these drains on resources. With just a little creativity and cooperation, a project team can design its own wall-Gantt-based metrics system with almost no added work for either the team leader or its members.

There remains a last critical topic to discuss: How does Visual Workflow Management work when a product development team is geographically dispersed? It is fine to consider the ideal situation of a

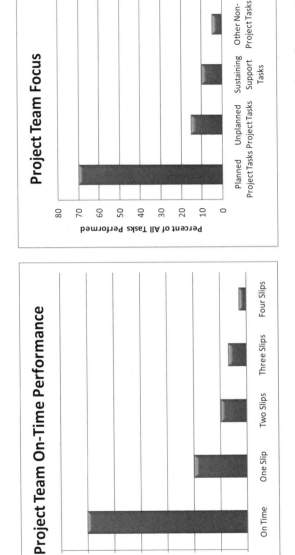

FIGURE 4.15: The above graphs display valuable team performance data which can be derived from the use of a wall-Gantt. As sticky notes are removed from the project board, they are placed into a loose-leaf notebook. Depending on how the colors of notes are defined, and the categories into which they are grouped after completion, a wide range of metrics can be tracked with virtually no additional time spent by either the team or the team leader.

collocated team with plenty of wall space for their visual board, but the reality of most project teams is that developers may be spread out over several time zones, and may also include outside contractors and key suppliers. Clearly a physical project board and stand-up meeting cannot service the needs of such a virtual team. Fortunately, many of the benefits of a physical implementation of Visual Workflow Management can be achieved using a customized virtual tool such as the one shown in Figure 4.16. In this case, a template was created in Visio that looks as much as possible like a physical wall-Gantt. A set of drag-and-drop stencils are available on the left side of the template for use by the team during their virtual stand-up meetings. To allow real-time interaction with this tool, stand-up meetings can be held using on-line webcast applications such as those available through GoToMeeting.com. In this way, each team member can interact with a common Visio template, and make their modifications (i.e., move, add, or remove sticky notes) in real time.

A virtual stand-up meeting should be facilitated in the same way as a collocated one. All team members log into GoToMeeting at the appropriate time, and as each takes their turn, they drag sticky-note icons to appropriate squares on the template and fill them out in the usual manner. If a task is complete, it is dragged to a "finished-tasks" section of the template for later disposition by the team leader. Once the meeting is over, it is possible to print out a physical copy of the template to post on the wall at all involved locations, if this is considered desirable. Otherwise, the virtual version should be posted on a team SharePoint site (or equivalent intranet site) so that all members can view the current version of the project board at any time.

Although this virtual approach comes as close as possible to approximating a physical implementation of a visual project board, a few words of caution are needed. First, there is no substitute for the personal interaction of team members with the wall-Gantt, whether real

FIGURE 4.16: An excellent example of an interactive "virtual project board." In this case, a Visio template has been used to create a realistic representation of a physical wall-Gantt. Through the use of interactive webcast applications, a geographically-dispersed team can update this template in real time, thereby capturing many of the benefits of having a collocated team and a physical project board.

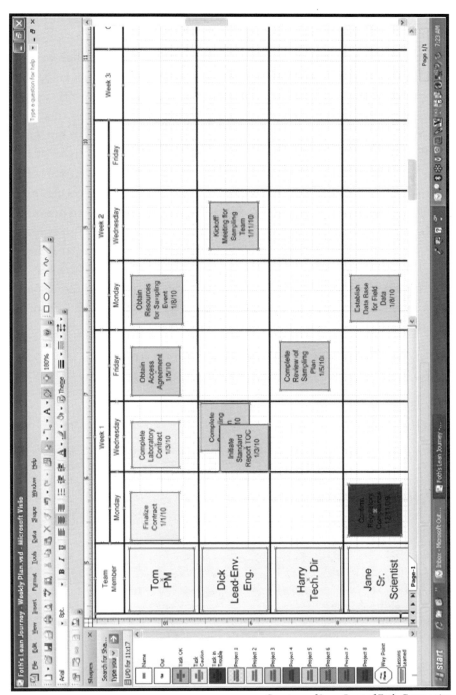

Courtesy of Jerry Berg of Foth Companies

or virtual. Just because the tool is in cyberspace, doesn't change human nature. Team members need to move and fill out their own "sticky notes" on the virtual template. If this is not enabled and enforced, much of the commitment and accountability that is the hallmark of visual management may be lost. Second, don't fall into the trap of "since we are going virtual anyway, let's just use an action list in SharePoint instead of a graphically-accurate project board." Action lists are better than nothing, but they don't come close to matching the clarity and interactivity of a wall-Gantt. Finally, use the virtual wall-Gantt sparingly, and only when a physical project board is just not possible. Gathering a project team together several times per week for face-to-face discussion and planning has benefits at many levels, not the least of which is the building of team identity and emotional commitment. As hard to define as they may be, a great team leader recognizes these intangibles, and makes the most of them whenever possible. A virtual project board may be easy, but having team members see each other face-to-face is the most powerful "visual" management tool there is.

Chapter References

Bicheno, J., 2004, *The New Lean Toolbox: Towards Fast, Flexible Flow*, PICSIE Books.

Bicheno, J., and M. Holweg, 2009, *The Lean Toolbox, 4th Edition*, PICSIE Books.

Galsworth, G. D., 1997, *Visual Systems: Harnessing the Power of a Visual Workplace*, American Management Association.

Grief, M., 1991, *The Visual Factory: Building Participation Through Shared Information*, Productivity Press.

Mascitelli, R., 2002, *Building a Project-Driven Enterprise*, Technology Perspectives.

Mascitelli, R., 2007, *The Lean Product Development Guidebook*, Technology Perspectives.

Pichler, R., 2010, *Agile Product Management With Scrum*, Addison-Wesley.

Poppendieck, M., and T. Poppendieck, 2003, *Lean Software Development: An Agile Toolkit*, Addison-Wesley.

Schwaber, K., and M. Beedle, 2002, *Agile Software Development With Scrum*, Prentice Hall.

Sekine, K., and K. Arai, 1994, *Design Team Revolution*, Productivity Press.

Shimbun, N. K., 1995, *Visual Control Systems*, Productivity Press.

Tufte, E. R., 1983, *The Visual Display of Quantitative Information*, Graphics Press.

Tufte, E. R., 1990, *Envisioning Information*, Graphics Press.

5

The Market Requirements Event

Background and Overview

The remaining chapters in this book describe the various LPD Events that constitute a lean product development process. Each chapter is modular and self-contained; you can read and implement one at a time, or take in the entire picture and then determine the best order for deployment in your firm. That being said, the Market Requirements Event is so fundamental to the success of any development project that it should be elevated in priority above the rest. In this first event, the needs of the marketplace are translated into high-level design requirements, and the key differentiators that will determine the success of your business case are clearly identified. Of equal importance is the communication of a common vision for the new product: All critical functions will be aligned toward the same goal with the same well-defined scope of work.

In recent years, I've become frustrated with the mystery that surrounds the so-called fuzzy front-end of new product development (for several perspectives, see Belliveau, et al (2002)). It is just a process, like any other, with steps to follow and tools to use. The fuzziness is a result of a lack of information to feed the process, not due to the process itself. Hence, it is worthwhile spending some time considering

113

how markets react to new product introductions, and in particular, how customers determine which products to purchase and how much to pay. While this knowledge will not guarantee success, it will help your organization focus its information-gathering efforts in preparation for the Market Requirements Event, and hopefully eliminate some of the fear factor.

Let's begin at the beginning. Customers pay for solutions to problems. If you cannot define the problem(s) that your new product solves, then you shouldn't initiate a development project. As obvious as this might seem, there are countless new products introduced every year that are nothing more than polished versions of previously available solutions. While this might be an easy road to take, it is not the path to high margins and increased market share. The problem that your new product solves may be of a practical nature (e.g., a new machine tool that can hold tighter tolerances with increased throughput), or somewhat more frivolous (e.g., a great handbag to complement a new dress). In every case, the amount of money that will change hands is determined by two factors: the importance of the problem to a customer's well-being, and the degree to which they are satisfied with currently available solutions. If a customer does not perceive that they have a problem, or if the problem you are solving is unimportant to them, they will not pay. Likewise, if customers are satisfied with currently available solutions, your new product won't raise an eyebrow. Successful new products close the gap between what's available and what is desired. If there is no gap, then there is no opportunity, other than to provide the current solution at a lower price (i.e., the market for your new product has become commoditized).

It is a fortunate company that has customers pounding on their doors demanding specific solutions to their very important problems. In rapidly changing markets, this is often the case. It didn't take a marketing genius to recognize that a faster microprocessor was a good idea back in the 1980's, or that a car with exceptional gas mileage would be a success at the time of this writing. Unfortunately, if a problem is so obvious that a solution would be a "sure thing," then every company on the planet is in a race to make that easy money. The true art of new product development is in the identification of *unarticulated needs*: Customers may not know that they have a problem until they see the solution, whereupon they reevaluate their current level of well-being and decide to open their wallets (see Leonard-Barton (1995)). What this implies is that you have some control over how your product will be *perceived*... and this is truly the operative word. Customers do not calculate the value of a new product in some objective and analytical way, they perceive value, using all five of their senses, and both halves of their brains. If an obvious problem does not exist in your marketplace, then it is up to you to craft your customer's perceptions such that they recognize they have a problem, and are (or should be) dissatisfied with currently available solutions. I'm fairly sure that few people realized that they had "restless-leg syndrome" before television ads made it clear that a twitching leg represents a malady that warrants prescription drug treatment. Similarly, (and without the need for hypochondria) we all managed to get by with land lines until mobile communication became available, at which time we completely changed our perception of needs and well-being to a degree that could never have been fully anticipated.

Since perception is the key to unlocking new market opportunities, we must understand how customers react to various attributes of a product. The four categories of perceived value listed in Figure 5.1 provide insight into how emotion and intellect play a role in a customer's buying decision. The most obvious dimension of perceived value is the performance and features that a new product delivers. How well a product performs its intended function(s) is clearly at the core of many purchases...but not all. The buyer of a machine tool, for example, is far more likely to care about hard-nosed performance than the person who brings home a designer purse. Yes, a purse must hold things. However high-fashion handbags are all about glamour, not practicality. There is emotion involved in every buying decision, and that subjectivity can override even the most obvious disparity in performance.

Another left-brain oriented category of perceived value is the cost of ownership and long-term reliability of a new product, represented by the retained-value column on the right of the figure. In some cases, the retained value of a product can be explicit: Can the product be resold after years of use, thereby allowing customers to recapture some of their investment? The use-life cost and resale value of a product are important in many situations, particularly when the motivation for purchasing the new product was to save money. If the resale of a product doesn't make sense, then that product is a "consumable," but must still last its full intended lifespan without failure. In either case, both initial performance and long-term economics will play a role in almost every buying decision.

Now it is time to give the right brain its due. The two middle categories highlight aspects of human nature that have become powerful drivers in the marketplace. If a product is perceived to be scarce, it will immediately take on an elevated importance over readily available solutions. We always want what we cannot have. If each new i-thing that Apple introduces were to be made available in massive quantities at your neighborhood retailer, some of its cache would be lost. Likewise, during almost every holiday season there is at least one toy that manages to become an obsession with parents. Generally this has little to do with the appeal of the toy, but rather the fact that it is in short supply. Your children might not have given the toy a second look, but once they hear that it won't be available, they will immediately begin the relentless badgering that results in sleepovers outside of toy stores. In extreme situations, such as the ones mentioned above, the scarcity is overt and often "manufactured." For almost every product, however, there is an opportunity to capture the perceived value of scarcity, in the form of differentiation. If your firm is the only one in the marketplace with a desirable set of attributes, it will develop pricing power over more commoditized solutions. From a different perspective, the increased demand for highly customized solutions over the past several decades is a manifestation of this category of perceived value. It is up to your firm to bring the relative scarcity of your new product to the forefront of your customers' minds.

The final category is the most intriguing, and holds the greatest untapped opportunities. How does your product impact a customer's self-esteem; in other words, how does it make them *feel*? For lifestyle products, this connection is obvious. A new sports car might make a

FIGURE 5.1: There are four categories of perceived value that customers will consider (at least subconsciously) when making a buying decision. The performance and retained value of a new product appeal to the logical side of a customer's brain, whereas the relative scarcity of a product and the esteem it imparts will influence the emotional side. A great product maximizes value in all four of these categories.

Product Examples	Categories of Perceived Value				Relative Market Price
	Performance	Esteem	Scarcity	Retained Value	
Paper Clip					
Gold Tie Clasp					
Tap Water					
Imported Bottled Water					
Decorative Wall Poster					
Original Oil Painting					
Tickets to Local Movie Theater					
Tickets to See Bruce Springsteen					
Magnetic Compass					
Portable GPS Locator					
Generic Office Software					
Fully Customized Office Software					
Digital Alarm Clock					
Swiss Grandfather Clock					

buyer feel successful, young, or attractive, or may stimulate their adrenal glands sufficiently to make them feel excited or thrilled. A new electronic gadget may impart a "coolness" factor to its owners, despite their obvious lack of cool. Even pragmatic products have a significant emotional content. The purchase of a new IT system or software application is often driven by risk-aversion; the supplier that has the best brand reputation can often charge more for their products than the new kids on the block. This added pricing power comes from the confidence that a leading firm inspires in its customers. Whether it be the reduction of fear or the enhancement of cool, the emotional content of a new product cannot be ignored, and can often allow a lesser product to conquer its betters in the competitive marketplace.

Once you are armed with opportunities to differentiate your new product, it is time to consider your opponents. How do the offerings of your competitors compare to your new product vision? Most important, is there some "high ground" in the competitive landscape that you can defend against all comers? This brings us to the most critical aspect of marketing; the *positioning* of a new product (see Nadler, et al (1997) and Mello (2002)). You can think of the marketplace as a volume defined by three axes, as shown in Figure 5.2. The first axis represents the performance and features that a product delivers (including all four of the perceived-value categories described above), the second reflects the level of quality achieved, and the third axis represents the price that a customer must pay. Within this volume there are limitless possible combinations of these three factors, with each combination identifying a unique market position. Naturally, your competition lives in this same space, and has staked out positions for themselves. Your goal is to identify *uncontested space* (see Kim, et al (2005)): A differentiated product must be positioned such that no other product directly competes with it. If two or more products occupy the same position, then there is no discernable difference between them, and that product has become commoditized. Ultimately, to break the stalemate among equals, one competitor will cut its price, followed by another, resulting in a death spiral of desperate cost-cutting and shrinking margins.

A well-crafted positioning strategy is the key to ensuring that your new product avoids such an ignominious fate. Actually, there is a great

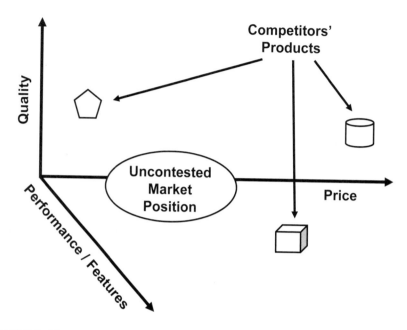

FIGURE 5.2: The competitive landscape can be characterized as a three-dimensional volume defined by three axes: performance / features, quality, and price. For a product to achieve high margins and a substantial market share, it must be positioned such that it occupies an uncontested space in the marketplace.

deal of uncontested space within the competitive landscape (e.g., if you offer a product with poor performance and low quality at a very high price, you will have little competition). What you are seeking is a position that will yield a compelling business case. For example, the differentiating attributes that you have identified might allow you to offer better performance than your competitors at a somewhat higher price. Alternatively, there may be an open position for a scaled-down version of an existing product that offers somewhat lower performance, but is more affordable to customers. Some of history's most successful products have achieved their greatness through clever positioning. Who would have thought two decades ago, for example, that there would be a huge global market for incredibly expensive "designer" coffee? At the other end of the spectrum, Wal-Mart has achieved leviathan status by providing goods at a price that cannot be matched by any competitor. Whether you decide to push the upper or lower limits of a positioning dimension (e.g., the highest quality, the lowest cost, the best performance, etc.), or find a nice comfy spot in the middle that has been ignored by your competition, without an uncontested position, you don't have a viable new product.

Unfortunately, like all other aspects of front-end product planning, developing a positioning strategy is hard work. Hence, most companies take the easy road; they just keep doing what they have previously done and hope (or even assume) that it will continue to work. Suppose that your firm has always delivered the most reliable products in your market segment. Each new generation of products that you have launched has followed this same trajectory: more robust, more reliable, longer life. Inevitably there will come a time when your customers will become saturated, meaning that they will be completely satisfied with the reliability of your products, and will not pay a penny more for further improvements along that trajectory. Owning a product that will last a lifetime may be a nice ideal, but is that what your target market segment really needs? For example, a professional cabinetmaker might pay top dollar for a power tool with exceptional reliability, but the typical do-it-yourselfer would be completely satisfied with a cheapo that will stand up to only occasional use. If your new product surpasses the saturation point of your target customers, you will overshoot their needs, as shown in Figure 5.3. The result will be an increase in cost to develop and manufacture the product, without an associated increase in price (since customers will only pay for perceived benefits). Hence, there is a sweet spot with respect to performance, features, and quality that balances the complete satisfaction of your customers with the profit margin that a product can achieve. In the figure, you should note that this sweet spot is just slightly to the right of center. This shift provides a safety margin with respect to customer satisfaction: You don't want to risk undershooting some customers' needs in the interest of squeezing every last dollar of profit from a product.

Before initiating a new product development project, ask yourself some hard questions. Have you considered all four categories of perceived value and selected differentiating attributes that customers will truly value? Is your new product positioned relative to the competition such that price, performance, cost, and sales volumes represent a viable business case? Finally, are you being completely objective about your

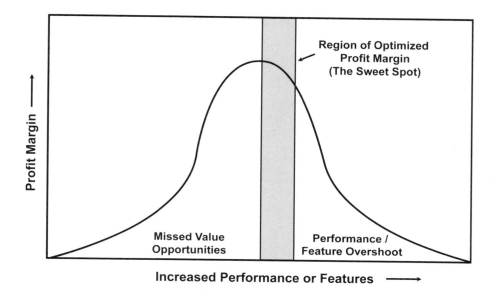

FIGURE 5.3: Any product that delivers performance or features that go beyond the needs of its target customers will experience a decline in profit margin: The cost of those improvements will not be matched by an associated increase in price. The sweet spot on the above curve represents an ideal balance between fully satisfying all customers, and avoiding design overshoot.

customers' level of dissatisfaction with existing products, or will your new product potentially overshoot their needs? Once you are confident that a robust business case can be achieved, it is time to schedule your Market Requirements Event, and begin the process of turning a great idea into a successful new product.

General Description of the Market Requirements Event

As with every lean product development (LPD) Event, the first step in executing the Market Requirements Event is *preparation*. Each event carries with it standard work for preparation, execution, and closeout. The specific format and formality of the standard work you create is entirely up to you, however at a minimum there should be a guideline or template that identifies the mandatory inputs to the event. The amount of time and effort invested in preparatory work should be scaled to the nature and complexity of the product being developed. A straightforward line-extension project will require far less preparation time than would be necessary for a major new product platform. Frequently a product idea has been banging around a firm for months or years prior to receiving serious attention from management. If this is the case, much of the preparation for the Market Requirements Event may have already been completed on an informal basis, and would only need to be consolidated before the event can be held. One word of caution: Don't shortchange the preparation time for this or any other event. If an event cannot be completed successfully, it should (indeed *must*) be repeated. This iteration will likely take far longer than it would take to get it right the first time.

An overview of the Market Requirements Event is provided in Figure 5.4, and the position of this event in the Event-Driven Lean Product Development process is shown in Figure 5.5. Since this is the first event of a lean product development process, its successful completion starts the clock for time-to-market. This does not mean that accelerating idea generation and business-case development is not important, but without a clear set of requirements (the output of this event), there is little point in forming a cross-functional project team. In fact, that team may come together for the first time at this event, making it the *de facto* kickoff for their project. The duration of the event itself is scalable, as always, but a full day is a reasonable minimum, with several days often required for complex, system-level products. The event is considered closed once all follow-up action items are completed.

In the next section, I will use a simulated case example to illuminate the specifics of how the Market Requirements Event unfolds. This is not just a literary device to keep the reader (and the author) interested: One of the most important factors in the success of any LPD Event is effective facilitation. Through the use of a fictional company, product, and team, I can share with you some of my experiences regarding what works, what doesn't, and how to handle the rough spots. In the simulation that follows, I've elected the project team leader to be the facilitator of this first event, but this is not essential. Not every great team leader is a great facilitator, although this is certainly a desirable trait. Without strong facilitation, an LPD Event can devolve into wasteful squabbling and indecision. If you need to bring in a designated hitter to be the facilitator, then go for it. Nurturing effective facilitation skills within your pool of team leaders takes time, and there is no time to waste when there is money to be made.

The Market Requirements Event

Objective: To transform voice-of-the-customer (market) data into a prioritized list of product design requirements that maximize customer value, market acceptance, and profits.

Inputs:
- Market Requirements Brief
- Market research data, surveys, direct customer inputs
- Early concepts, ideas, competitors' products, etc.

Outputs:
- Engineering requirements template
- Actions required for event closeout

Attendees (typical):
- Team leader
- Core team members (cross-functional development team)
- Marketing manager / director
- Engineering manager / director
- Sales / service / field-support representatives
- Others (strategic suppliers, supply chain, quality, etc.)

Agenda (typical):

8:00 – 9:00	Review of Market Requirements Brief / market data
9:00 – 12:00	Part 1 – Identify top-five key differentiators
1:00 – 3:00	Part 2 – Prioritize requirements and features
	- Round 1 Lean QFD (high level)
	- Compare outputs to market data
	- Round 2 Lean QFD (refine)
3:00 – 4:00	Complete engineering requirements template
4:00 – 4:30	Identify actions required to close out the event
4:30 – 5:00	Management outbriefing / learning opportunities

FIGURE 5.4: An overview of a typical Market Requirements Event. The details of how this event unfolds, along with some important tips on facilitation, are provided in the next section.

Event Simulation: SpeedFreaks Watercraft, Inc.

The back-story for this fictional case example is a familiar one: An enthusiast with an entrepreneurial flair becomes frustrated with the products available on the market, and decides to create his own solution. Back in the early 1980's, Tom Craft, an avid boater and unabashed adrenaline junky, began tinkering with designs for a revolutionary speedboat. At first, he thought only of himself: To keep the endorphins flowing, he needed more power, more agility, and most of all, more speed. A prototype boat, fabricated by hand in his garage, morphed into several custom orders from other speed addicts, which in turn evolved into a first, and then a second generation of world-class speedboats. Alas, as Tom matured and his testosterone level declined, he lost his hunger. Along with the success of his firm came other responsibilities and other interests, and pretty soon his brainchild, SpeedFreaks Watercraft, Inc., settled into a safe and comfortable rut. The pace of new product introductions slowed, and a culture of risk-aversion emerged. Why take chances when you are the market leader?

A few years ago, Tom retired to allow more time for fishing (his new passion), leaving the company to be run by his son, Chris. Now Chris was no adrenaline junky, but he was keenly aware of the decline of his father's firm over the past three decades. After cleaning out some dead wood from the executive team, Chris was ready to revitalize his family's firm. But how was he to foster innovation and risk-taking in a company that had become complacent?

His solution was simple: Go back to the drawing board with a hand-picked team and create a breakthrough new watercraft just like his father had...from scratch. Fortunately, virtually all the employees at SpeedFreaks enjoyed watersports, so Chris engaged every member of the firm, from the V.P. of marketing to the boat builders on the production floor, in his quest for new thinking. Each individual was asked to talk to friends, attend boat shows large and small, take test drives of competitors' products, mine the blogosphere, and interview suppliers, distributors, and retail outlets. What was new, different, and exciting? What was generating a positive buzz? Most important, what was missing? Where were the shortfalls in performance, features, appearance, and

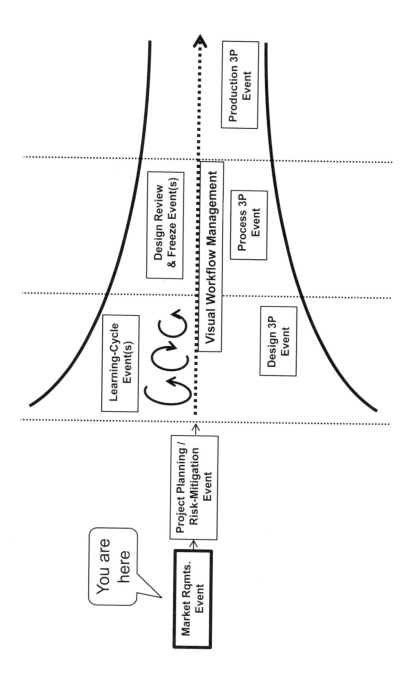

FIGURE 5.5: The Market Requirements Event represents the first of a series of events that make up the Event-Driven Lean Product Development process.

convenience that might be addressed by the newly christened Tigershark Model 45? With the marketing department at the helm, all voice-of-the-customer inputs were gathered and organized...but not fully digested. Chris did not want to dictate the solution to his project team; he wanted their ownership of the new product, and even more important, their collaborative insights.

To provide a clear starting point for the team, Chris asked the marketing group to generate a Market Requirements Brief, as shown in Figure 5.6. This one-page synopsis was intended to provide a snapshot of the company's vision for the new product. Since brevity is the key to successful communication, the marketing group worked hard to condense the vital details onto a single sheet of paper. Backup research was organized into files by topic, and would be available to the team during the upcoming Market Requirements Event. In addition, all invitees to that event (and in particular, the newly selected project team) were encouraged to speak with individuals from outside their own functional areas to gain a heuristic sense of what might constitute a revolutionary new product. To reinforce this request, each participant was asked to create a brief "user story" about the new TigerShark speedboat. This user story would describe the experiences that a typical customer might have with the new product from a very personal perspective. What attributes brought them joy? How did they interact with the product? Why would they recommend the new boat to other watersports enthusiasts? One week prior to the event, the Market Requirements Brief, agenda, and supporting documentation were distributed to all attendees, with a mandate to *be prepared*. As a final step, Chris selected a brilliant and dynamic nautical engineer to be both the project team leader and the facilitator for the event, a young man named Harry Hornblower (with apologies to C. S. Forester).

At last, the day of the event arrived. Chris had decided to limit the duration of this first meeting to a single day, with the understanding that once a high-level vision for the overall system had been agreed upon, additional deep-dive events would be held to address critical subsystems, such as the engine, thrusters, and hull configuration. To encourage the total focus of event participants, an off-site conference center was selected as the venue (this is not essential, but can help avoid

---

Market Requirements Brief
Revision 0 – 5/13/11

1. Product designation: *Tigershark Speedboat Model 45*
2. What specific customer problem(s) does the new product solve?
       Need for a more aggressive watercraft than is currently available.
3. Who are the target customers?
       Young, affluent outdoor enthusiasts who enjoy multiple watersports.
4. "Most likely" sales volumes:
       Year 1 = *500*   Year 2 = *1000*   Year 3 = *1500*
5. Target market price: *$150,000 USD*
6. Target manufacturing cost: *$100,000 USD*
7. Target market entry date: *1st Quarter, 2013*
8. Key differentiators:
       i. *Higher top speed than any other watercraft in its class.*
       ii. *Faster 0 – 40 mph acceleration than any other watercraft in its class.*
       iii. *Attributes that directly support multiple watersports and recreational*
              activities.
9. Critical physical characteristics:
       i. *Less than 10,000 lbs.*
       ii. *Length: 25' to 30'*
10. Critical performance requirements:
       i. *Capable of tight-radius turns at full throttle and at top speed.*
       ii. *Capable of maintaining stability under high surf conditions.*
       iii. *Torque-to-horsepower ratio greater than one (ft. lbs. / hp.).*
11. Critical features:
       i. *Advanced GPS navigation system.*
       ii. *Servo-controlled azimuthal thruster(s).*
12. Other critical requirements or constraints:
       i. *Must meet all state and local regulations for the towing of watercraft.*
       ii. *Should be compatible with Model 32 standard trailer.*

FIGURE 5.6: The above template is an example of a brief, one-page summary of the vision for a new product, in this case the TigerShark speedboat. This represents only a starting point for the Market Requirements Event, and may be revised several times throughout the development project as the team learns more about customer needs and technical solutions.

distractions, and may be warranted for large-scale projects). At precisely 8:00 a.m., Harry was introduced and the proceedings began. After brief introductions, each participant was asked to share their user story. Harry kept comments and questions to a minimum during this process, and then moderated a lively discussion about the participants' user stories once all had been shared. The goal of this warm-up activity was to begin forming a picture of what the new product might look like. To avoid giving the impression of management control, neither Harry nor Chris (who attended the event as an observer) influenced this discussion, except to answer questions and avoid wasteful tangents. Market data was introduced as needed, and when necessary the Market Requirements Brief was referred to, but only as a guideline. The new TigerShark product would be developed in "layers," meaning that the vision and even the details of the new boat would be allowed to evolve over time as the team discovered new knowledge about both their target customer and possible technical solutions.

After about an hour of open discussion, Harry proposed that their dialog would be better served if they used a lean tool to organize their thinking and test some of their assumptions regarding market needs. The tool that the team used is shown in Figure 5.7. The column on the left provides space to capture ideas for potential "key differentiators." A key differentiator is an attribute of the new product that is unique in the marketplace, and of significant value to target customers. Without several key differentiators (or at least a single powerful one), a new product will struggle to gain a foothold in the market and will have little pricing power. Once a healthy and diverse list of possible differentiators is developed, each is assessed based on two important metrics: the relevance of the differentiator to the target customer's buying decision, and the degree to which customers are satisfied with currently available products. Relevance to the buying decision (on a scale from 1 to 3, with 3 being high) reflects how customers perceive the impact that an attribute has on their well-being. A high score implies that the attribute would be fundamental to the customer's choice among alternatives, a medium score indicates significant impact on both choice and price, while a low score represents a nicety that might, at best, be a tiebreaker.

The second metric attempts to quantify the current degree of satisfaction in the marketplace, both with your firm's existing product (if

FIGURE 5.7: The "key differentiator" tool is designed to capture ideas for possible new product attributes, and determine if they have the potential to strongly influence the target customer's buying and pricing decisions. The "D-score" reflects the differentiation potential of an attribute, while the "P-score" indicates how important it would be to match the competitions' performance or features.

Possible Key Differentiators	Relevance to the Buying Decision (R)	Degree to Which Market Needs Are Totally Satisfied (N = 10% to 100%)			Differentiation Opportunity (D = R / Max. N)	Need for Parity (P = R x [Max. (N2, N3) - N1])
		Your Current Product (N1)	Competitor A Product (N2)	Competitor B Product (N3)		

Brainstorm on these!

3 = High
2 = Medium
1 = Low

Best estimates based on market data and team's knowledge

Focus on the "Top Five"

High scores imply need for parity

129

applicable), and with several market-leading competitors' products. The scale ranges from 10 percent, implying that the given attribute is not currently available on any product, to 100 percent, indicating that the target market segment is completely satisfied with the currently available choices. Although these two metrics are, at best, semi-quantitative (good market-research data can help refine these scores), they collectively answer a critical question: Is there a "gap" in available offerings that can form the basis for a highly differentiated product? In mature and stable markets, gaps are few and far between. However, in dynamic markets (or in mature ones that have been rocked by some unexpected change), the relevance and satisfaction scores will quickly shift, resulting in a temporary opportunity for a new product to fill that void (see Christensen (1997) and (2003), and Moore (1991)). For example, when gas prices were relatively low, monstrous vehicles were the order of the day. The differentiating attribute of "high gas mileage" had declined in relevance to a two (or even a one for some purchasers of land tanks). Likewise, the level of satisfaction with the gas mileage of available vehicles was fairly high. Hence, only a minimal opportunity to differentiate existed. However, with the dramatic increase in the price of oil came a sea change in the automobile market. Almost overnight the relevance of gas mileage to the buying decision shot up to a three-plus, while satisfaction with available offerings was at an all-time low. This huge gap was so compelling that an entirely new category of car emerged...the hybrid vehicle. Gaps don't last forever; market forces will act to close them as soon as they appear. Your firm's opportunity lies in identifying them as early as possible, and being the first (or at least the second) to fill that gap and reap the benefits.

The two remaining columns are outputs of the tool: a ranking of the differentiation potential of a proposed product attribute, and the degree to which "parity" must be considered. The first output, the D-score, increases as an attribute's relevance to the buying decision grows, and also increases as the market's satisfaction with existing products (from all providers) decreases. When these two effects are combined, the resulting score represents a measure of the gap we are seeking. Although there are no rules regarding what constitutes a high D-score, I've found that scores of three or higher indicate a solid opportunity to differentiate your new product. The second output, the P-score, represents the gap between

The Market Requirements Event

your existing product's performance and features, and the currently available offerings of competitors. If this score is high (e.g., greater than one), you may be compelled to match a competitor's performance or feature just to avoid a negative perception in the marketplace. In a sense, the D-score tells you where you can gain a market advantage, while the P-score tells you where you need to plug a hole.

One final note before returning to our event simulation. The key-differentiator tool shown in Figure 5.7 *is a discussion tool, not a decision tool.* This distinction is important. A decision tool is intended to form a final verdict on whatever issue is being addressed. The assumption is that once a decision is made, no further discussion or evaluation will be needed. A discussion tool, on the other hand, provides a template for collaborative thinking, and allows a group to capture and evaluate their ideas in real time. The output of the tool above is a prioritized list of the most promising differentiators, along with critical mandates to achieve parity. This output will be refined and reevaluated as the event (and indeed, the project) progresses. Ultimately, decisions will have to be made and attributes frozen, but this should happen only after the project team has spent substantial time investigating design alternatives and their ramifications. We are looking for a consensus starting point for development, not a final answer.

Back at the ranch, Harry and the event participants began brain-storming on possible key differentiators. The first few were easy; the old standbys of top speed, rapid acceleration, and the like. After the low-hanging fruit was captured, the team began reviewing the user stories they had created to harvest any promising features that might delight their customers. One story in particular received a great deal of attention. A participant from the sales department had described the experience of a scuba-diving enthusiast who used the increased range that the new TigerShark provided to reach prime dive spots that would not otherwise have been accessible in a single day. This alternative-use perspective spawned a number of possible differentiators that might be included in the TigerShark to support its use as a scuba-diving platform. After a time, the brainstorming began to wind down. Although a few new ideas had been proposed, there was little that was truly "out of the box." Just as Harry was about to close the discussion and move on, the founder of the company walked into the room, having just returned from a deep-sea fishing trip. After the pleasantries, the elder Craft threw out his own differentiating suggestion: Why not include features to support deep-sea fishing? After receiving blank stares from the group, he went on to justify his idea. Sport-fishing enthusiasts had the same need for range as scuba divers; if a fisherman could get to the prime fishing spots quickly, he (or she) could do more fishing in better spots than would be possible with a slower craft.

"Just add a couple of deep-sea pole mounts and a top-notch fish-finder radar and you'll have a boat that fishing nuts would die for," Tom said confidently.

Despite their skepticism, and out of respect for the founder, a fish-finder radar was added to the list. After this final addition, the team began scoring each possible differentiator with respect to the two metrics: relevance to the buying decision and market satisfaction. As the scoring proceeded, Harry assured the group that any number could be changed at any time, provided that a consensus of the participants agreed. Market data was trotted out to help anchor some of the numbers, in particular regarding the competitions' products. After much tweaking of scores, it was agreed that the entries were as close as could be achieved with the currently available information. The final result, including the calculated D- and P-scores, is shown in Figure 5.8.

Once the template was complete, the attendees found themselves startled by the results. Certainly, some of the obvious differentiators had received appropriately high scores; high top speed, rapid acceleration, and great appearance. In addition, features that would support scuba-diving received a relatively high score, indicating that this might be a valuable path to follow. However, the number-one-ranked key differentiator was the fish-finder radar! Did this make any sense? After some rigorous discussion, the group realized that there were actually

FIGURE 5.8: Results of the TigerShark team's analysis of possible key differentiators. Note that the traditional (i.e., low-risk) differentiating opportunities, along with a surprising "wild-card" feature, are identified by high D-scores. There is also evidently a need for parity (indicated by a high P-score) with respect to the new boat's navigation system.

Possible Key Differentiators	Relevance to the Buying Decision (R)	Degree to Which Market Needs Are Totally Satisfied (N = 10% to 100%)			Differentiation Opportunity (D = R / Max. N)	Need for Parity (P = R x [Max. (N2, N3) - N1])
		Your Current Product (N1)	Competitor A Product (N2)	Competitor B Product (N3)		
High Top Speed	3	0.3	0.4	0.4	7.5	0.3
Rapid Acceleration	3	0.4	0.5	0.5	6.0	0.3
High Towing Capacity	2	0.7	0.8	0.8	2.5	0.2
Gas Mileage	1	0.7	0.7	0.8	1.3	0.1
Appearance	3	0.3	0.4	0.4	7.5	0.3
Safety	2	0.7	0.6	0.8	2.5	0.2
Next Gen. GPS Navigation	2	0.1	0.1	1	2.0	1.8
Advanced Two-Way Radio	1	0.1	0.5	0.5	2.0	0.4
Low Maintanence Cost	2	0.5	0.5	0.6	3.3	0.2
Fish-Finder Radar	1	0.1	0.1	0.1	10.0	0.0
Supports Scuba-Diving	2	0.3	0.4	0.4	5.0	0.2
Supports Water-Skiing	3	0.5	0.6	0.7	4.3	0.6

two possibilities: There was either a real opportunity to access a large and untapped market segment (i.e., deep-sea sport fishermen), or the high D-score was a spurious result. This high score was caused by the complete lack of a fish-finder radar on any currently available speedboat. It is possible that no competitor had recognized the opportunity, or it might be because there just isn't any market interest. The group decided that this potential key differentiator would require immediate investigation and additional market research, but out of deference to the founder, they kept it in the mix. Finally, one attribute stood out as representing a parity issue (the highest score in the right-hand column). SpeedFreaks' current watercraft products had not kept up with advanced GPS navigation technology, and this shortfall would have to be addressed in the new TigerShark to avoid facing negative perception in the marketplace.

It was time to move on to the next step in the Market Requirements Event agenda; developing a high-level set of design requirements that could deliver the key differentiators identified by the group. This translation process would be performed using another lean tool that helps align technical requirements with the voice-of-the-customer. The so-called Lean QFD shown in Figure 5.9 is a simplified version of the classic Total Quality Management (TQM) method that is variously referred to as Quality Function Deployment (QFD) or House of Quality (see Terninko (1997)). For the Market Requirements Event, I've chosen to simplify the standard QFD process to increase its value-added / time-spent ratio. Traditional QFD sessions can be painfully long and tedious, caused in part by excessive detail. I won't suggest that the reader abandon this powerful tool; however I believe that you can get 80 percent of the benefits in 20 percent of the time by using the simplified Lean QFD. It should be noted that if your customers are highly technical, this activity might not be necessary. The Lean QFD translates differentiators that are stated in the customers' language into design requirements that are stated in the language of a product development team. If your customers speak the same technical language as your developers, then you may be able to bypass this activity and move directly to building a high-level requirements matrix. I will illustrate the use of the Lean QFD tool by returning to our simulated case example.

	Key Differentiator #1	Key Differentiator #2	Key Differentiator #3	Key Differentiator #4	Key Differentiator #5	Cumulative Weighted Score	Priority Ranking of Feature / Requirement
	D1	D2	D3	D4	D5		

Possible Features / Requirements That Could Deliver Key Differentiators

FIGURE 5.9: The purpose of the Lean QFD tool shown above is to help translate desirable key differentiators (in the language used by target customers) into technical design requirements (in the language used by developers). Note that if your customers speak the same language as your engineers and designers, this tool may not be necessary to arrive at a high-level set of design requirements.

Harry displayed the Lean QFD template on the conference room's projection screen, and began entering the five highest-scoring key differentiators from the group's previous activity. Below each differentiator he added the associated D-score for that attribute. As he typed, he explained that the D-scores would be used as weighting factors (i.e., multipliers) for the scoring process that would follow. Once all five selected differentiators were in place, Harry asked the group to discuss each one in turn and suggest design requirements that might deliver differentiating benefits to their customers. Each key differentiator yielded one or more possible design requirements, as shown in the completed Lean QFD in Figure 5.10. In some cases, a single requirement was all that was necessary: If a fish-finder radar was to be included as a feature of the new TigerShark speedboat, the best on the market was the Model 865 Side-Scan unit. In other cases, several competing requirements were

135

proposed, with the Lean QFD serving as a filter to help the group select the best of these alternatives. Unlike the terse brainstorming that was encouraged during the first activity, entries into the Lean QFD matrix were discussed at some length to ensure that the collaborative insights of the team were fully represented in the requirements list.

Once a complete list of possible design requirements was formed, Harry explained the scoring system that would be used. Each potential product requirement would be evaluated based on how strongly it supported each of the five key differentiators (i.e., how well it delivered the desired benefits to target customers). Although the suggested requirement was initially intended to support only a single key differentiator, it might also have an impact on other desired differentiators. This "interaction effect" could be positive or negative. Product design is fundamentally about optimizing a trade-space. In some instances, a design requirement might be synergistic among several design attributes (e.g., a requirement for light weight would support both the desire for high top speed and rapid acceleration for the TigerShark speedboat). On the other hand, a proposed requirement might actually subtract value from other differentiating attributes (as might occur if an appearance-based requirement caused the speedboat to be less hydrodynamic and therefore more sluggish). Due to the interaction effect, the scoring for each proposed requirement would span a range from +5 (indicating very strong support of a given differentiator) to -5 (implying a strong negative effect on a differentiator). A zero score would apply if the proposed requirement did not have any impact on a specific differentiator.

Again Harry made it clear that the purpose of the lean tools used in the Market Requirements Event was to facilitate discussion and collaboration, not to make hard-and-fast decisions. With discussion thus encouraged, there was much debate over the scoring, and several times the requirements list and the scores were changed to reflect the best thinking within the group. Finally, with both conversation and the attendees themselves exhausted, a version of the Lean QFD emerged that was agreeable to most members of the group. The completed Lean QFD for the TigerShark Model 45 speedboat is shown in Figure 5.10.

		Fish-Finder Radar	High Top Speed	Appearance	Rapid Acceleration	Supports Scuba-Diving	Cumulative Weighted Score	Priority Ranking of Feature / Requirement
		10	7.5	7.5	6	5		
Possible Features / Requirements That Could Deliver Key Differentiators	Model 865 Side-Scan Radar	5	0	0	0	2	60	3
	Max. Speed = 60 mph	0	2	0	1	5	46	X
	Max. Speed = 70 mph	0	4	0	2	5	67	X
	Max. Speed = 80 mph	0	5	0	3	5	80.5	1
	2-Color Gel-Coat Finish	0	0	2	0	0	15	X
	3-Color Gel-Coat Finish	0	0	5	0	0	37.5	4
	Dual-Hull Configuration	0	-3	2	-3	2	-15.5	X
	Single-Hull / Carbon Fiber	0	4	2	3	0	63	2
	0 - 40 mph in 10 seconds	0	0	0	3	0	18	X
	0 - 40 mph in 8 seconds	0	0	0	5	0	30	5
	Custom Scuba Storage Holds	0	0	0	0	5	25	6
	Onboard Tank Compressor	0	0	0	0	2	10	7

FIGURE 5.10: The completed Lean QFD for the TigerShark Model 45 development project. Note that in some cases, a proposed design requirement supports more than one key differentiator, and in one case (the dual-hull configuration) there would actually be a negative effect on other differentiators. The numbers listed just below each differentiator are simply their D-scores from the previous lean tool, and are used as multiplicative weighting factors for each differentiator.

After an emergency caffeine and sugar infusion, the group reviewed their findings thus far. The highest-scoring product requirement was, not surprisingly, an aggressive top speed. In fact, several alternative top-speed requirements were proposed, and after weighing risks versus benefits, the group agreed that they should push the limits. Thus, an 80 mph goal was selected, and the other alternatives for a high top-speed requirement were down-selected (indicated by an "X" in the right-hand column). The potential for negative interaction was exemplified by a proposed requirement for a dual-hull configuration. Although the dual-hull design would be esthetically pleasing, the added drag and reduced maneuverability would cause unacceptable negatives among other desired attributes. On the other hand, an all-carbon-fiber, single-hull design could be made very stylish, yet would strongly enhance several other key differentiators. Finally, features that support scuba-diving and deep-sea fishing came through with reasonably high scores, indicating that they should be added to the initial TigerShark requirements matrix.

With the insight provided by the Lean QFD tool, the group was ready to craft their final output; a preliminary design requirements matrix for the new TigerShark speedboat. Before the group got started, however, Harry suggested some ground rules:

"What we have created thus far," he stated, "is a wish list of features and requirements. This is just not enough to provide a valid starting point for our development team. There are two additional considerations that must be added to the mix: *risk* and *priority*. We have struggled in the past with these issues, and rather than repeat our mistakes, we are going to bring both of these factors to the forefront on this critical project."

Harry went on to explain his thinking through a brief tutorial, which I will summarize here for the reader's benefit. Each proposed product requirement or feature has three different categories of risk associated with it: cost risk (can the requirement be achieved in a cost-effective manner), schedule risk (will the requirement cause an unacceptable delay to product launch), and technical risk (does the development team sufficiently understand the technology needed to meet the proposed requirement). Each category of risk should be addressed in the requirements matrix that will guide the efforts of the development team sufficiently; the team should immediately focus on the highest-risk requirements, with the goal of mitigating those risks aggressively and proactively. Indeed, some or all of the initially defined requirements may need to change once they have been thoroughly investigated by the project team. Hence, for each requirement or feature the estimated level of risk in all three of the above categories should be included in the design requirements matrix, using a high / medium / low scale.

In addition to the consideration of risk, a development team also needs guidance as to which requirements are the most important, and which can be adjusted or even eliminated to achieve an on-time product launch and an acceptable profit margin. Traditionally, requirements for a new product are stated in a one-dimensional manner: Everything is a "must-have" with no latitude for tradeoffs or compromises. This over-simplified way of thinking is not representative of market perceptions, and can impose severe and unnecessary limitations on designers. As

138

challenging as it might be to accomplish, all product requirements (in fact, all aspects of a development project) should be assigned a relative priority. I have found that a simple language works best, both from a communication and an execution standpoint. The three classifications that I recommend are *must-haves, should-haves,* and *could-haves,* as shown in Figure 5.11. A must-have requirement or feature is defined as critical to the business case. If this requirement is not met, the product will suffer significantly in the marketplace and its success will be placed in jeopardy. A should-have requirement is deemed to be important to a large subset of customers, and could have a substantial impact on sales and price, but it is less constrained than a must-have and therefore allows more flexibility during the design process. Finally, a could-have feature or requirement represents a nicety or option that might be a tiebreaker for some customers, but will have minimal impact on the business case. Indeed, could-haves can be either reduced or eliminated if necessary to meet cost and schedule targets. Based on this three-tier priority system, the general structure of product design requirements is shown in Figure 5.12. Note that "basic requirements" form a foundation upon which differentiating attributes are added. In general, it is not necessary to review basic requirements during the Market Requirements Event, since it is reasonable to assume that a diligent cross-functional development team can handle these more mundane aspects of product design without the need for a formal event.

Defining must-haves, should-haves, and could-haves early in the development process allows product designers to perform tradeoffs in a more nuanced and effective way. More important, as the project progresses and cost and schedule constraints begin to take their toll, the developers (with the agreement of management) have the option to adjust or even eliminate lower-priority features or requirements to achieve the desired product launch date and target manufacturing cost. The could-haves, in particular, represent a "shock absorber" for the project team, allowing mid-course corrections to be made without compromising the business case of the new product, as shown in Figure 5.13.

	Must-Have	Should-Have	Could-Have
Product Versions	Basic configuration to meet majority of customer needs	Configurations to meet needs of other important segments	Configurations to meet all potential customer needs
Product Features	Platform product with no options or extra features	Limited options and features available	Broad range of options and features
Prototype Testing	Verify performance on a single pre-production unit	Performance and extended-life testing on five units	Full performance and life testing on large sample size
Documentation	Provide only critical documentation and instructions	Generate additional service and support documentation	Capture learning from new design for future projects
Development Tasks	Complete critical-path tasks on schedule	Complete important value-creating tasks not on critical path	Identify and implement process improvements

FIGURE 5.11: A simple language of prioritization can be applied to virtually every aspect of new product development. Must-haves are defined as being vital to a project's success, while should-haves are important but somewhat more flexible. A could-have is desirable but optional, and can be either delayed or eliminated if necessary to meet project schedule and cost targets.

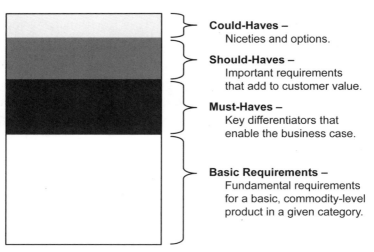

Could-Haves – Niceties and options.

Should-Haves – Important requirements that add to customer value.

Must-Haves – Key differentiators that enable the business case.

Basic Requirements – Fundamental requirements for a basic, commodity-level product in a given category.

FIGURE 5.12: The totality of product requirements begins with a foundation of basic requirements, upon which differentiating attributes are added. The focus of the Market Requirements Event is on identifying these differentiating and unique attributes, while basic requirements are left to the cross-functional design team to define outside of the formal event.

140

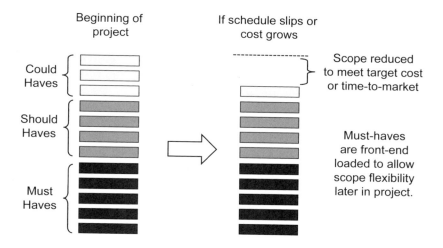

FIGURE 5.13: One of the greatest benefits of prioritizing product design requirements is that the could-haves represent a "shock absorber" for a project team: They can be reduced or even eliminated to correct for schedule slips or unacceptable cost growth as the project progresses.

With Harry's tutorial on risk and prioritization complete, the attendees at the TigerShark event set to work creating the design requirements matrix shown in Figure 5.14. This represented the desired output of the event, and captured the group's best thinking with respect to the new speedboat product. As can be seen in the figure, several of the design requirements and features were determined to have a potentially dangerous mix of high risk and high priority (as represented by an "H" in any of the three risk categories, along with must-have priority). It was clear to the group that before any significant design effort could begin, these issues would have to be addressed. In fact, the first activity of the cross-functional development team would be to identify ways to mitigate high-risk issues that were vital to the product's business case. (How this is accomplished is discussed in Chapters 6 and 7.) As a closing activity, the event attendees agreed upon several critical action items that would be completed immediately after the event, including some quick-and-dirty market research on fish-finder radars, and identification of potential strategic suppliers for carbon-fiber composite materials. At last, the event was adjourned.

Once the last of the attendees had left the room, Harry and Chris remained behind to reflect on the day's proceedings. Although the event had been exhausting, and the discussion at times had been contentious, they both agreed that this was the first time in the history of the company that a project team had been given such a clear and thorough starting point. Over the next few weeks the action items from the event would be completed, and the project team would be ready to establish a project budget and schedule, and define a detailed plan for risk mitigation. In other words, they would be ready to hold the Project Planning / Risk-Mitigation Event (see Chapter 6).

■ ■ ■

Alas, we must now leave the TigerShark project team, never to return. Different simulated case examples will be used in the remaining chapters, primarily to allow me to best illustrate the execution of the remaining LPD Events. For those of you who require closure, suffice to say that SpeedFreaks, Inc. went on to glory and success with their revolutionary speedboat. One of the great benefits of simulated case examples is that, unlike the real world, they always have a happy ending.

Advanced Topic: Developing a New Product in Layers

During the previous event simulation, the team leader proposed that the TigerShark speedboat product would be developed in *layers*. This concept implies that as the product development project progresses, and as new knowledge is gained with respect to both customer needs and technical solutions, the requirements can (and should) evolve to reflect the new learnings of the team. This seems to fly in the face of traditional thinking: Design teams need firm initial requirements to permit efficient execution, and any changes downstream will cause turbulence and delays. Actually, the goal of layered development is to avoid unnecessary changes downstream by allowing a development team enough latitude up front to steadily converge on an optimal solution.

142

Design Requirements	Differentiator / Parity / Basic (D, P, B)	Risk Assessment			Priority		
		Technical (H, M, L)	Schedule (H, M, L)	Cost (H, M, L)	Must-Have	Should-Have	Could-Have
Maximum Speed	D	M	M	H	80 mph	85 mph	90 mph
Acceleration	D	M	M	M	0-40 in 8 sec.	0-40 in 7 sec.	0-40 in 6 sec.
Model 865 Side-Scan Radar	D	L	L	L	X		
3-Color Gel-Coat Finish	D	L	L	M	X		
Single-Hull - Carbon Fiber	D	M	H	H	X		
Custom Scuba Storage	D	L	L	L		X	
Onboard Tank Compressor	D	L	L	H			X
Next Gen GPS Navigation	P	L	L	M	X		
XYZ S-to-S Radio	P	L	L	L		X	
UL Cert. on Electronics	B	L	L	L	X		
Model SB32 Drive Train	B	M	L	L		X	
Use Standard Trailer	B	H	L	L			X

FIGURE 5.14: The completed design requirements matrix for the TigerShark speedboat product. Note that for each requirement or feature the three categories of risk are assessed and a must / should / could priority is assigned. Situations where a requirement is both high risk and high priority must be immediately addressed by the development team to ensure that the product's business case can be realistically achieved. Also note that several basic requirements have been included near the bottom of the matrix to emphasize that these items would be added by the project team after the Market Requirements Event is complete.

One way to understand layered development is to visualize a narrowing funnel, as shown in Figure 5.15. At the inception of a product development project, a set of desired high-level requirements are defined. These initial requirements are stated as attributes or goals, rather than as predetermined solutions. In some cases, the requirements might be defined by ranges rather than specific numbers (e.g., boat length must be between 27 and 30 feet), thereby allowing designers a larger trade-space in which to work. In the early stages of the project, the development team will systematically investigate the highest-priority requirements or features, particularly where the associated risk is considered to be high as well. As they discover the feasibility of each requirement, how long it will take, and what it will cost, they will begin to converge on an optimal product design concept. In this way, the funnel begins to narrow. As each learning cycle is completed (see Chapter 7), the design requirements matrix will be revised to reflect the team's recent learning. If the requirement changes are minor, they may fall within the purview of the team to implement themselves. For more significant changes (such as the modification of a must-have requirement) an approval cycle would be required. In extreme cases, it might even be necessary to hold a follow-up Market Requirements Event to reconsider the entire product concept and revalidate the business case based on the new information.

As the project progresses, there will come a time when some requirements must be frozen (see Chapter 9). These staged-freeze points are driven by schedule demands, such as the lead time required for ordering prototype parts or production tooling, regulatory submission points, or even critical trade-show deadlines. Once frozen, a requirement cannot be "defrosted" without a compelling reason, and only with management approval. In this way, the funnel should steadily and continuously narrow, until a finalized design emerges that is ready for transition to production. This layered model for product development may seem like a recipe for uncertainty and delays, but it comes with an excellent pedigree. The Toyota Product Development System is based on the premise of delaying design decisions as long as possible to allow development teams the time to consider multiple design alternatives, and explore creative possibilities (see Ward, et al (1995)). Likewise, the highly successful Agile Software Development methodology is fundamentally based on layered development, wherein requirements are not explicitly defined up front, but rather evolve in parallel with the evolution of the software design itself (see Poppendieck (2003)). The goal of layered development is to harness the learning of a development team as the project progresses, rather than establishing an etched-in-stone set of requirements up front and blindly executing to these initial goals. You will see in Chapter 7 that this rather uncomfortable concept can be implemented in a practical and efficient way. I can only ask that you keep an open mind until that chapter arrives.

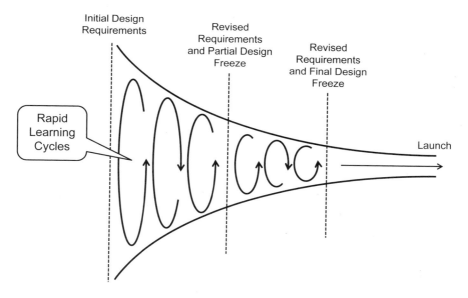

FIGURE 5.15: A narrowing-funnel approach to new product development allows a development team to steadily converge to an optimal product design solution. Rapid learning cycles provide opportunities to harness the team's new knowledge, and as their understanding increases, product requirements are revised and rationalized. Staged-freeze points within the process are necessary to address production lead-time issues and other external schedule constraints.

Chapter References

Belliveau, P., et al, 2002, *The PDMA Toolbox for New Product Development (Vols. 1 & 2)*, John Wiley & Sons.

Christensen, C. M., 1997, *The Innovator's Dilemma*, Harvard Business School Press.

Christensen, C. M., and M. E. Raynor, 2003, *The Innovator's Solution*, Harvard Business School Press.

Cohen, L., 1995, *Quality Function Deployment: How to Make QFD Work for You*, Addison-Wesley.

Kim, W. C., and R. Mauborgne, 2005, *Blue Ocean Strategy*, Harvard Business School Press.

Leonard-Barton, D., 1995, *Wellsprings of Knowledge*, Harvard Business School Press.

Mello, S., 2002, *Customer-Centric Product Definition*, PDC Professional Publishing.

Moore, G. A., 1991, *Crossing the Chasm*, HarperBusiness.

Nadler, D. A., and M. L. Tushman, 1997, *Competing by Design*, Oxford University Press.

Phillips, P. L., 2004, *Creating the Perfect Design Brief*, Allworth Press.

Pilloton, E., 2009, *Design Revolution: 100 Products that Empower People*, Metropolis Books.

Poppendieck, M., and T. Poppendieck, 2003, *Lean Software Development: An Agile Toolkit*, Addison-Wesley.

Terninko, J., 1997, *Step-by-Step QFD: Customer-Driven Product Design*, St. Lucie Press.

Verganti, R., 2009, *Design-Driven Innovation*, Harvard Business School Press.

Ward, A. C., Liker, J. K., Cristiano, J. J., and D. K. Sobeck II, 1995, "The second Toyota paradox: how delaying decisions can make better cars faster," *Sloan Management Review*, Vol. 36, No. 3, pgs. 43-61.

6

The Project Planning / Risk-Mitigation Event

Background and Overview

General Dwight D. Eisenhower once famously observed, "Plans are nothing, but planning is *everything*." While I might take exception to the first half of this statement, the second half is undeniably true: The act of creating a project plan represents the single greatest opportunity for a product development team to control its own destiny. It should therefore come as something of a surprise that the vast majority of new product development projects follow virtually no plan at all. To understand this apparent contradiction, we must return once again to the project / process duality that was first discussed in Chapter 3. A large number of firms have adopted some form of a phase / gate development process, under the assumption that this standardized structure represents an adequate roadmap for successful project execution. It does not. Whereas a phase / gate process (or any other governance process) provides guidance as to the "what" of product development, in most cases it does not address the "how." How does each activity within a project depend on its predecessors? How will lead times and resource availability impact project execution? How can the critical path of a project be optimized to reduce time-to-market? How will team members be matched with roles and responsibilities? How will non-recurring

147

and recurring costs be managed? How will knowledge gaps be closed? And perhaps most important, how will risks be identified and mitigated to guarantee a successful outcome? To answer these questions, a team should meet at the very beginning of their project to establish an execution and risk-mitigation plan. In short, they should hold a Project Planning / Risk-Mitigation Event.

Some readers may argue that while the creation of a project-specific schedule, resource plan, and risk-mitigation strategy is indeed necessary, these activities are best performed by a trained project manager (or at least by a team leader with project management skills). This view is reinforced by an increasingly arcane body of knowledge that defines the project management discipline (see Project Management Institute (2008)). Certainly one should not expect the average developer to understand this complex and sophisticated field. It takes an "expert" to build a successful project plan, right? Nothing could be further from the truth. After thirty years of experience as a project manager and educator, I can assure you that the few critical skills needed to plan a development project can be learned and understood by any competent professional. In fact, I believe that the democratization of project management knowledge is vital to successful project outcomes. A project plan that is developed unilaterally by a team leader (even with solicited inputs from team members) is no substitute for a team creating that plan themselves, with all of the emotional commitment and buy-in that such collaborative involvement entails. If a team owns the plan, understands it thoroughly, and agrees upon its viability, the chances of meeting a project's objectives are dramatically increased.

In my "perfect world," every team member would understand the basics of project management: how to define project deliverables, estimate task durations, determine resource requirements, and identify risks (for a traditional perspective on basic project management and risk identification, see Kerzner (2000) and Wideman (1992)). To achieve these goals, I've stripped the discipline of project planning down to its bare essentials (for more on the topic of Lean Project Management, see Mascitelli (2002)). Visual tools are used to build a project master schedule and optimize its duration. Resource-loading and constraint management are performed using rough estimating techniques. Simple brainstorming and scoring methods are employed to identify and rank project risks. Does this bare-bones approach to project planning result in the same quality of plan as one developed by a Project Management Professional (PMP)? Probably not. However keep in mind the words of Eisenhower...plans are nothing. In reality, it is impossible to create the perfect plan at the beginning of a project, since even the best plan won't be worth the paper it is written on after just a few short weeks or months. Striving for the perfect project plan is both futile and unnecessary. All that is needed at the inception of a project is a valid starting point, some well-defined critical milestones, and a flexible approach to real-time planning as the project progresses. The Visual Workflow Management techniques described in Chapter 4 create just such a flexible environment for dynamic adaptation of a project plan.

At this point, some of you dyed-in-the-wool lean practitioners might be wondering how value-stream mapping can be applied to the planning of new product development projects. Indeed there are several valuable books on this very topic (see, for example, Locher (2008) and Rother, et al (1999)). As you will soon learn, I've borrowed significantly from this process-mapping methodology to create my simplified project planning approach. In fact, you could rightly observe that the Project Planning / Risk-Mitigation Event is, at least in part, nothing more than a project-specific value-stream-mapping event. While there is an important place for value-stream mapping in the context of new product development, it also has some fundamental limitations. I will discuss the relationship between value-stream mapping and project planning, and describe opportunities to create a standard-work project plan, in the final section of this chapter.

General Description of the Project Planning / Risk-Mitigation Event

Like the members of a successful project team, LPD Events depend upon one another. The outputs of each Event represent inputs to the next, from the initial definition of product design requirements through to the final design review that enables the freezing of a production-ready product configuration. Thus, the timing of the Project Planning / Risk-Mitigation Event is driven by the finalization of outputs from the Market Requirements Event (see Chapter 5), as shown in Figure 6.1. In most situations, only a few weeks should separate these first two meetings; just enough time to close out action items from the first event and adequately prepare for the next. This preparation includes some soul-searching on the part of each project team member with respect to their role and responsibilities, the scope of work that the project will entail, and the potential pitfalls that could jeopardize a successful outcome. Since team members will be expected to estimate the duration of project tasks during this event, an effort should be made to mine past history: how long have similar projects taken to complete, where was that time spent, and what lessons can be learned from their successes and failures?

The attendee list for the Project Planning / Risk-Mitigation Event should include all team members who will have direct value-creating responsibilities, along with functional supervisors and / or resource managers, as shown in Figure 6.2. The latter are not essential, but their presence will bring additional history and insight to the event, and their buy-in on resource commitments and the timing of activities will become critical as project execution proceeds. The event itself is typically facilitated by the project team leader, but as always, a "designated hitter" may be advisable if the team leader lacks either the experience or personality to keep the event on track. (Actually, if this is the case, one might question the selection of the team leader, since an event is just a microcosm of the project itself.) The duration of this event is highly scalable: While minor projects might be planned in an afternoon, any project of substance will require at least a full day. In fact, for a complex system product, a tiered series of events will be necessary, beginning with the creation of a system-level master schedule, followed by additional events to create plans for each subsystem development effort based on overall integration milestones.

FIGURE 6.1: The Project Planning / Risk-Mitigation Event should follow closely after successful completion of the Market Requirements Event.

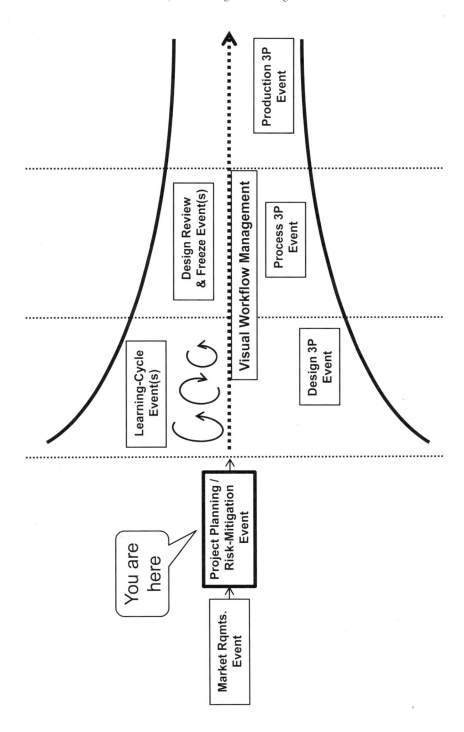

The Project Planning / Risk-Mitigation Event

Objective: To generate a realistic project plan, including a high-level master schedule, launch date, budget and resource plan, and to perform proactive risk identification and mitigation for the project.

Inputs:
- Market Requirements Brief (updated)
- Engineering requirements matrix
- Lessons learned from previous projects (risks and death threats)

Outputs:
- High-level project master schedule
- Estimated product launch date
- Resource estimates and project budget
- Prioritized list of project risks
- Actions required to close out event

Attendees (typical):
- Team leader
- Team members (cross-functional development team)
- Functional supervisors / resource managers
- Others (strategic suppliers, supply chain, quality, etc.)

Agenda (typical):

8:00 – 9:00	Review of business case and engineering requirements
9:00 – 12:00	Create a basic project plan / master schedule
1:00 – 2:00	Establish a resource plan and budget
2:00 – 4:00	Identify and prioritize project risks
4:00 – 4:30	Identify actions to close out event
4:30 – 5:00	Management outbriefing / learning opportunities

FIGURE 6.2: An overview of the Project Planning / Risk-Mitigation Event. This event should typically be scheduled just a few weeks after the Market Requirements Event has been successfully closed out. A sample agenda for a one-day event is provided, but the duration is scalable based on the complexity of the product under development.

As in the previous chapter, I will describe the details of how the Project Planning / Risk-Mitigation Event unfolds through the use of a simulation. However, before we begin our fictitious case example, a word of warning is required. The process of creating a project plan is somewhat like the making of sausage: While the final result might be great, the steps required to get there can be pretty unappetizing. In particular, the planning approach that I recommend begins with the development of an open-ended project schedule, which will subsequently be optimized to (hopefully) meet management's expectations. Should a senior executive walk into the conference room before this optimization has taken place, they may be horrified by what they see (i.e., a project duration well beyond their expectations). In fact, I've personally experienced some rather tense moments due to this exact circumstance. Unfortunately, it can be career-limiting to bar upper management from your meeting, as tempting as this might be. I therefore recommend that whoever is responsible for your planning event take the time to educate executive stakeholders as to how the process will proceed, and provide assurances that the team will ultimately arrive at a reasonable project duration and launch date. This way, should managers decide to drop by, their heads won't explode. Beyond this caveat, all that is needed to hold your planning event is a conference room with open wall space, a roll of white butcher paper, and (as always) a large pile of sticky notes.

Event Simulation: Lazy Rider Corp. and the Electric Bicycle (Part 1)

Launching a startup company is no easy task, yet Lance Leydon had accomplished this feat in record time. After years of working for one of the world's leading lithium-ion battery companies, he had become obsessed with the potential for this amazingly compact energy source to improve the way people lived their lives. With support from several environment-minded investors, he had gathered a small but talented team of engineers and designers to harness this potential in the form of an electric-powered vehicle. At first, Lance focused his team's efforts on the development of a new generation of high-efficiency golf carts. With profits rolling in from this initial success, it was time to look for new opportunities. Then it hit him: Why not address a form of transportation that had long been neglected – the lowly bicycle? Actually, there were already products on the market that claimed to be powered bicycles, but some careful market research uncovered several large gaps in market satisfaction. In particular, there was a strong need for a product that serviced the fastest-growing demographic in the United States;

overweight, undermotivated people who would only exercise if the task was well-masked by fun and enjoyment.

Once their initial market research was completed, the newly christened Lazy Rider Corp. held a Market Requirements Event to define the requirements for this new form of electrified transportation. After several iterations and adjustments, Lance felt confident that they had arrived at a valid list of must-haves, should-haves, and could-haves, and it was time for the team to build a project plan. In preparation for their Project Planning / Risk-Mitigation event, he called a pre-meeting to establish expectations. With the team assembled, Lance drew two concentric circles on the whiteboard at the front of the conference room, similar to those shown in Figure 6.3. After noting the quizzical looks on most attendees faces, he began his explanation.

"The most important aspect of project planning is defining the scope of work," he stated. "Imagine that you are a contractor that has been hired to paint someone's house. Naturally you would be expected to provide an estimate before starting work. How would you generate this estimate? Would you just write down on your proposal form 'paint house' along with a price? What do you think could go wrong if this is all that you provided to your customer?"

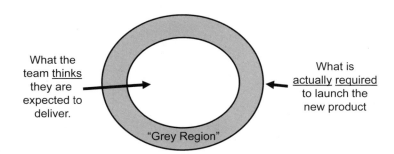

FIGURE 6.3: Establishing an accurate project scope is the first critical step in building a project plan. Without careful definition of project deliverables and customer expectations, there is the potential for scope-creep, as represented by the grey region in the above figure.

Several hands went up, and in each case the response was similar. The statement "paint house" was inadequate to define the work that was expected. Would you be expected to sandblast and scrape the surfaces? How many coats of paint? What would be done to protect the customer's property from paint splatter? And so on. Clearly a much more detailed list of expectations would be required to avoid having this painting project turn into a disaster, for either the customer or the contractor. Back to the concentric circles on the whiteboard. Lance pointed out that the inner circle represented a project team's understanding of their scope of work, while the outer circle represented the expectations of their stakeholders (e.g., management, investors, customers). The grey region between the two was the danger zone. If the team and its stakeholders were not absolutely clear about the details of the project, it was likely that the team would miss critical expectations, and find themselves with a bad case of scope-creep. The inevitable result would be a constantly slipping project schedule. To have any chance of meeting schedule commitments and satisfying stakeholders, a project's scope must be defined in great detail, including every deliverable that would be generated by the team and delivered to their customers. In short, the two concentric circles must merge into a sharp line that is agreed to by both the value creators and the recipients of that value.

"Before our Project Planning / Risk-Mitigation Event in two weeks," Lance continued, "I want each of you to think through what your responsibilities will be on this project. You are all experienced engineers, designers, and production specialists, so harness that background. Think about how this project will be similar to, or different from, previous efforts. Specifically, what *deliverables* were you expected to create on past projects, and what will be needed for this project. A deliverable is any tangible and transferable item: simulations, drawings, prototypes, tooling, documentation, and so on. For each deliverable within your area of responsibility, think about the tasks required to create it. How long will they take? How many and what type of resources will be needed? What could go wrong that might cause schedule slips, performance shortfalls, cost growth, or quality issues? I expect each of you to be prepared to answer these questions, and to commit to an initial project schedule and resource plan at our upcoming event."

Not surprisingly, the team members had concerns. How could they commit to a schedule without having any idea about the design concept that would be developed? Lance addressed this issue by suggesting that each responsible individual should consider a "worst-case / best-case" estimate of time and resources.

"The worst-case estimate should embody all of your concerns about risks and uncertainty, while the best-case scenario should represent a reasonable but optimistic assessment of what might be possible," he said. "Don't think of the plan we will create as being etched in stone. It will give us a reasonable starting point for project execution, but will no doubt evolve over time. Every project schedule has risks associated with it: risk that we will misinterpret the customer's needs, risk that the technology won't deliver the performance that we require, risk that resources won't be available, etc. The difference between your optimistic and pessimistic task-duration estimates is a manifestation of these risks. If the difference is small, this indicates that you perceive the risk for that task to be low. The larger the difference, the greater the perceived risk. All I ask is that you come to the event with a general understanding of your tasks and deliverables, and the ability to discuss and defend your schedule estimates. We will work as a group to arrive at a schedule that balances risk with time-to-market; one that you all believe is aggressive but achievable."

With that, Lance tried to adjourn the meeting, but was met with one last question. A highly experienced mechanical engineer pointed out something that had not yet been discussed.

"This product may be a bicycle, but it isn't simple," the engineer noted. "There are major elements of the design that must work together in perfect harmony to deliver the performance needed to be a market success. It may not be a jet aircraft, but it is still a system, and should be treated like one. My question is how are we going to plan a project that has so many interdependent elements?"

Indeed this was a significant omission on Lance's part. Relatively straightforward, component-level products can be treated as a single entity, without the need for systems thinking. However, this product was far too complex for the team to take that easy path. With a sigh of resignation, Lance proceeded to create a system-decomposition diagram, similar to the generic version shown in Figure 6.4. (Note to reader: For this event simulation, I have presented simplified, generic versions of each planning template, rather than accurately representing the ones created by our fictitious project team. This allows me to describe the creation of a relatively complex project schedule while maintaining visual clarity in the figures.) A system diagram illustrates how a complex product can be partitioned into multiple modules (aka, subsystems), thereby allowing a development team to address each module as a separate entity. System-level requirements are budgeted to each subsystem, such that when all subsystems are integrated, the product will come together seamlessly to meet customer needs. A last critical step in system decomposition is defining the interfaces between the modules. These interface definitions will allow the parallel development of multiple modules, thereby substantially reducing the overall project schedule. All that is required to achieve these schedule gains is careful attention to maintaining the integrity of the subsystem interfaces, and the inclusion of tasks within the project schedule to integrate and test the final system. Lance recognized that to meet the financial targets that his investors had established, a systems approach would be essential.

"It looks to me like our electric bicycle can be logically divided into four subsystems," Lance continued, "the chassis and wheels, the drive train, the power module, and the control electronics. When we get together in two weeks, we will begin by creating a system-level master schedule, and then deep-dive into each of these four subsystems to ensure that the goals of the master schedule can be achieved. This will probably require some iteration, but the time-to-market gains will be worth the effort. As you are preparing for the event, please keep these subsystems in mind, and be thinking about what will be required to integrate them into a final product and validate overall system performance. Now if there are no other questions, let's get to work, and I'll see you all in two weeks."

■ ■ ■

On the day of the Project Planning / Risk-Mitigation Event, Lance and his admin arrived early to prepare the conference room. On one blank wall, they taped a large sheet of white butcher paper, and began drawing parallel lines that spanned the full length of the sheet, resulting in a series of "swim lanes." A swim lane was created for each function or discipline that would contribute deliverables to the project, along with a few extras in case something had been missed. At the top of the sheet, space was allowed for the project timeline. Initially, however, this space was left blank: At first the team would develop an open-ended project schedule, meaning that they would not be constrained by a predetermined end-date. With this preparation complete, Lance began greeting the event's attendees, handing each of them a pad of sticky notes as they entered the conference room.

The meeting began with a brief overview of the most recent version of the project's Market Requirements Brief and the prioritized list of engineering design requirements. Once all questions were answered, the planning process began.

"You will notice that each of you has been allocated a swim lane on the sheet up on the wall," Lance said. "These swim lanes represent the functional disciplines that will contribute to the project. Some of you will be task-team leaders, meaning that you may have several engineers or designers working with you to create your assigned deliverables. Others may work alone. In either case, if a deliverable is placed within your swim lane, you are responsible for its successful completion. Now I want each of you to take your pad of sticky notes and start writing down the deliverables that you have identified as necessary to complete your portion of the project. I suggest you begin with the final deliverables that must be in place to commercialize our electric bike, and then work backwards to define the intermediate deliverables that will be needed to yield those final outcomes. Keep the level of detail to a minimum at first: We can always drill down if necessary."

Lance went on to describe how the swim lanes should be populated. Each team member was asked to place their deliverables within their swim lane in roughly chronological order, from the earliest items that must be completed, to the final deliverables that would enable product launch. While the team was working on their swim lanes, Lance drew two vertical lines down the planning chart. These lines represented critical "external milestones" that would influence the project schedule. External milestones are factors that are beyond the control of the project team,

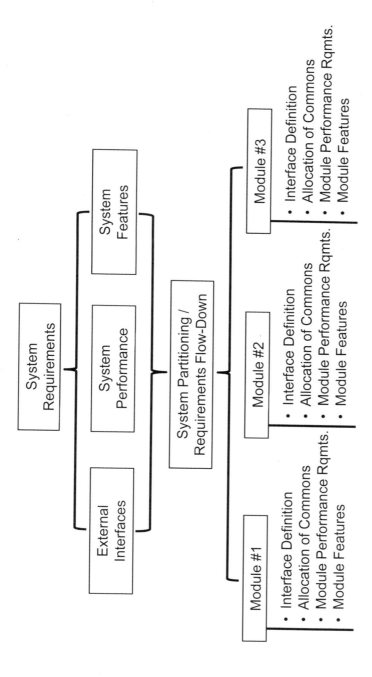

FIGURE 6.4: A complex product should be treated like a system, following the decomposition approach shown above. Each module or subsystem is allocated a budget for shared (aka, "common") system requirements, and has its own set of performance and feature goals. The subsystems are linked together through shared interfaces that must be carefully defined to ensure successful integration of the final system.

and in most cases are beyond the influence of the firm itself. Examples include delivery dates that are defined by external contract customers (for customer-specific products), regulatory submission dates, trade shows, investor-imposed deadlines, retail buying-windows, and so on. For the Lazy Rider electric bicycle, Lance identified two such external milestones: a major bicycle trade show that was scheduled for March of the following year, and the submission of their product to Underwriter's Laboratory for safety testing. As the team members placed their sticky notes on the plan, they were told to consider where their deliverables would fall relative to these two external milestones. After some discussion by the team to ensure that no critical deliverable was missed, the result was a "deliverables roadmap" that displayed what must be accomplished by the team, who was responsible for each item, and approximately when those items must be delivered, as illustrated by the generic version shown in Figure 6.5. This represented Step 1 in the project planning process.

After the team took a break to catch their breath, it was time to begin Step 2. Lance established his expectations for the next round of planning.

"Our next step will be to transform the deliverables roadmap you have created into the beginnings of a project schedule. This means that we will be adding durations and dependencies to the deliverables you have identified. Remember that a deliverable is an outcome, not a task. Hence, for each deliverable I want you to think through the task or tasks required to generate it, and how long those tasks might take. Your goal is to assign an overall duration to each deliverable. To do this, you have to keep in mind two things. First, any duration estimate must be based on some assumptions about resource-loading: Is a full-time person required to achieve your estimate, a part-time individual, or several individuals working in parallel? Make sure you capture your resource assumptions; we will need them for the final step in the planning process. Second,

FIGURE 6.5: A generic version of how the visual planning tool used in the Project Planning / Risk-Mitigation Event would look after completion of Step 1 in the process. In its current form, this template represents a "deliverables roadmap" in which all high-level deliverables for the project are assigned to swim lanes that indicate which function or discipline will be responsible for their creation. Note that this illustration does not align with the case example described in the text, thereby allowing the reader to easily visualize how the planning template evolves throughout the event.

Externally Driven Milestones

Core Team Members	(before Milestone 1)	◇ 1	(between Milestones 1 and 2)	◇ 2	(after Milestone 2)
Team Leader	Project Plan / Schedule		Revised Project Plan / Schedule; Product Delivery Sched.		Revised Product Delivery Sched.
Marketing	Market Requirements Brief		Revised Market Requirements Spec.		Final Product Documentation Package; Final Product Launch Plan
Design Engineering	Prelim. Eng. Design Specification; Prelim. Design Approval		Final Eng. Design Specification; Final Design Approval		
Test Engineering			Validation Test Data; Validation Test Report		Qualification Test Data; Qualification Test Report
Manufacturing Engineering			Fabricate Prototypes; Fabricate Prototypes		
Quality	Validation Test Plan		Qualification Test Plan		Release to Production

any duration estimate must take into account risk. I propose that our goal should be to develop a project schedule that has an 80-percent confidence level. This means that if we were to perform the project ten times, eight of those times the project would be completed on schedule. Hopefully, you have generated best-case and worst-case estimates for the work you will be expected to perform. Here's where you will make use of that range of estimates. Consider the realistic conditions under which this project will be executed, and use your best / worst case estimates to arrive at a duration that you believe can be achieved eight out of ten times. Once you have your estimates, write them on the appropriate sticky note for each deliverable."

The team began this process, with much discussion and debate taking place about who and what would actually be required to create the deliverables they had identified. It was clear to all of the participants that this was a rough-cut process, but with past history as a guide they were able to generate durations that seemed to make sense, and that had a reasonably high probability of being achieved. Once all deliverables had been assigned a duration, Lance explained how these outputs would be linked to one another.

"Now that we have durations assigned, we must consider dependencies. Most deliverables on a project depend on one or more previous deliverables for their successful completion. Likewise, those deliverables will likely provide a vital feed to other downstream deliverables. These dependencies will ultimately determine the overall duration of our project, so getting them right is pretty important. I want all of you to work together to determine the dependencies among our defined deliverables. Move sticky notes as necessary to get the order of dependency right, and separate them by the approximate durations you have estimated. As you are doing this, consider the two external milestones I've identified, and order the deliverables such that they reconcile with the needs of each milestone. Again, this is an iterative process, so take your best initial cut, and then we will work as a team to refine and adjust. Draw dependencies on the schedule in pencil so that we can easily make the inevitable changes that will be necessary."

After several rounds of refinement, the team agreed that what was shown on the wall seemed like a reasonable ordering of activities at the system level, and that the durations and dependencies appeared to be achievable. As a sanity check, the team held a deep-dive discussion on the specifics required to complete each of the four subsystems that must be integrated into the final product. Some additional adjustments were made to accommodate sufficient subsystem and system testing, and at last the team believed that their schedule was reasonably accurate. The resulting plan was similar to the generic example shown in Figure 6.6. With Step 2 of the planning process complete, it was time for the big question to be answered: How long would the electric bicycle take to develop and launch? Lance traced through the dependant tasks and identified the longest pole in the schedule tent; the critical path of the project. When tasks occurred in serial, their durations were added directly. When there were several parallel paths, he selected the longest one. When he was done, he added all of the durations and announced the result: In its current state, the development of the electric bicycle product would take approximately twenty-two months, with roughly an 80-percent confidence level. Unfortunately, although the overall dura-tion of the development project was not unreasonable, it seemed that appearing at the trade show next spring was out of the question. After much discussion, it was agreed that the company would be better served by showing up the following year with a completed and refined product, rather than making a desperate attempt to attend the upcoming show. A generic example of what a project plan might look like after the critical path has been identified is shown in Figure 6.7.

It was now time to complete the final step in the visual planning process; allocating resources to the project schedule that the team had created. While the team was on a break, Lance added a monthly calendar to the top of the schedule template that they had collaboratively devel-oped, starting with the agreed-upon end-date and working backwards to create roughly equal spaces for each month. When the group returned, Lance handed out sheets of colored sticky dots to each team member, and proceeded to explain how they would be used.

"You each have a sheet of red and a sheet of yellow sticky dots. We are going to take advantage of visual communication to create a resource-loading plan for our project. Each red dot represents a full-time person for a period of one month. The yellow dots represent a quarter-time person for the same period. I want each of you to work your way across your swim lane and estimate roughly how many resources will be needed in each month to complete the deliverables you will be responsible for. If the durations of deliverables overlap, then take this into account and include additional resources if necessary. These estimates should be based on the assumptions you made when creating your initial task durations. If you need to represent a half-time person for a month, use two yellow dots, three dots for a three-quarter-time person, and so on. I recognize that these will be approximations, but they will be more than adequate to answer some critical questions, as you'll see once the dots are all in place."

With that, the team went to work, converging on the wall mural that they had created, with dots in hand. Lance played ringmaster as the melee proceeded, pointing out missed items and questioning assumptions. Ultimately the activity subsided, and what was left behind looked like a postmodernist work of art. An illustration of the process that the team used is shown in Figure 6.8, and a photograph of a typical completed visual planning template is provided in Figure 6.9. It was now time for Lance to demonstrate the utility of those simple colored dots.

"Now I want each of you to stare at the template you have created," Lance said. "What do you see? Where there are clusters of colored dots, the project activity will be most intense, with red dots indicating the highest levels of resource-loading. If a cluster appears within your swim lane, ask yourself whether there are enough people available in your functional area to realistically meet the demand during that period. Remember that this is not the only project that we will be working on over the next two years, so any resource conflict among projects could become a constraint that will cause potential schedule slips. Now quickly add up the dots across your swim lane from beginning to end. The total head count you arrive at will determine your functional area's resource

FIGURE 6.6: After Step 2 in the visual planning process, the template will include the dependencies among the various deliverables, along with estimated durations required to create each of these outputs. An effort should be made to order the deliverables correctly, and to reconcile them with any external milestones that have been identified. Remember that the duration estimates must always be based on both an assumption of resource-loading, and an assessment of the risk that each activity will experience.

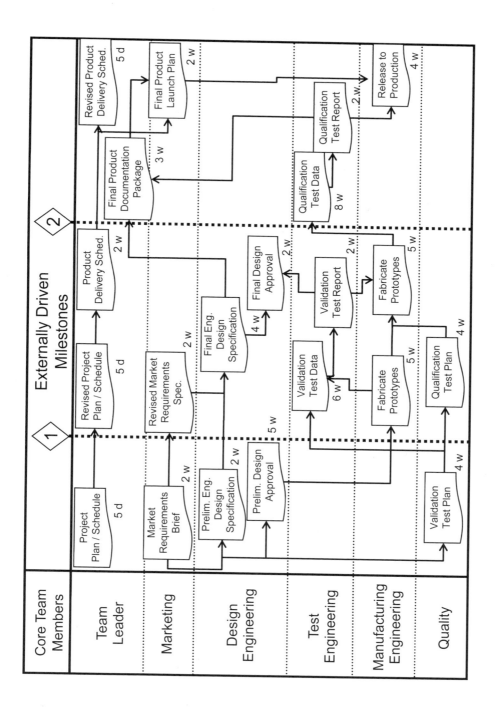

budget for the project. You can also easily calculate the monthly "burn rate" for the project by adding all of the dots in any vertical column. Finally, by totaling either all columns or all rows, and multiplying that number by the cost of a full-time-equivalent person, you will arrive at an estimate of the non-recurring cost of developing our electric bicycle."

At last, the first day of the Project Planning / Risk-Mitigation Event was complete. After expressing congratulations and thanks to the team, Lance sent them all off for a good night's sleep; they would be back in the morning to begin identifying project risks and assigning priorities for mitigation. Before heading home himself, Lance took high-resolution digital pictures of the visual planning tool. Within the next week, he would work with his admin to convert the plan into a Gantt chart and resource-loading matrix. These electronic versions would be distributed to the event's attendees, along with the digital pictures and a request to vet the final outcome. Ultimately, the cleaned-up and verified plan would be published as the electric bicycle project's roadmap for execution. Time for some well-deserved rest before the next day's activities begin.

Intermission: Optimizing the Duration of a Project Schedule

Although Lance was satisfied with the estimated duration of his electric bicycle project, you will likely not be satisfied with your team's initial estimate. In this section, I will describe some effective techniques for compressing a project's duration without significantly increasing its schedule risk. First, let me state the obvious: You never get something for nothing. To shrink a project's duration, you must alter the balance within the project. The only way you can accelerate the launch of a product without increasing risk is by either adding resources (where they would

FIGURE 6.7: The same template as shown in Figure 6.6, with the critical path for the project highlighted. The critical path is the longest series of dependant tasks or activities, and represents an approximation of the total duration of the project. Again, the duration shown in the above example does not align with the case example described in the text.

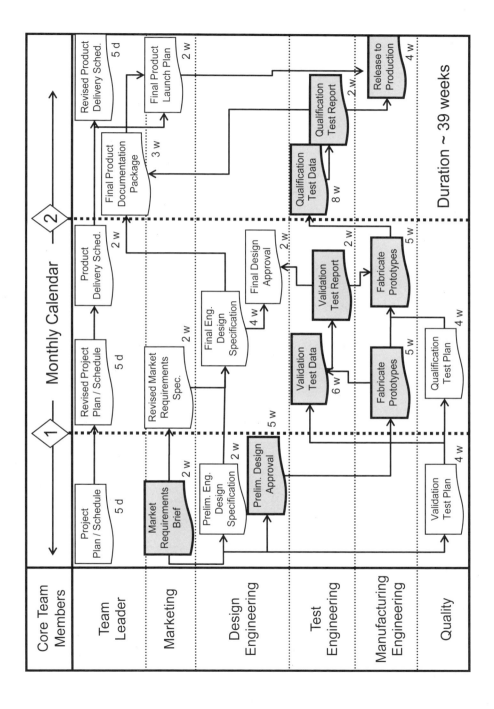

directly benefit the critical path) or by reducing the scope of the project. Assuming that neither of these options is in the cards for your project, the next best opportunity would be to alter the flow of tasks in some way. For example, you could take two serially-dependant, critical-path tasks and move them into parallel. The benefit would be a reduction in overall project duration. The price would be increased risk, since the knowledge needed to perform the downstream task would not be available if the tasks were performed simultaneously. At best, you could minimize this negative impact by ensuring that there is constant communication between the two parallel tasks, so that the necessary knowledge flow can occur in real time.

There is, however, a trick we can borrow from lean manufacturing. One of the hallmarks of a lean factory is the reduction of setup and changeover time. Toyota and other lean firms employ a technique to accomplish this goal that can be adapted for use on development projects; the defining of "internal" and "external" activities (for more on the general topic of single-minute exchange of die (SMED), see Shingo (1985)). An internal activity is one that must occur in a dependant order for value to be created with low risk. An external activity could occur at other times during a project without significantly increasing risk. In a sense, we are looking for activities that are currently on the critical path

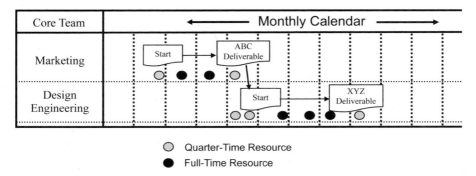

FIGURE 6.8: The final step in the visual planning process involves the assignment of resource-loading assumptions to each deliverable. A simple visual technique that employs colored sticky dots allows the entire team to clearly see the total resource requirements for each swim lane, the total monthly resource-loading (aka, the "burn rate") for the project, and to identify any potential resource bottlenecks that might jeopardize the project's end-date. Note that only a portion of the schedule template is shown for clarity.

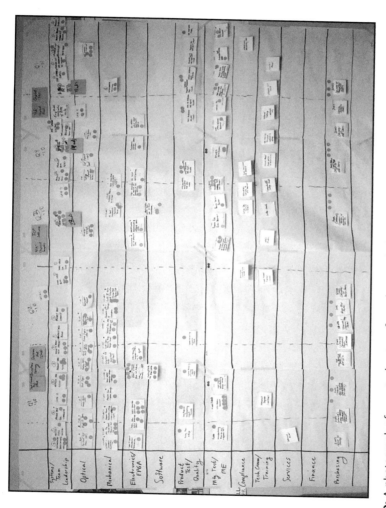

FIGURE 6.9: A photograph of an actual output from the visual planning process. Unfortunately, the black-and-white photo fails to capture the information content of the full-color version (not to mention its artistic appeal). Although this methodology can be challenging for the team, the result is easy to understand, and more important, was created by and agreed to by the team members themselves. Once the event is complete, this template should be captured as a Gantt chart and provided to the team as the project's initial master schedule.

that don't need to be there. If we can identify these types of external activities, we can move them into parallel with other project tasks without taking unnecessary chances.

For example, suppose that your project includes a task that involves the testing of a prototype, as shown in Figure 6.10. It is likely that during your initial planning process, this task might resemble the one shown at the top of the figure. However by "parsing" the task into three segments, an opportunity reveals itself. In reality, "testing of a prototype" is really three separate activities: preparing for the test, performing the test, and writing the final test report. In its current state, your critical-path schedule is paying the price of all three of these activities. Yet only one of them is actually dependant on the predecessor task; performing the test. You could, with minimal risk, prepare a test fixture, write test procedures, and gather the required test equipment without actually having the prototype in your hands. These external steps could be performed prior to the availability of the actual prototype with manageable risk. Likewise, the final test report is really not what is needed to move on to the next critical-path task; all that is required is just the raw data derived from the test. The writing of a formal test report is also an external activity that could be performed in parallel with the critical path at minimal risk. By removing these external activities from the critical path, you can decrease your overall project duration in relative safety.

A good analogy is to imagine a relay race. The first runner begins the race holding a baton. As he or she approaches the end of the first leg of the race, their teammate begins running to match the speed of the first runner. The baton is exchanged with both runners at a full gallop, so that no time is lost in the handoff. A similar situation occurs in project work; you want to "hit the ground running" on each successive task, without any unnecessary delays. By identifying low-risk opportunities to parse the critical path of your project, you can take weeks or months out of your project duration, provided that you can identify enough resources to staff the parallel activities that you have added to the plan.

One final note before returning to Lazy Rider's Project Planning / Risk-Mitigation Event. In the first half of the event, Lance and his team created a high-level master schedule. You might be wondering how this plan translates into action on the part of the team. There are basically

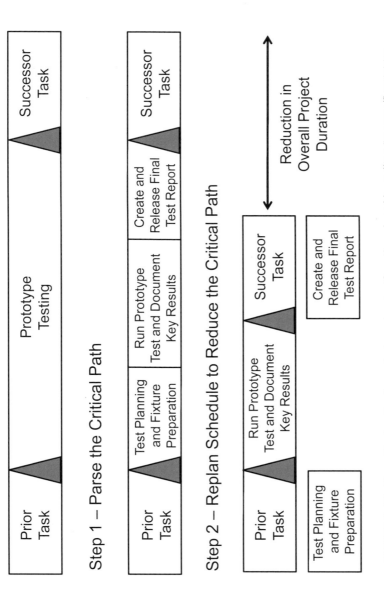

Step 1 – Parse the Critical Path

Step 2 – Replan Schedule to Reduce the Critical Path

FIGURE 6.10: The critical path of a project can be significantly reduced by pulling "external" activities into parallel with "internal" activities. The goal of this technique is to parse the project schedule such that each schedule-critical task "hits the ground running" in relation to its predecessor task(s).

three steps to converting a master schedule into project workflow, as shown in Figure 6.11. The first, of course, is to finalize the master schedule. The second is to expand the first few months of that high-level schedule into a somewhat more detailed intermediate plan. The result of this second step is a list of planned tasks that must be completed by the team to keep the project on schedule. As each month of the project passes, the intermediate planning window rolls forward, such that you are always looking a few months ahead at upcoming tasks. The final step in the execution of a project master schedule is the planning of day-to-day activities over an even shorter time-horizon. These latter two steps are already in your LPD toolbox, provided that you have read (and remember) Chapter 4. The visual project-board format that I recommend includes both the planned-work task list and the day-to-day activity plan (the wall-Gantt). Hence, you are now able to connect the dots. The long-term project master schedule created during your planning event is expanded to populate an intermediate-term task list, which is ultimately executed through the use of a visual two-week action plan. In this way, the time spent on planning is minimized (no detailed planning and replanning of the entire project duration), and the linkage between the master schedule and the daily activities of team members is clear and unambiguous. Now back to our regularly scheduled case example.

Event Simulation: Easy Rider Corp. and the Electric Bicycle (Part 2)

The electric bicycle project team was back in the conference room for the second day of their Project Planning / Risk-Mitigation Event. Again, Lance got everyone's attention by drawing two graphs on the whiteboard, similar to the ones shown in Figure 6.12. An explanation followed.

"In previous development projects, we have suffered mightily due to unforeseen risks that have caused significant launch delays," he began. "Yet, in most cases, these risks could have been avoided if we had taken the time at the beginning of the project to identify and mitigate them. Let's not make that same mistake again. We may not be able to anticipate

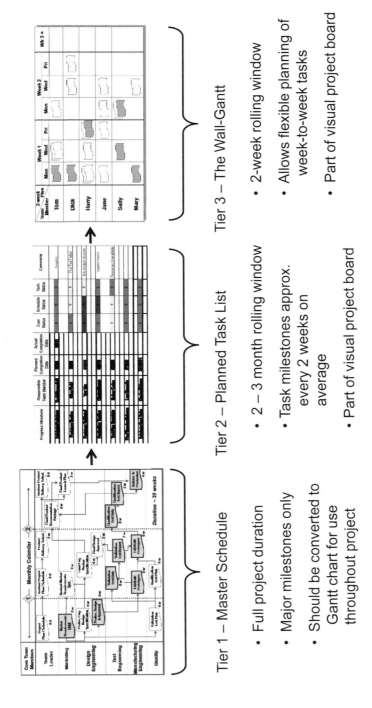

Tier 1 – Master Schedule

- Full project duration
- Major milestones only
- Should be converted to Gantt chart for use throughout project

Tier 2 – Planned Task List

- 2 – 3 month rolling window
- Task milestones approx. every 2 weeks on average
- Part of visual project board

Tier 3 – The Wall-Gantt

- 2-week rolling window
- Allows flexible planning of week-to-week tasks
- Part of visual project board

FIGURE 6.11: The long-term master schedule created during the Project Planning / Risk-Mitigation Event can be translated into team actions through the use of the visual project board described in Chapter 4. The master schedule is expanded into an intermediate-term task list (included on the visual board), which is subsequently converted into day-to-day team activities through the use of a two-week wall-Gantt.

every possible project risk, but at least we can use our knowledge of past history to avoid known issues and protect ourselves from likely obstacles. The two graphs I've drawn illustrate how critically important this is. The curve on the left shows how a typical project progresses. The team's effort ramps up at a leisurely pace, until the first disaster occurs. Then the team goes into react mode. Additional resources are pulled in to try to get the project schedule back on track, while other unexpected problems begin popping up right and left. Ultimately, the project end-date slips despite these reactive measures, and we wind up losing revenues and profits."

"On the other hand, if we proactively identify risks and immediately attack the most critical ones, we have a chance at avoiding catastrophe. Make no mistake; this represents a paradigm shift. Rather than back-end loading a project with resources, we are going to front-end load the project's efforts, as shown in the right-hand curve. Any risk that has the potential to become a death threat will be mitigated through rapid learning cycles in the earliest stages of concept development. These learning cycles (see Chapter 7, and for examples from software development, see Beck (2001)) will continue until all perceived risks have been reduced to acceptable levels. Hopefully this new philosophy will ensure that project risk decreases over time, with the final stages of development being nothing more than a relaxed stroll to the finish line."

Lance had to pause to let the laughter subside. Indeed, even he was skeptical that this new knowledge-based approach to development would work as advertised. However something different had to be done; Lazy Rider's last major new product launch had felt like a sixteen-month-long root canal. Since the disbelief in the room was palpable, Lance decided to share a story from his personal experience that had left him with some serious scar tissue.

"You guys all know that in my previous life, I worked on advanced battery technology. One of the biggest problems in commercializing those powerful lithium-ion batteries was that we never knew when a new technology left the world of "research" and was ready for "development." In fact, I began to hate the term R&D, since this implies that research and development are essentially the same thing. Wrong. I have come to recognize that research should represent the investigation of non-product-specific technologies, with the goal of proving feasibility

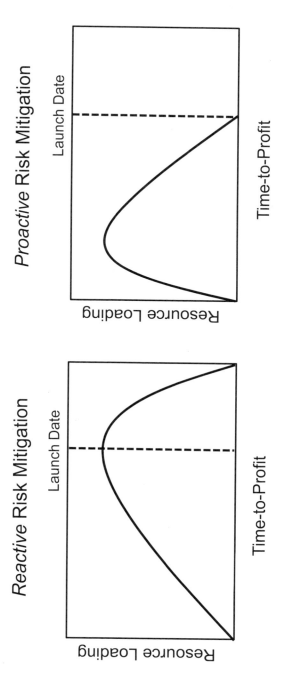

FIGURE 6.12: A reactive approach to managing project risk will likely result in schedule slips, since unanticipated negative events often must be addressed when there is precious little time and money left on the project. Hence, the planned launch date is often missed, as shown in the graph on the left. Performing proactive risk identification and mitigation at the very beginning of a project can reduce the schedule impact of potential risks, resulting in a greater probability of meeting the planned launch date, as shown in the graph on the right.

for commercialization. On the other hand, development is the process of incorporating those feasible technologies into commercial products. The main difference between these two activities is *risk*: Research projects often have open-ended schedules due to their inherent uncertainty, whereas a development project must meet a specific launch date for its business-case goals to be met."

To illustrate this point, Lance drew a diagram on the whiteboard similar to the one shown in Figure 6.13. Research projects should lay the groundwork for development by proving the feasibility of new technologies for commercialization. The objective of research should be to build a "supermarket" of feasible technologies that developers can browse when designing a new product. Mixing research and development on the same project will cause the potential for schedule slips to increase astronomically. The biggest challenge for any technology-driven company is to recognize the difference between the "R" and the "D," with the operative word here being *feasibility*. Lance shared with the team how his previous employer had dealt with this issue.

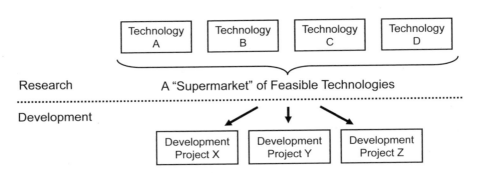

FIGURE 6.13: The intent of a research project is to demonstrate the feasibility of non-product-specific new technologies. Once feasibility has been proven, these technologies can populate a "supermarket" of available concepts for inclusion in development projects. In this way, the high degree of schedule risk associated with research activities is segregated from the more predictable world of product development.

"The problems associated with mixing research and development on a single project came to a head with the launch of a new cell-phone battery that our firm created. The potential performance of this battery represented a breakthrough, and the market pull was tremendous. As a result, shortcuts were taken at every step in the development process to accelerate time-to-market. Unfortunately, the advanced technology we were utilizing was unproven and highly unpredictable. We could get a prototype to work on the test bench, but couldn't achieve repeatability. Moreover, under certain conditions the batteries would heat up to unacceptable levels. After some hurried experiments, the decision was made to go to market without completely understanding these issues. The result nearly sank our company. Almost immediately we heard complaints from the field about cell phones overheating and even smoking. Furthermore, the factory was forced to scrap hundreds of batteries due to variability in the manufacturing process. It was a nightmare."

"After the smoke cleared, we decided that we could not let this happen again. One of our engineers had worked on several NASA projects, and was familiar with a feasibility model that they used to manage risk in new technology development. We adapted their model to our products, and immediately saw the benefits that this *language of feasibility* could provide. Here is the model we used." Lance handed out a sheet of paper to each attendee which explained the five levels of feasibility shown in Figure 6.14, and then continued. "I want you all to read the definitions of the five feasibility levels and tell me where we might have concerns with our electric bicycle product." After a couple of minutes, the first hand went up.

"Well, I think it is safe to say that the bicycle chassis and wheels are at Level 5," one of the industrial designers offered with a smile. "Similar products have been in production for over a century."

"Yeah, and the motor is also pretty mature. I think that meets the criteria of Level 5 as well," noted a manufacturing engineer.

"Okay, I have one," Lance interjected, noting that his team was missing one of the elephants in the room. "We are considering the idea of using proportional control of the power system through pressure sensors on the bicycle's pedals."

One of the revolutionary concepts that had been proposed for the new electric bicycle was a feature that would encourage exercise while still providing a "power assist." As the rider increased pressure on the pedals, the control electronics would respond by delivering proportionally higher levels of power to the wheels. In this way, a rider could get exercise on flat terrain, but feel like Superman when going up steep hills. The assist level would be adjustable from "no assist" to "full power," with the latter eliminating the need for pedaling entirely. Immediately upon mentioning this innovative feature, several team members responded.

"I think that idea is only at Level 1," stated a mechanical designer. "As far as I know, you are the only one in our firm that really understands how that's going to work, Lance."

"I disagree," said a new voice from procurement. "We have had several in-depth conversations on this topic, and I've identified a product in a different market that uses almost exactly the same concept. I think it's at least at Level 3."

And so it went. The conversation continued, but Lance had already accomplished his goal. His team was substituting the five levels of feasibility for their normal imprecise vocabulary, and as a result the discussion was far more objective and fruitful. An idea at Level 1 is really just a gleam in the eye of a designer or developer. There is no tangible evidence that it will work in a real-world product application. The next step is to convene a group of subject-matter experts and review the idea for viability. If the concept passes this test, it is considered to be at Level 2. The first real challenge is the development and testing of a proof-of-concept prototype. If the prototype achieves the desired performance, it moves to Level 3. (Note that a concept can be elevated to Level 3 if it is either in use by a competitor, or by another industry in a similar application. Just be sure that the extrapolation to your proposed new product is accurate.)

The most difficult level to achieve is Level 4; proving the repeatability of results. It is common for new technologies to display a high degree of variability in performance. Before an idea is ready for use in development, it must show acceptable performance over multiple samples, while being tested in a realistic product environment. This might take several design iterations, with a statistical sampling of prototypes being tested after each iteration. Once a stable design concept has been demonstrated and Level 4 has been achieved, the final step is to review the new technology with production specialists (and possibly with strategic suppliers)

Levels of Feasibility		Definition
Level 1	Unproven Technology	Concept is immature. Typically the result of a brainstorming session. Concept appears to have potential, but has not been reduced to practice – never tested by analysis or prototyping.
Level 2	Consensus of Experts	Concept is documented and presented to a "panel of experts" within firm. Experts agree that the concept has potential for successful implementation in a development environment. Proof-of-concept testing is defined by panel.
Level 3	Proof of Concept	Proof-of-concept prototype is fabricated (or accurately simulated), and tested under representative product-application conditions. Level 3 may be satisfied by referring to the use of the concept by other firms in similar product applications.
Level 4	Repeatable and Stable	Sufficient feasibility testing and analysis has been completed to convince the design team and "panel of experts" that the technology is repeatable and stable. Typically this requires the fabrication and testing of a statistical sampling of prototypes.
Level 5	Producible and Cost-Effective	Manufacturability and process-related issues have been considered, and verified by testing or analysis where appropriate. Production represent-atives have reviewed the concept and have estimated the cost impact in a realistic product application. Concept is ready to exit feasibility; risks are considered acceptable.

FIGURE 6.14: The five levels of feasibility defined above are based on a similar NASA model. A new technology must achieve Level 5 before being ready, from a risk standpoint, for inclusion in a product development project.

to determine its cost and quality implications. If transitioning the new concept to a manufactured product is considered to be low risk from a cost and quality standpoint, then the new technology achieves Level 5, and is ready to be placed on the "supermarket shelves" for use on the next development project. Lanced used the ongoing discussion of feasibility as a segue into the last critical activity of the Project Planning / Risk-Mitigation Event.

"Alright, time to capture some of this great discussion in a usable format. So far, we have been focused on technical risks, in the form of new and unproven technologies. Keep in mind, however, that there are other forms of risk that could become potential death threats to the project. In fact, I suggest that there are actually four categories of risk that we must consider to ensure that our new product is protected from hidden dangers. The first category is market risk. Here is where our understanding of the customer's perceptions and needs is tested. Do we really know what customers will buy? Are our pricing and volume assumptions correct? Will distributors embrace the new product, or will they see it as more trouble than it is worth? Without focusing some of our upcoming brainstorming on market risks, there is a good chance that these and other critical issues will be missed."

Lance continued to describe the other three categories of project risk, as shown in Figure 6.15. The second category identified in the figure is the most obvious one: technical risk. This would include any feasibility issues identified during initial discussions, along with other potential project killers, including a lack of capable suppliers, testing and integration concerns, new manufacturing process technologies, and so on. The third category to be addressed is schedule risk. Of course both market and technical risks can cause schedule slips, but we have already accounted for these issues in the previous two categories. What we are looking for in this third focus area are schedule challenges that have not already been captured: resource constraints, regulatory submissions, long lead times, availability of prototyping facilities, etc. Finally, the fourth category includes risks to cost and quality. Is the product's target manufacturing cost achievable, or is it just wishful thinking? Are production processes precise and accurate enough to meet the new product's design tolerances? How will the product be supported in the field?

Collectively, these four categories span the space of potential risks. By focusing on each of them as a separate brainstorming activity, you can be assured that nothing critical will be missed.

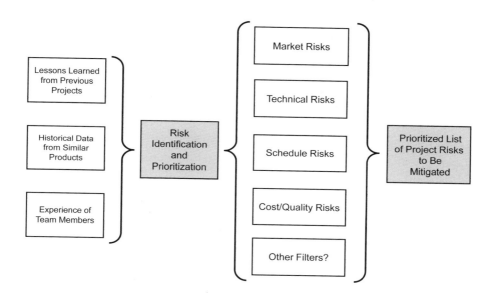

FIGURE 6.15: There are at least four categories of project risk that should be carefully considered when performing your risk-identification activity. Feel free to add additional categories if you believe they are important. Note that in all cases, the team should harness past history and lessons learned to provide a valuable feed to the current project's risk-assessment efforts.

In all cases, the team should be actively considering lessons learned on previous projects, as well as any other history and experience that each member brings to the table. One of the best ways that I've found to harness this valuable organizational knowledge is through the use of "trigger lists" such as the generic ones shown in Figure 6.16. After each project is completed (and even during project execution, if you have the discipline), a lessons-learned meeting should be held that is entirely focused on capturing new and relevant knowledge in appropriate organizational learning tools. The trigger list represents one of these tools, and is particularly well-suited to the archiving of known project risks. After being updated during a lessons-learned meeting, the list then becomes the basis for subsequent projects' risk-mitigation activities, and so it goes, with each generation of trigger list becoming increasingly comprehensive and robust. Note that the point of these lists is not to delve into great detail on how a possible risk might manifest itself. This is better accomplished through knowledge briefs (see Chapter 7). The purpose of a trigger list is to stimulate discussion and remind a project team of what might be lying in wait for them as they begin their efforts.

With trigger lists in hand, Lance and the electric bicycle team began brainstorming on possible project risks, beginning with a focus on market-related threats. Whenever the discussion began to wane, Lance (or another team member) would point out one of the items on the trigger list that hadn't been considered, and a new discussion would ensue. After roughly thirty minutes of capturing market risks on a flip chart, the discussion moved on to technical risks, and so on. In no time, the morning was spent, and so was the team. A solid list of risks had been identified for each of the four categories, with technical risk (not surprisingly) dominating the other categories in terms of sheer number of issues raised. After a long lunch to allow time for urgent calls and e-mails, the event entered the home stretch. Lance rallied the group for one final step.

"Okay guys, you've done an awesome job so far," Lance said with as much cheer as he could muster. "All we have left to do is to rank our list of risks in terms of their priority for mitigation. To do this, we'll use a simple scoring system, based on two 1-to-5 scores." As he was talking, he flipped a slide up on the projector screen that resembled Figure 6.17.

"The first score we will use represents an estimate of the *impact* that a risk could have on the success of our project, should it actually come to pass. For this impact rating, a "5" indicates a potential death threat to the project – significant damage to the business case would occur. On the other extreme, a "1" implies that even if the risk were to occur, it could be absorbed by the project with no impact on the business case. The second 1-to-5 score we will use is an assessment of the *probability of occurrence* of a risk. In this case, a "5" would indicate that the chance of the risk actually occurring is approaching a certainty, whereas a "1" would reflect a very small chance of occurrence."

Market	Technical	Schedule	Cost/Quality
• Under / over estimated volumes	• Failure to meet rqmts.	• Disruptive rqmts. changes	• Exchange rates
• Related projects failed or delayed	• Stability and repeatability	• Availability of resources	• Process yields
• Market downturn	• Incorrect materials	• Dependencies on other projects	• Process time
• Better competitor products	• Incorrect test methods	• Missing competencies	• Raw-material prices
• New technologies	• Environmental issues	• Long lead-time items	• Tolerance stack-up
• New markets / customers	• Capability of manufacturing processes	• Prototyping capacity	• Raw-material variability
• Incorrect pricing	• Supply-chain issues	• Force *majour*	• Extremes of use environment
• Late to market	• …	• External approvals	• Reliability issues
• …		• Conflicting priorities	• Worker competencies
		• …	• …

FIGURE 6.16: Generic examples of trigger lists for the four categories of project risk. Note that your trigger lists should be based on past project history and lessons learned, and should be used during risk brainstorming to stimulate discussion and ensure that nothing critical is missed.

183

Impact (1-to-5 scale) –

1	-	Very minor risk – no significant project impact
2	-	Minor risk – can be managed without mitigation
3	-	Medium risk factor – may require mitigation
4	-	High risk factor – significant impact on cost / schedule
5	-	Very high risk factor – can be a "project killer"

Probability of Occurrence (1-to-5 scale) –

1	-	Very low probability – not worth considering
2	-	Low probability – very unlikely to occur
3	-	Medium probability – realistic chance of occurrence
4	-	High probability – likely to occur
5	-	Very high probability – almost certain to occur

FIGURE 6.17: A simple 1-to-5 scoring system is used to rank the criticality of project risks. The first score reflects the impact a risk might have on the success of the project, while the second score indicates the probability of that risk actually occurring. The product of these two scores provides a Risk Priority Number (RPN) that is useful in focusing the team's attention on possible death threats to their project.

With the scoring system fully explained, the team began working down their list of brainstormed risks, ranking each one in turn. To keep the process moving, Lance asked for a show of fingers: The number of fingers shown on a raised hand reflected a person's 1-to-5 score for that risk. It was then relatively easy for him to take an approximate average of all the team members' inputs. (Note that this tool is not intended to be precise; just accurate enough to segregate the potential project killers from far less threatening obstacles.) After each risk was scored, Lance multiplied the impact and probability numbers together to arrive at a Risk Priority Number (RPN) that would be used to prioritize all of their brainstormed issues for future mitigation. A sampling of the team's output is shown in Figure 6.18.

Before closing the event, Lance put one more graphic up on the projector screen. A five-by-five matrix of colored dots was displayed on the slide, with one axis of the matrix representing "impact" and the other denoting "probability," as shown in Figure 6.19. In this visual way, the

Potential Risks to Project	Subjective Score		Ranking (P x I)
	P	I	
Retailers reject our electric bicycle and refuse to display them	3	5	(15)
Our price-point should be lower due to import competition	4	2	8
Proportional assist power system – feasibility	5	5	(25)
Miniaturizing control electronics to fit bicycle form factor	2	3	6
Lead time for UL submission and possible design corrections	3	3	9
Availability of critical environmental-testing lab equipment	2	4	8
Cost of tooling for injection-molded power-system enclosure	4	2	8
Supplier capability to provide source inspection of motor assy.	3	2	6
Too many features – added complexity will reduce reliability	2	4	8
Bicycle frame not ridged enough to support power assist	1	5	5
Product will be perceived as being for "sissies"	2	4	8

FIGURE 6.18: A sampling of the risks that were identified by the electric bicycle project team during their Project Planning / Risk-Mitigation Event. The highest-ranking risks will be the focus of an upcoming Learning-Cycle Event that will provide the tools to mitigate risk issues and close any critical knowledge gaps.

message of the scoring system became clear: Risks that had been given a high score for both probability and impact deserve all of the team's initial attention. The dots that were colored red (i.e., RPN scores of 15, 16, 20, and 25) would be addressed immediately, using a standardized set of risk-mitigation and problem-solving tools. Finally, it was time to adjourn the event and release the team.

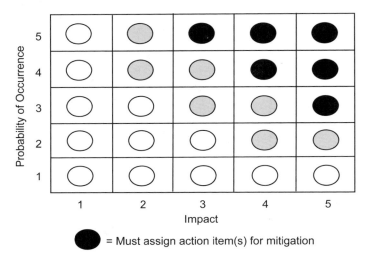

= Must assign action item(s) for mitigation

FIGURE 6.19: A graphical representation of the 1-to-5 scoring system used to rank the criticality of project risks. The upper-right corner of the graph indicates those risks that should receive immediate attention by the team (black in the figure, but colored red in the real world). Lower-scoring risks cannot be ignored: They should be monitored over time to ensure that they do not grow into significant threats.

"Well, we made it," Lance enthused once all of the scoring was done and the "reds" had been identified, "time to go and rest our synapses. Over the next few weeks, I want all of you to be thinking about action-able ways in which we can mitigate the highest-ranking risks. Keep in mind that a risk can be mitigated either by reducing its potential impact and /or by reducing its probability of occurrence. After years of working in new product development, I've come to believe that an ounce of prevention really is worth at least a pound of cure. Let's take that trite old saying to heart, and be ready to attack the potential project killers at our upcoming Learning-Cycle Event. See you all in a few weeks."

Advanced Topic: Value-Stream Mapping and Standardized Schedule Templates

At the beginning of this chapter, I commented on the application of value-stream mapping to product development process improvement. It is time to expand that discussion and provide you with some suggestions for creating and using standardized schedule templates. First, let me offer a disclaimer. I personally use value-stream mapping only occasionally, as a method for refining a recurring process embedded within the overall product development landscape. There are, in fact, a number of these recurring processes: the release of drawings, the execution of an Engineering Change Notice, and many others. From a process improvement standpoint, these are the low-hanging fruit. In each case, the process remains (or should remain) consistent and repeatable, regardless of the nature of the project itself. Hence, we can refine the daylights out of these opportunities without fear of suboptimizing the overall development process, or needlessly constraining project teams. Since these recurring loops are often executed several times during a given project, the benefits of honing your approach can be dramatic.

That being said, I've seen more time wasted on attempts to use value-stream mapping to force-standardize the end-to-end product development process than I care to think about. There are two fundamental reasons why these efforts often fail to meet expectations. The first is the inherently non-recurring nature of product development. Imagine a manufacturing line in which every unit produced is substantially different from the previous one: different order of processes, unique steps required for each individual unit, substantially more or less complexity, etc. You get the picture. Now consider how you would value-stream map that little slice of heaven. To be sure, some of the steps would be common to all of the products, but only a precious few. In most cases, the differences will outweigh the commonality, resulting in a value-stream map with finger-like tendrils winding their way in various directions, along with conditional decision points, if / then statements, and so on. How would you optimize such a value stream, let alone put it to use as a roadmap for production flow?

This is the reality of new product development projects, again harkening back to the project / process duality of this vital activity. To the degree that your development projects are identical, you can use value-stream mapping effectively. However, as the differences among projects increase, this tool becomes exponentially more cumbersome and ineffectual. In all cases, some amount of process mapping can be used, but the level of detail that can be "standardized" will depend on the commonality among all of your projects. For firms with products that are very similar from project to project (e.g., the auto industry in general, and Toyota specifically), value-stream mapping can be very powerful. For a high-mix producer of low-volume medical devices, however, the tool provides little value for the time spent. These types of firms (and I would argue that they are in the majority) will be better served by the standardized schedule templates described below.

The second fundamental reason that value-stream mapping is less than effective in the world of new product development is more subtle. When a *kaizen* team develops a future-state value-stream map for a production line, they are making a basic assumption that the line will be staffed in a consistent way. Once operators are trained and assigned to stations, these resources will be predictably available to perform the tasks they are responsible for. This is not, and in fact *cannot*, be the case in new product development. Each project has a somewhat different scope of work, requiring a different mix of skills. Moreover, the order of tasks, number of iterations, and scale and complexity of tasks is also, in most cases, somewhat variable. To make matters even worse, development projects are generally initiated at different and unpredictable times, causing a complex overlap of project activities and resource demands. The bottom line is that the fundamental assumption of value-stream mapping, that a stable workforce can be applied to a well-honed process map, rarely occurs.

This is the reason that I've chosen to use the Project Planning / Risk-Mitigation Event to create what amounts to a simplified, project-specific value-stream map. The master schedule created by a project team during this event represents a reasonably well-optimized process map for their project's unique requirements. Add to this the advantage of having the team members develop their own map, as opposed to inheriting a map created by some disembodied improvement team, and you get a far better solution to the complexity of new product development. The only disadvantage to the approach I advocate is that perhaps the pendulum has swung too far in the other direction: It is likely that each project team is repeating the work done by previous teams, at least for those portions of their project that are similar to others completed in the past. It appears that we are caught between two extremes: a one-size-fits-none value-stream map on the one hand, or expecting every team to, at least in part, reinvent the wheel.

To resolve this paradox, we can use the project / process duality of new product development to our advantage. Over time, it is likely that your firm will recognize that certain categories of project have very similar master schedules. For example, special-order projects have more in common with each other than with a new platform development project. As these categories of similar projects are identified, a standardized schedule template can be created by simply merging the common attributes of schedules from several completed projects within that category. This standardized schedule template can then be made available to future projects of this type as a starting point for their Project Planning / Risk-Mitigation Event. It is still critical that each new project team reassess the standard template, and be encouraged to make any necessary changes to meet their project's goals. However, much time will be saved and the accuracy of new schedules will likely improve over time. If a given category of project occurs frequently within your firm, you should consider investing in a value-stream-mapping event to optimize that category's standardized schedule template. In this way, we can come full circle. The advantages and power of value-stream mapping can be brought to bear without fear of constraining future project teams from making the adjustments needed to be successful.

You can choose to embrace the dual nature of new product development, or you can fight against it. Unless your projects are virtually identical to each other, imposing a detailed, standardized process will likely fail to do more than frustrate your project teams. Likewise, although creating project-specific plans can be effective, it can also be wasteful if taken to an extreme, and can fail to benefit from organizational learning.

189

The ideal answer is to determine the similarities and differences among your development projects over time, and to optimize each of these realms using the best tool for the job.

Chapter References

Beck, K., and J. Fowler, 2001, *Planning Extreme Programming*, Addison-Wesley.

Fleming, Q. W., and J. M. Koppelman, 2000, *Earned Value Project Management, 2nd Edition*, The Project Management Institute.

Kerzner, H., 2000, *Applied Project Management*, John Wiley & Sons.

Lewis, J. P., 1999, *Mastering Project Management*, McGraw-Hill.

Lientz, B. P., and K. P. Rea, 1999, *Breakthrough Technology Project Management*, Academic Press.

Locher, D. A., 2008, *Value Stream Mapping for Lean Development*, CRC Press.

Mascitelli, R., 2002, *Building a Project-Driven Enterprise*, Technology Perspectives.

Project Management Institute, 2008, *A Guide to the Project Management Body of Knowledge*.

Rother, M., and J. Shook, 1999, *Learning to See*, The Lean Enterprise Institute.

Shingo, S. and A. Dillon, 1985, *A Revolution in Manufacturing: The SMED System*, Productivity Press.

Wideman, R. M., 1992, *Project & Program Risk Management*, The Project Management Institute.

7   The Learning-Cycle Event(s)

Background and Overview

Throughout much of human history, the wealth and power of both individuals and states has been determined by their hoard of treasure. This treasure usually took the form of large piles of precious metals, and those entities that possessed the biggest piles were a force to be reckoned with. In fact, our past is largely driven by attempts to find treasure, steal treasure, and in the case of alchemists (the R & D scientists of their day), to create treasure from non-treasure. In our current times, precious metals still retain their luster, but by far the more valuable treasure is *knowledge*. Firms that can efficiently harvest the knowledge of their employees will excel in the marketplace. Those companies that are also adept at harvesting knowledge from outside sources, including their competition, will fare even better. However, it is the alchemists, those enterprises that are capable of *creating* knowledge, that will achieve a sustainable competitive advantage.

The idea that knowledge itself is the true source of competitive advantage is a relatively new concept. In the early 1990's, two landmark books formed the genesis of what has become an accepted reality. The first, entitled *The Fifth Discipline* (see Senge (1990) and (1994)), brought the term "learning organization" into the business lexicon.

Organizations that can learn from both themselves (e.g., their past experiences) and from others (e.g., their competitors, different industries, academia, etc.) are best positioned to solve customer problems and develop valuable new products. At approximately the same time, two Japanese investigators proposed an entirely new perspective on how collaboration among innovative individuals can actually create knowledge from whole cloth in *The Knowledge-Creating Company* (see Nonaka, et al (1995)). While each of these books stands as an achievement on its own, they wouldn't have received much attention from the pragmatic business community had it not been for the thrashing that Western industry had suffered at the hands of the Japanese during the previous two decades. During this same time period, a number of investigators (see Sobek (1998) and (1999), and Ward (2007)) had independently concluded that Toyota, Honda, Sony, Matsushita, and other giants had achieved greatness through a robust culture of learning. Thus, these two rivers of thought had their confluence: Success in new product development (as well as all other aspects of the enterprise) is fundamentally dependant on a firm's ability to create, transform, and retain knowledge.

Every product-based firm must be capable of transforming knowledge, however the challenges associated with this transformation vary greatly. A large percentage of new products are simply manifestations of repurposed knowledge: Little or no new knowledge is required to generate minor line extensions, or to fulfill special orders that demand straightforward customization of existing product designs. For these low-risk projects, knowledge is nothing more than grist for the mill. A firm with a reasonably effective knowledge management system and a talented staff of developers can survive and even prosper in this environment. However, once the bar is raised to the level of high-risk, innovative (i.e., highly differentiated) products, the creation of new knowledge becomes essential. While it is certainly true that firms from many nations have introduced highly innovative products, studies of Japanese industry icons have shown that their approach to knowledge creation is fundamentally different from traditional Western methods. This disparity first came to light in a study of Toyota's Product Development System by Dr. Allen Ward and others (see Ward (2007)). The differences between these two systems can be summarized in the contrasting philosophies of "design-to-test" versus "test-to-design."

A typical U.S. design team, for example, would address the challenge of developing a high-risk new product by rapidly converging on a single conceptual design, fabricating a relatively sophisticated prototype, and then performing tests to determine the validity of their initial concept. In gambling terms, this is similar to placing a very large wager at long odds. If the proposed concept is successful, the firm wins, and the new product can be launched without delay. However, if the prototype test results fail to meet expectations, as is often the case, the firm loses. A time-consuming design iteration (perhaps several) will be required to converge on a successful concept, and the product's launch date will be significantly delayed. A graphical representation of this design-to-test approach is shown in Figure 7.1. In a sense, the development team "doesn't know what it doesn't know" until these knowledge gaps are painfully uncovered far down the development pipeline. (Actually, the proper quote by Mark Twain is even more apropos: "It isn't what you don't know that hurts you; it is what you think you know that isn't so.")

The problem with a design-to-test methodology is that learning takes place in excessively long time batches. Substantial time and resources are wasted uncovering knowledge gaps that could have been identified much earlier. I'll share a personal example that makes this point abundantly clear. I am an avid woodworker. Recently, I decided to try a new finishing method that would complement a formal dining-room table that I had built. Not having any experience with this new finish, but armed with magazine articles and a false sense of security, I spent the better part of three days applying this multi-step finish. Near the end of this tedious process, I discovered to my horror that two of the materials I had been using were incompatible. The result was a terrible case of "fisheye" (a very bad thing), and a ruined finish. Another three days were required to strip the table, solve the problem, and achieve a successful outcome.

The irony of this story is that all of that wasted time could have been easily avoided. If I had started with a sample board of the same wood and my finishing materials, I could have performed a test case in just a few hours, and learned the same lesson without the pain. Even better,

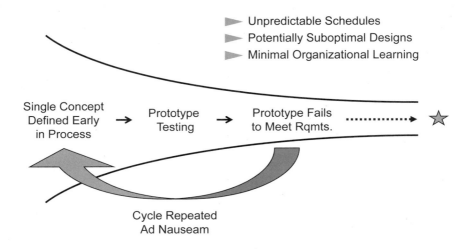

FIGURE 7.1: The traditional approach to developing high-risk, innovative new products involves a "design-to-test" methodology. A single conceptual design is identified early in the project, a fully-formed prototype is fabricated, and testing is performed to validate this initial concept. If the prototype fails to meet product requirements, as is often the case, then long iterative loops must be executed to eventually converge on an optimal design. These extended learning cycles represent time batches that can cause significant delays to product launch.

I might have created a set of sample boards and applied variations of the finish on each. By carefully recording my learning on each sample, I would have established a robust knowledge base that would have enabled me to identify a truly optimized finish. As the Pennsylvania Dutch often say, "Too soon old, too late smart." This far more sensible approach represents a fundamentally different way of solving problems; a test-to-design methodology that front-end loads learning through the use of rapid learning cycles, as illustrated in Figure 7.2. Rough prototypes and quick-turn experiments are used to explore a set of possible design alternatives, establish a deep understanding of the challenges being addressed, and ultimately yield an optimal concept. In a sense, this philosophy encourages designers to cast a wide net, and through a Darwinian process, separate the weak from the strong. In the literature, this wide-net approach has come to be known as "set-based design" (aka, set-based concurrent engineering, see Sobek (1999) and Ward (2007)) and the natural-selection part is often referred to as performing "rapid

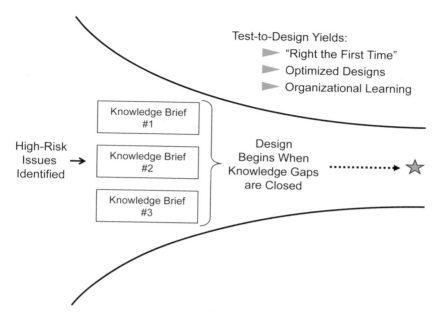

FIGURE 7.2: Toyota and other iconic Japanese firms have adopted a "test-to-design" methodology that front-end loads learning and closes critical knowledge gaps before any detailed design work is performed. In this way, risks are mitigated early in the project, and once design work begins, it can proceed with a high degree of confidence in obtaining a successful outcome.

learning cycles" (see Kennedy (2003), Kennedy, et al (2008) and Schipper, et al (2010)). Collectively, I'll refer to the combination of set-based design and rapid learning cycles as "knowledge-based development."

Before we begin exploring this new paradigm, it is important to note that there is both a strategic and a tactical aspect to the creation and management of knowledge. The Learning-Cycle Event described in this chapter is intended to aggressively pursue the tactical dimension; achieving economic success for a specific new product opportunity. This event is, however, part of a larger picture, and can offer a much greater opportunity for maximizing your firm's competitiveness. The strategic aspects of rapid learning cycles will be addressed in the final section of this chapter. For now, we will use the Learning-Cycle Event as a tool for mitigating project risks, closing knowledge gaps, and accelerating new product development through aggressive front-end learning.

Mitigating Risk through Rapid Learning Cycles

The final activity of the Project Planning / Risk-Mitigation Event described in Chapter 6 is the creation of a prioritized list of project risks. In the same chapter, a compelling case was made for immediate, proactive mitigation of the highest-ranking risks; literally the first thing a development team should focus on once a project plan is in place. The mitigation of risk (i.e., the reduction of either the probability of occurrence and / or the impact of a risk) can be divided into two categories:

- Immediately Actionable: The root cause(s) of the risk are clearly understood, and the steps necessary to mitigate the risk are apparent and straightforward. In this case, action items and responsibilities can be assigned without delay.

- Knowledge Gaps: The root cause(s) of the risk are not evident, or an optimal solution cannot be immediately identified. In this situation, new knowledge must either be found or created to close the knowledge gap and thereby mitigate the risk.

It is the latter type of risk that is the most pernicious. A lack of knowledge cannot be mitigated through a set of action items: A methodical process must be used to systematically identify root cause(s), gather or create the required knowledge, and select an optimal course of action for the development team. A knowledge gap exists whenever there is a disparity between the current situation with respect to team knowledge and the desired state, as shown in Figure 7.3. If a team does not face any knowledge gaps on their project, then there may not be a need to hold a Learning-Cycle Event to mitigate their risks. A brief team meeting to assign action items and due dates may be all that is needed to achieve a high confidence-level in their project's success. However, if knowledge gaps are identified, and in particular if those knowledge gaps impact must-have features or requirements, a much more powerful and aggressive approach is warranted. In this situation, a series of rapid learning cycles can be used to gain the required knowledge in the shortest possible time.

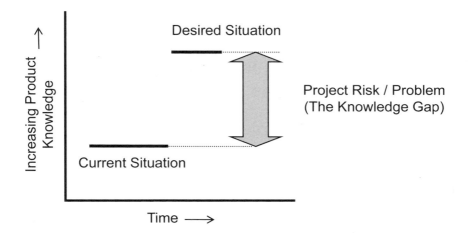

FIGURE 7.3: A knowledge gap exists whenever there is a disparity between the current knowledge of a development team and the desired knowledge necessary to achieve a low-risk, optimized product design.

A learning cycle is basically a mini-project in which the team establishes a plan for learning, defines a set of quick-turn experiments, and agrees upon a target date for integrating the new knowledge and reassessing their situation. The duration of a learning cycle is dependent on the nature of the product and the type of knowledge required, but the goal should be a cycle of no more than one month, and preferably less. After each cycle is complete, the team determines whether all critical knowledge gaps have been closed. If this is the case, the team is unleashed to design the new product with a high assurance of first-time success. If knowledge gaps persist, a new cycle of learning is planned, and the process continues until the required knowledge has been gained. For a relatively simple new product with only a manageable few knowledge gaps, all learning may be accomplished in one or two cycles at the beginning of the project. On the other hand, for complex system products it may be necessary to first execute several system-level learning cycles, develop an optimal system concept, and then proceed to perform additional learning cycles at the subsystem and component levels. For these more challenging products, the learning process may continue well into the project, as shown in Figure 7.4.

197

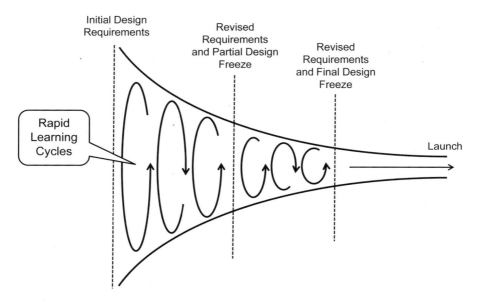

FIGURE 7.4: Rapid learning cycles allow a development team to close knowledge gaps and mitigate high-ranking risks early in a project. For the case of a complex, system-level product, however, learning cycles must first be executed for the overall system design, and subsequently for each major subsystem, and even for critical components. In this situation, learning cycles may persist well into a project's duration.

From a practical standpoint, the Learning-Cycle Event described in the next section is a means to an end. On any given project, the goal of this event is to achieve an optimal product design in the shortest possible time. However this narrow view ignores the strategic elephant in the room. If a development team learns vital lessons, creates precious new knowledge, and then disbands after launching their highly successful product, much that has been learned will be lost to the entropy of organizational "tribal knowledge." On the other hand, if that same team captures their learning, and that new knowledge is system-atically integrated with the learnings of other project teams, then each subsequent development team can stand on the shoulders of all those who preceded them. In this way, future learning cycles can be shortened or even eliminated, project-killing risks can be avoided entirely, and new product development will accelerate at an ever-increasing pace. As you will soon see, we can address the near-term tactical needs of project teams, while building a strategic knowledge base for future projects, and all without sacrificing speed and efficiency.

General Description of the Learning-Cycle Event

I sense through the pages of this book that you, the reader, are skeptical. Have I not made a compelling case for learning before doing? Is it not reasonable that by performing quick and rough experiments to close knowledge gaps early in a project, the probability of success can be dramatically increased? I suspect, though I cannot be sure, that your discomfort is more emotional than intellectual. Dramatically different ideas evoke basal emotions, not the least of which is fear. The path to conquering your fear is through an understanding of scalability. I have emphasized throughout this book that Lean Product Development Events are inherently scalable. This means that the duration of events can and should be adapted to the needs of each unique project, such that they always deliver high value for time spent. For previous events, however, we were talking about, at most, several days of time invested by a development team. Now we are considering learning cycles that could demand weeks or even months. If you fail to properly scale a one-day event, perhaps a few hours will be wasted. However, if you miss the mark on learning cycles, you could squander unnecessary weeks of precious schedule, a potentially career-limiting miscalculation. I will, therefore, describe in some detail how to adapt and scale the Learning-Cycle Event.

A general description of the Learning-Cycle Event is provided in Figure 7.5, and the timing of this event within the Event-Driven Lean Product Development process is shown in Figure 7.6. The vital inputs to this event are a prioritized list of project risks, along with updates to the guiding scope and requirements documents for your project. The desired outputs will be described in detail below. Participants for the event may be limited to just the core development team, or can be expanded to include support functions, strategic suppliers, and additional subject-matter experts from both inside and outside your firm. Your choice of participants should be based on the type of risks

---

The Learning-Cycle Event

Objective: To focus the collective knowledge of a cross-functional team on the mitigation of critical project risks and the elimination of knowledge gaps prior to executing a new product design.

Inputs:
- Market Requirements Brief (updated)
- Engineering requirements matrix
- Prioritized list of project risks

Outputs:
- Risk-mitigation action list for critical project risks
- Knowledge briefs documenting tradeoffs and solutions to knowledge gaps
- Archived learnings of the team, including performance, curves, concept selection matrices, etc.

Attendees (typical):
- Team leader
- Team members (cross-functional development team)
- Others (strategic suppliers, supply chain, quality, etc.)

Agenda (typical):

8:00 – 9:00	Review prioritized risks and select critical issues
9:00 – 11:00	Sorting of risks into "immediately actionable" and "knowledge gaps"
11:00 – 12:00	Create / revise plan for development of knowledge briefs
12:00 – 4:00	Collaboratively discuss knowledge briefs and assign responsibilities and dates for next learning cycle
4:00 – 4:30	Identify actions to close out event
4:30 – 5:00	Management outbriefing / learning opportunities

FIGURE 7.5: An overview of the Learning-Cycle Event. The agenda shown is typical for a project of moderate complexity. It is important to keep scalability in mind when planning your own events; the duration of both the event itself and the learning cycle that follows should maximize the value-added for time spent.

that the project faces; a broad spectrum of risks mandates a more comprehensive list of invitees. The agenda for the event is where there is the greatest degree of variability from project to project. In all cases, the first action on the agenda will be to review the prioritized list of risk issues for the project, followed by a discussion of which risks must receive immediate attention before design work can begin. Where this line is drawn is important: Your goal should be to address the death threats to the project, rather than attempting to mitigate every possible issue that could arise throughout execution.

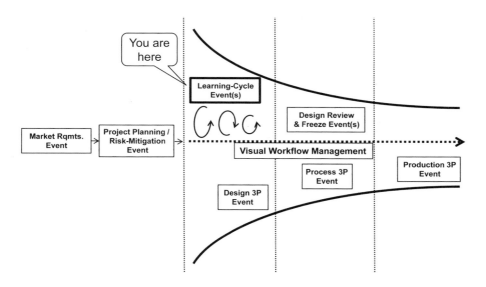

FIGURE 7.6: The Learning-Cycle Event serves as a risk-mitigation planning session, and should be scheduled almost immediately after the successful completion of the Project Planning / Risk-Mitigation Event.

Once the potential project killers have been identified, the next action on the agenda for the Learning-Cycle Event is a sorting process, as shown in Figure 7.7. If a given risk is fully understood, and a course of action to reduce that risk is evident, then it would fall into the "immediately-actionable" category, as described in the previous section. However, if the risk or issue is not well-understood, and in particular if the root cause(s) of the risk are not certain, then it would be designated as a "knowledge gap." It is important to perform this sorting process wisely, since the time invested by the team in addressing a knowledge gap is substantially greater than would be required to take immediate action. Some examples may help make the distinction between these two categories more clear.

There is definitely not a one-to-one correspondence between risks and knowledge gaps, and it is entirely possible that a project would not have any knowledge gaps that are worth the time to pursue. The following are some examples of risk issues that would be immediately actionable:

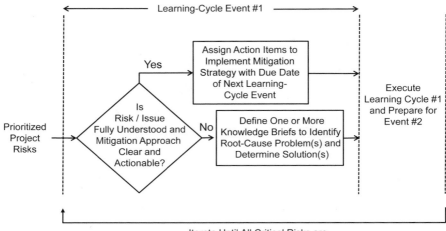

FIGURE 7.7: Major risks to a project's success are sorted during the early stages of the Learning-Cycle Event. Those risks or issues that are well-understood can be addressed through immediate action, whereas knowledge gaps require a more robust process for risk mitigation.

- A key customer has not yet been consulted regarding the desired features and performance of the new product. Action: Assign an appropriate team member to meet with the customer and solicit their inputs.

- Another firm has introduced a competing product that has not yet been analyzed by your team. Action: Procure a sample of the product and perform tests to determine how it might impact your proposed product's business case.

- A commercial component might be useful for the proposed new product, but the supplier has not yet been qualified by your firm. Action: Ask procurement and quality assurance to begin the certification process for the new supplier.

- A key technical resource within your firm is currently over-booked on other projects. Action: Meet with management to determine if priority can be given to your project, or if another appropriate resource can be identified.

- The cost of a desired material or component is not known. Action: Investigate the cost of the item, and gather several quotes from suppliers along with samples of their material.

In all of these situations and many more, there is a clear course of action that can be followed without delay. There will certainly be a need to provide feedback to the team, and unquestionably there will be learning involved. However, the knowledge to be gained is narrow and specific in scope, and therefore is not worth the time required to perform a formal trade study or employ systematic problem-solving. It may, nonetheless, be worth documenting the results of these actions for use by future development teams. Indeed, there are many projects whose high-ranking risks can all be addressed through immediate action. As I mentioned above, minor line extensions and customized special orders will often have a sufficient existing knowledge base to allow execution to proceed with confidence.

There will, however, be times when a robust and systematic approach to risk mitigation will be essential. Some examples include:

- There is no low-risk approach for meeting a desired performance target or implementing a needed product feature.

- Existing technology has never been tested under the use conditions of the proposed new product.

- The choice of materials or components depends on design factors that are not well-understood.

- Customer or market needs are divergent, unclear, or simply unknown.

- The feasibility of a new technology for integration into a commercial product has never been proven.

- There are significant and complex tradeoffs among several design variables, with the overall product performance being driven by the balancing of these variables.

- The root causes of a technical (or other) risk are not known, and therefore a straightforward solution cannot be defined without the potential of "unintended consequences."

In these and other circumstances, there is a clear knowledge gap that must be closed. Furthermore, these types of risks are likely to manifest themselves on future products, and therefore would justify the application of systematic problem-solving to establish a solid knowledge foundation for all products that will follow. A standard-work approach will be used for these situations, based on a proven Toyota methodology now in widespread use in many companies; the so-called A3 template (named for the size of the sheet of paper involved – A3 is the European equivalent of an 11" x 17" page). Personally, I prefer the term "knowledge brief" (see Kennedy (2003)). This method will be described in detail later in this section, but first I will finish describing the agenda for the Learning-Cycle Event.

Once the sorting of risks has been performed, the remainder of the Learning-Cycle Event is focused on establishing a plan for the first learning cycle. Who will be responsible for performing immediate risk-mitigation actions? What will be the topics of the first knowledge briefs to be developed? Who will own them, and what supporting materials, information, or critical resources will be needed to begin their creation? How are the planned knowledge briefs time-phased; can they all be developed in parallel, or are there interdependencies that may demand a staggered approach? (For an excellent description of how multiple parallel learning activities can be effectively planned, see Schipper, et al (2010).) Finally, what is the optimal duration for the first learning cycle, based on the nature and complexity of the knowledge briefs that will be created? Once a plan for the first learning cycle has been agreed upon, it is time to adjourn the Learning-Cycle Event and begin the first rapid learning cycle.

The activities that take place during each learning cycle should be tracked through the use of Visual Workflow Management, as described in Chapter 4. Frequent team stand-up meetings provide a perfect forum to discuss progress on quick-turn experiments, and to gain collaborative input on future directions. When the agreed-upon period for the first learning cycle is complete, it is time for an abbreviated repeat of the Learning-Cycle Event, as shown in Figure 7.8. This subsequent event is intended to integrate the learnings from the previous cycle, and determine whether an additional cycle is required. There are two possible

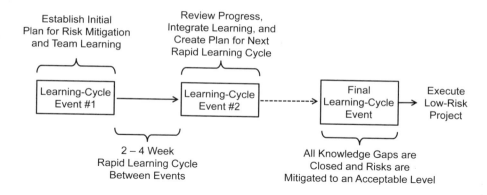

FIGURE 7.8: Each Learning-Cycle Event is followed by a short-duration learning cycle in which quick experiments and rough prototypes are used to generate a rapid increase in the team's knowledge. The number of iterations of these learning cycles depends on the magnitude and severity of the knowledge gaps.

outcomes to this follow-up learning event: either the team concludes that all critical knowledge gaps have been closed and the product design effort can proceed, or the team believes that an additional learning cycle is necessary to fully address any remaining issues. Again, the number of follow-up events, and the associated number of learning cycles, is scalable to the complexity of the project and the type and severity of risks involved.

Before launching into our fictitious Learning-Cycle Event case example, I'll briefly describe the format and contents of a knowledge brief. This is one of those topics that has developed an air of mystery about it, creating the impression that generating a knowledge brief is more difficult than it actually is. A knowledge brief is simply a single (albeit oversized) sheet of paper that identifies a risk-inducing problem, provides an analysis of its root cause(s), and then documents the solution to that problem in a clear and visual way. The goal is to tell a story, from beginning to end, of how new product-related knowledge has been gained. Why not just generate a multi-page report and file it away for future reference? You can probably answer this question yourself: If new knowledge is not captured in a brief, visual, and easily accessible format, it won't be used by future development teams. The knowledge brief is intended to reduce the barriers to knowledge reuse, a common weakness in virtually all knowledge management strategies.

Theme	Ownership
Problem Statement	Countermeasure Selection
Problem Analysis (Current-State Definition)	
	Verification Method(s)
Goals	Implementation and Follow-up Plan
Alternative Evaluation	

FIGURE 7.9: A straightforward template for creating a knowledge brief. This A3-sized format is intended to tell a story, from beginning to end, of how a problem has been identified, analyzed, and ultimately solved. Note that a knowledge brief should not be finalized until a follow-up activity has been completed to verify that the selected countermeasure(s) have effectively mitigated the identified problem.

The template that I recommend is a slight variant on the standard Toyota approach (see Shook (2008) and Sobek, et al (2008)), as shown in Figure 7.9. The top sections of the form are intended to identify the general theme of the brief, along with who is responsible for the brief and who must approve the solution before the problem-solving process can be considered closed. The theme statement is nothing more than a string of keywords that will allow rapid search and retrieval once the knowledge brief has been archived. (The topic of storage and retrieval will be covered in the final section of this chapter.) The ownership section should identify the individual who is responsible for creating the brief, along with approval line(s) and a place for revision control. Knowledge briefs should be developed in layers: Many changes can be made before a final solution is identified. Hence, careful revision control is important.

The remainder of the knowledge-brief template contains sections that flow from an initial statement of the problem under consideration (upper left) to a plan for implementing the identified countermeasures (lower right). I will use a simulated case example to illustrate the details

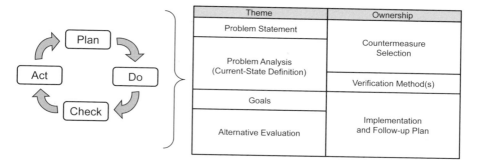

Theme	Ownership
Problem Statement	Countermeasure Selection
Problem Analysis (Current-State Definition)	
	Verification Method(s)
Goals	Implementation and Follow-up Plan
Alternative Evaluation	

FIGURE 7.10: The knowledge brief provides a structured method for implementing the Plan / Do / Check / Act cycle of continuous improvement.

of how a knowledge brief is created, but it is worthwhile pointing out the primary difference between my format and the typical Toyota-based approach. In my experience, one of the most important aspects of problem-solving is verifying that a proposed solution actually mitigates the problem. It is all too easy to jump to an answer, even when using this rigorous process, and assume that a quick test is all that is needed to validate a solution. It is my view that just as much emphasis should be placed on verification as is expended on root-cause identification. Hence, I have added an explicit section in my knowledge-brief template to define the verification method(s) that will be used, including quantitative acceptance metrics, tolerance bands, and the number of samples to be tested and verified. A rigorous problem-solving process deserves an equally rigorous verification effort.

In reality, the knowledge brief is yet another manifestation of the old Shewart cycle for continuous improvement, as shown in Figure 7.10. The first two sections, defining the problem statement and performing root-cause analysis, correspond to the "Plan" step of the cycle. The "Do" step consists of the establishment of goals, the evaluation of multiple alternatives, and the selection of preferred countermeasures, while the "Check" part is explicitly addressed in the verification section of the knowledge-brief template. Finally, we arrive at the "Act" step, which is addressed by documenting and executing an implementation and follow-up plan. Again, there is nothing mystical here; just a well-crafted methodology that yields a highly readable and reusable packet of valuable knowledge.

The simulation example that I will employ has been intentionally simplified to focus on a new product with only a single knowledge gap. While this may not be a realistic scenario for most development projects, it will allow me to illustrate how the above template can be used efficiently and effectively. Admittedly, my case example gives short shrift to one of the most challenging aspects of creating a knowledge brief: The identification of the root cause(s) of a risk or problem. Several of the references cited earlier in this chapter have invested many pages on this topic, so I will commend the reader to these sources for an expanded perspective. However, I will describe two classic methods for the identification of root causes, to provide you with a solid starting point for your own efforts.

When the topic of root-cause identification is raised, someone with lean training will undoubtedly mention the "Method of Five Whys." In this overly-simplistic approach, the question "why" is asked several times to push beyond superficial symptoms and ultimately uncover the true root cause of a problem. Unfortunately, in most situations, the Method of Five Whys just doesn't work. Before you accuse me of blasphemy, allow me to defend my position. Asking "why" several times is an excellent way to explain the concept of root-cause analysis, but it suffers from a fundamental flaw; it assumes that each time the question is answered, there is a 100-percent probability that the response is the only possible answer. This is rarely, if ever, the case. In the real world, problems are almost always a manifestation of multiple contributing factors. In other words, you could ask the same "why" question of multiple individuals, and would likely receive different answers. To assume a linear progression from the first "why" to the fifth is naïve, and will likely yield, at best, an incomplete perspective.

Fortunately, there is a technique that is far more effective; the venerable fishbone diagram, as shown in Figure 7.11. A set of "bones" is defined for the fish, based on the nature of the problem to be solved, with each bone representing a likely category of root cause. An individual or team then brainstorms on specific root causes that might correspond to each bone. Once a comprehensive set of possible causes has been identified, the fishbone diagram represents a robust starting point for problem

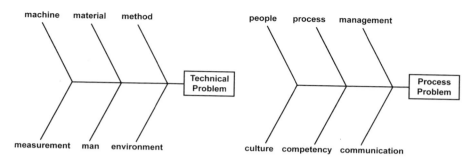

FIGURE 7.11: The classic fishbone diagram provides an effective means of decomposing a problem into its potential root causes. The left-hand diagram has "bones" which correspond to a typical technical problem, while the version on the right would apply to an organizational or process problem. These are just suggestions; your bones may be different.

analysis. The most probable causes are then selected for further investigation. If you are of a rigorous bent, you can use a simple probability calculation to isolate the most promising avenues to pursue. Each bone of the fish can be assigned a relative probability, based on its likelihood of containing the dominant root cause. This is, of course, a subjective assessment, but if a group of experts contributes to the assignment of probabilities, the result will be surprisingly accurate. You may recall from your summer-semester probability and statistics course in college that all probabilities for a given event must add up to 100 percent. Hence, you must divvy up the probabilities such that all bones add up to a certainty. Now, for each bone, you proceed to assign probabilities to the specific root causes in that category, again with all possibilities adding up to a certainty. You can then determine the most promising candidates for further investigation by simply multiplying the probability of a bone, times the probability of each possible cause along the length of the bone. Naturally, you might have missed something, but at least you will have a logical approach for focusing your investigative efforts. If all of this math is making your head hurt, you can just pick the most likely candidates by intuition and proceed with your problem analysis. We will now begin our fictitious case example, so you can see how the creation of a knowledge brief unfolds.

Event Simulation: Woodchuck Custom Closets (Part I)

Norm Abraham was muttering to himself as he made his way to the back of the workshop. In front of him was the object of his frustration; a floor-to-ceiling cabinet module, surrounded by a semicircle of chairs. At first glance, it was a handsome piece; high-quality cherry hardwood, with a nice dark stain and a lacquer finish. Upon closer inspection, however, it was evident that several of the drawers near the bottom of the cabinet were held in place by duct tape.

"What a disaster," he grumbled, as a small group gathered around him. "I've never been so embarrassed in my life."

The humiliation he was referring to had resulted from a recent visit by a potential customer. Norm's company, Woodchuck Custom Closets, had grown steadily over the past several years due to a thriving market for modular closet cabinetry. His point of entry into that market had been at the bottom; ready-made shelving, drawers, and storage, built entirely of plastic-laminated MDF (medium-density fiberboard). Beginning with private residences, he expanded his business into commercial properties, ultimately gaining the lion's share of that market in the Las Vegas area. In recent months, however, growth had stalled, and Norm had decided to move his firm up-market. The beautiful but flawed cabinet in front of him had been Woodchuck's first foray into that arena, and it might well be its last.

"Hey boss, I think if we just added a couple of staples to the sides of the drawers, these drawer fronts would hold just fine." The brave soul who had spoken was Verner Panton, the craftsman who had fabricated the prototype. Verner was a fine workman, but had no real experience with hardwood cabinetry, and his lack of knowledge had resulted in a fundamental flaw: The drawer fronts on the prototype cabinet were weakly joined to the drawer sides. Unfortunately, this defect had been uncovered by a prospective customer – one of the drawer fronts had literally come off in the customer's hands. Hence, it was back to the drawing board with a healthy dose of humility.

"I appreciate the suggestion, Verner," Norm said, with all the patience he could muster, "but I think it's time we take a step backwards and understand the problem before we try to fix it." With that, the group took their seats, and an informal meeting began. "My goal for this meeting is simple. If we are going to have a chance at the high-end closet market, we have to offer cabinetry that is the equivalent of fine furniture. All of our experience is based on the assumption that we can use screws, staples, nails, or any other fastener that works. Our new target customers just won't accept those kinds of clumsy solutions. They expect to see high-quality joinery, and for what these cabinets will cost them, that joinery should last a lifetime."

One of the attendees, a young designer named Raycine Eames, was eager to dig in.

"I think the problem is pretty obvious," she stated. "We used a simple butt joint along with a thin line of glue, and expected it to hold up under pull stress and racking stress. No fine woodworker would use a joint like that." Although her comment wasn't very diplomatic, it got the discussion going. As the dialog continued, Norm pulled out an oversized sheet of paper and handed it to Raycine.

"I heard about this tool from a friend of mine at the local MEP center," Norm said. (Note to reader: The Manufacturing Extension Partnership is a real-world agency that offers subsidized consulting and support to small-to-medium sized firms throughout the United States.) "He said that the problem with most companies is that they fail to solve problems effectively. Rather than actually understanding the root cause of a failure or design issue, they just keep shotgunning solutions in the hope of getting lucky. This really rang a bell for me. If we are going to be successful in this new market, we need to learn rapidly and effectively. We cannot afford another mess like this, so we are going to build a knowledge base of proven solutions to cabinet design problems, starting with this darn drawer-face joint."

With that, Norm began explaining the process they would use. The first step was to clearly state the problem that must be solved. Verner provided an input to that discussion.

"Yesterday, I ran a simple test on one of the unbroken drawers. You had told me that the drawers had to be able to hold up to 100 pounds of load, so I put some weights in the drawer and gave it a hard pull. At first, it held up okay, but once I reached the 100-pound point, the drawer joints failed. I think that sums up our problem pretty well."

"That's great, Verner," Raycine said, "but what about racking load? I pulled out one of the drawers this morning and leaned on one corner. The drawer box distorted so badly that I couldn't get it to slide back in properly."

"Good," said Norm, "so we need to include both pull load and racking load in our problem statement." After some additional discussion, Norm felt it was time for the team to do some learning.

"Here's what I want you guys to do. Raycine, you are going to own this problem. I want you to come up with some quick experiments to test this sad drawer design to its limits. Don't waste time making things pretty. I want quick mock-ups and lots of them. Give me some statistics. I want you all back here in one week with the results, and we will then decide what our next steps will be." With that, the team's first learning cycle began.

One week later, the team was back in front of the ill-fated cabinet. This time, however, there was a pile of damaged and broken drawers lying in a pile by their chairs. Raycine wasted no time in sharing her results.

"Well, as you can see, you have to break a lot of drawers to make a good cabinet. Verner and I built and busted ten drawers, and recorded the results in a histogram." She handed out a graph of their data and began explaining her test method. "I set up a test jig to ensure that the results were consistent. You can see the jig I used over there." She pointed at a crude but effective setup that was clamped to a workbench nearby. "We put each drawer into the jig, and added weight in twenty-pound increments. At each increment, we gave the drawer a calibrated 'hard pull' and recorded the integrity of the drawer joints. As you can see from the data, all but one of the prototypes failed before the required hundred-pound load."

"Great job, both of you," Norm said enthusiastically, "now we have a baseline for improvement. But what about the problem of racking?" Again, Raycine was prepared.

"We're way ahead of you. I set up a simple experiment to test for racking on an additional five sample drawers. I placed a fifty-pound weight on one corner of each drawer while it was pulled out to full exten-sion. Verner and I felt that this was a reasonable requirement, similar to a person leaning on the side of the drawer. Every single drawer was distorted to some degree, and most of them were so out of square that they wouldn't return to the closed position." It was obvious by her tone that Raycine was quite proud of herself.

"Well, I think we are ready to revise our initial problem statement with some real numbers and facts," Norm said. "Now we need to understand the root causes of these failures. Why are the joints failing? Any ideas?" Raycine shot her hand up, acting for all the world like the teacher's pet.

"I decided to investigate the failure modes we were seeing by digging into some books on fine woodworking. What had really surprised me was that every single joint failed at the glue line." She picked up one of the broken drawers and pointed out the ragged line where the glue had obviously given way. "I had always heard that glue joints in hardwood were stronger than the wood itself. Obviously, either that truism is wrong, or we're not using the glue properly. It turns out that the latter is the case. Glue doesn't bond to the ends of boards the same way that it adheres to the long grain along the sides and edges. In fact, a glue joint at the end of a board is essentially useless, as we've just found out."

"So we now have at least one root cause of the failures: improper use of glue to join the sides and front of the drawer," said Norm. "Don't stop there. Are there any other contributing factors? Keep in mind that we have two failure modes: pull failures and racking failures. Does the poor glue joint explain both of these problems?" This time it was Verner who jumped in.

"Well, while Raycine was studying her books," he looked over at her with a satisfied grin, "I was learning from an expert. Over the weekend I spent a few hours with a world-class craftsman over in Henderson. This guy builds reproduction period furniture for museums and rich clients, and he knows everything there is to know about making strong drawers. He said the same thing about how glue joints work, but he also pointed out that for a drawer joint to be strong, it must have mechanical strength. Our butt joints just fall apart without glue. On the other hand, he showed me a drawer he'd just built for a nineteenth-century cabinet. It was solid as a rock under both pull and rack. What really amazed me was that the drawer he showed me wasn't even glued yet! The dovetail joints he used were so mechanically strong that they held together on their own. With a couple spots of glue, these joints would last forever." He then grabbed a sample from a nearby bench and passed the piece around.

"Well, now we have two root causes to deal with," said Norm. "We need to use glue properly, and we need a joint that has inherent mechanical strength. I'll add my two-cents worth to our learning. I called some potential customers, and asked them what they were looking for in high-quality cabinetry. They all said the same thing: Fine furniture uses joinery that is both robust and aesthetically pleasing. A couple of them mentioned dovetail joints specifically as a sign of quality, and one also mentioned a finger joint as being a good choice. I think we have three goals in this problem-solving exercise. First, we need a joint that uses glue properly. Second, we want a joint that has inherent mechanical strength. Finally, we need a visually pleasing joint that clearly communicates the quality of our work. So guys, I want to see some alternatives. Pick three or four different possible joints, and let's run another learning cycle. Fabricate five samples of each joint and run the same tests as before. Don't limit yourselves to just what we've talked about; come up with some additional alternatives as well. Consult your expert and your books, but I want you to cast a wide net. You've got two weeks to cobble together some quick samples and run your tests. We'll get back together on the fifteenth and see where we stand."

Intermission: Expanding Product Knowledge through Set-Based Design

The result of Woodchuck's problem-solving efforts up to this point is shown in Figure 7.12. Once they had identified the root causes of their problem, they had reached a crossroads. They could have just picked a better joint design and started making cabinetry again. While this singular solution might have worked, they would never know if there had been a better choice. There is an old saying: "Better is the enemy of good enough." I think this is backwards. It would be far more accurate to say that "good enough is the enemy of better." By settling on the first alternative that seemed to work, Woodchuck would have learned very little about how to make better drawers. On the other hand, if they pursued several alternative solutions, and used rapid experiments to determine the advantages and disadvantages of each, then they would not only find an optimal solution, they would gain a deeper understanding of drawer joints in general. That knowledge would serve them for years as their product designs expanded and evolved.

Theme: Drawer-Front to Drawer-Side Joint for Wooden Furniture

Problem Statement
Joint between drawer front and drawer sides fails prematurely when drawer is loaded to greater than 100 lbs. Joint is also susceptible to racking stress that causes distortion of drawer box, resulting in a poor fit.

Problem Analysis
Current butt-type drawer joint fails 90% of time when pull tested with a 100 lb. fill load, and 100% of time when rack tested with a 50 lb. shear load.

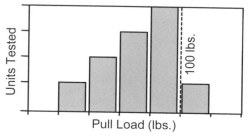

Root Causes
1) Butt joint has insufficient long-grain to long-grain surface area to enable a strong glue bond.
2) Butt joint has no inherent mechanical strength in pull or rack.

FIGURE 7.12: Illustration of the Woodchuck design team's initial inputs to their A3-formatted knowledge brief.

This idea of "casting a wide net" is the essence of set-based design. By identifying several alternatives that might address the root causes of a problem, you will gain an understanding of the benefits and disbenefits of each. Rapid experiments will help to separate the weak contenders from the strong ones, and will ultimately yield sufficient knowledge to select a winner. Moreover, the rejects for a current application may turn out to be the best options for future applications. This foundation of knowledge can be fed upon by design teams for many generations of new products. The general concept of set-based design is illustrated in Figure 7.13.

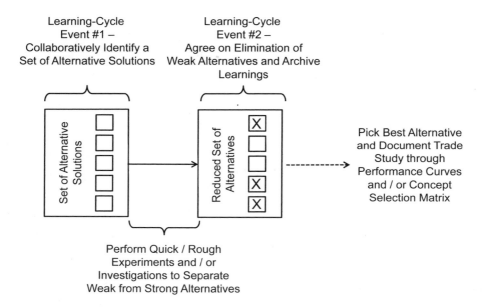

FIGURE 7.13: A set-based approach to product design involves considering multiple possible design alternatives and then systematically filtering these options until an optimal choice is identified. The Learning-Cycle Events and subsequent learning cycles represent a practical means to perform this filtering process.

The lynch pin of the set-based design approach is the method used to sort winners from losers. I have found that one of the most powerful trade-off tools available to product designers is something called the Pugh matrix (aka, the concept selection matrix, see Pugh (1991) and Mascitelli (2004)). This technique allows a group of collaborators to

Design Alternatives / Must-Have Criteria	4 Wheels	3 Wheels	Treads	Skids	Air Float	Casters	Handle	Backpack
Support 10 lbs.		S	S	S	-	S	- - -	- -
Minimal Friction		S	- -	-	+ +	S	+	+
Turning Radius		S	- -	S	+	S	+ +	+ +
Smooth Movement	Default Design	S	- -	- -	+ +	S	- - -	- -
Light Weight		+	- - -	+	+ + +	S	- - -	- -
Nice Appearance		S	-	S	+	S	S	S
Handle Stairs Easily		S	S	S	- -	S	- -	- -
Easy Assembly		+	- - -	+	+	S	+ +	+ +
Low Cost		+	- -	+	+	-	+ +	+ +
High Reliability		S	- -	+	+	S	+	+
Number of Parts		+	- -	+ +	+ +	S	+ +	+ +
Totals +	0	4	0	6	14	0	10	10
Totals −	0	0	19	3	3	1	11	8

FIGURE 7.14: A worked example using the Pugh matrix (aka, the concept selection matrix) to filter design alternatives for a canister vacuum cleaner. Note that a weighting column can be added just to the right of the "must-have criteria" column to provide a more accurate means of identifying an optimal design choice.

weigh the advantages and disadvantages of multiple design options, easily agree on the best alternatives, and capture the logic of their choices for future reference. An example of a Pugh matrix is shown in Figure 7.14. In this worked example, a set of eight design alternatives for a canister vacuum cleaner are weighed against a number of selection criteria. Although it is not essential, I've found that by designating one of the alternatives as the "default," and using it as a baseline for comparison to the other alternatives, you will achieve more accurate and consistent scoring. Typically, the default is either an alternative that is currently in use, or one that is deemed to be the lowest risk. The selection criteria should represent "must-haves," meaning that each criterion is potentially a showstopper: If a proposed design alternative cannot satisfy that criterion, then it may not be viable for the given application. Your objective in using this matrix is to filter out those alternatives that have a low probability of success, and highlight the ones (and there may be several) that have the best potential for meeting your design goals.

Once a set of alternatives has been identified, and the must-have criteria chosen, it is time to score each option. My preferred approach uses the nomenclature that was originally proposed by the tool's namesake. In each column, the associated alternative is compared to the default design. An "S" is used to designate that the alternative is the "same" as the default in meeting a specific must-have criterion. Pluses are given to an alternative that exceeds the default in meeting that criterion, with the number of pluses indicating the magnitude if its advantage (I suggest using a range of from 1 to 3). Similarly, minus signs are used to indicate that an alternative is worse than the default at meeting a given criterion. Ideally, you would engage a group of subject-matter experts to help determine these scores, with the discussion that ensues being one of the great advantages of this tool. Once the matrix has been completed to everyone's satisfaction, the columns are totaled. The "S" scores are ignored, since they fail to differentiate winners from losers. The pluses and minuses are totaled at the bottom of each respective column. Now all that remains is to interpret the results.

In general, we are looking for design alternatives that have pluses but no minuses (as is the case for the three-wheel design shown in Figure 7.14). These concepts have apparent advantages over the default, and hence should be investigated further by the development team. A second level of opportunity is indicated by a design alternative that has a robust number of pluses, but also one or more negatives. In these situations, the team should first consider how certain they are that the minus scores are accurate. If there is a reasonable doubt, then action items should be assigned to determine if the perceived negatives are real. Next, the team should look to other design alternatives, or their own ingenuity, to try and mitigate the negative scores. Perhaps a beneficial attribute from another alternative can be merged with the promising candidate to eliminate the negatives. In any case, if the negative scores can be mitigated, then the associated design alternative should pass through the Pugh-matrix filter and be further investigated by the development team.

It is critical that, wherever possible, the inputs to the Pugh matrix be data-driven. This is not always possible, particularly during the first iteration of using the tool. However, as with many other activities in Event-Driven Lean Product Development, the Pugh matrix should be

218

developed in layers. Once the team has taken an initial cut at filtering the design alternatives, they should consider their scores and identify those that should receive further thought and investigation. After a rapid learning cycle, the scores in the matrix can be refined and the results reconsidered. This process continues until the team is confident that the scores and conclusions displayed in the matrix are accurate. The finalized Pugh matrix represents an excellent communication and knowledge-capture device, offering a wealth of learning for both current and future projects. Always keep in mind that tools do not create knowledge: The team should always apply their intuition and common sense when evaluating a set of design alternatives. If the team wishes to gain a deeper understanding of how the must-have filtering criteria interact with their design options, they can add a weighting column just to the right of the must-have list in the Pugh matrix (I typically allow a range of weighting factors from 1 to 3). This "weighted Pugh matrix" is a far more nuanced tool, and can yield better results, but it will take additional time to refine the weighting factors, so I suggest using it only in cases where the differences among alternatives are subtle.

Armed with an understanding of set-based design and the Pugh matrix, we can now return to our simulated case example and see how the Woodchuck team's problem-solving process proceeds.

Event Simulation: Woodchuck Custom Closets (Part II)

The team was gathering again at the back of the workshop, but this time there were two piles of drawers set amidst their chairs: broken drawers on the left and unbroken drawers on the right. This was definitely a good sign. Norm began the meeting by sharing what he had learned during the previous two weeks.

"Well, as you can see, we are making progress," he said, gesturing toward the piles of drawers. "Just to review for everybody, we decided to investigate four possible countermeasures to the drawer failures we've been experiencing. The first was essentially a baseline. Verner suggested that we keep our old butt joint and try a better glue – an epoxy adhesive that is much stronger than the yellow glue we used initially. The second alternative was to use a rabbet joint to attach the drawer front to the sides. A simple joint to execute, but one with better gluing properties. The last two choices were the ones suggested by experts and discerning customers: the finger joint and the dovetail joint." He paused to hand around samples of each type of joint for the team to examine.

"My assignment during this past learning cycle was to get some feedback from potential customers on the aesthetics of our choices. Well, the voting was unanimous. Of the five customers I polled, all of them preferred the dovetail joint hands down. Several indicated that the finger joint was attractive and would be acceptable, but their eyes really lit up when they saw that fancy dovetail. I think we are ready to add our first inputs to the Pugh matrix that I shared with you last week."

With that, he pulled out a Pugh-matrix template that he had constructed, based on conversations with the team over the past two weeks. He then asked each attendee to suggest how many pluses or minuses each joint should receive for aesthetics, based on his findings. After some haggling, the team agreed that the dovetail should receive three pluses, the maximum number allowed. They then assigned two pluses to the finger joint, since it had gotten good reviews. The rabbet and glue joints were deemed to be aesthetically the same as the default, and were given an S-score. With one row of their matrix complete, it was time for Raycine to contribute.

"Verner and I had an interesting two weeks," she began. "After spending several frustrating days getting our new commercial jig to work properly, we started spitting out joints right and left. It turns out that making rabbet joints is easy; a shop-made jig works fine. But without the commercial jig, making finger and dovetail joints would be prohibitively time-consuming. Anyway, we made five joints of each type and subjected them to the torture test we agreed upon. The epoxy glue joint was really no better than our old joint. It seems that the glue just can't hold on to the end grain, as we suspected. The rabbet joint did somewhat better, but still we had a premature failure on one drawer, and all of them failed when loaded just beyond our specification of 100 pounds. It's better, but still not acceptable."

"The remaining two joints were amazing. Both the finger and dovetail joints held up under load-testing and rack-testing until we ran out of weights. Not a single joint failed, even with up to a 200-pound load!" She made her point by picking up one of the dovetail samples and whacking it with her hand. "The finger joint seemed to be more susceptible to racking stress, but the dovetail was rock solid. If we can make these joints at production rates, we'll never have a complaint from a customer."

Based on these findings, the team was able to complete the remainder of their Pugh matrix, as shown in Figure 7.15. Clearly using a better glue was not a viable option. Although the rabbet joint had some minor advantages over the baseline, the improvements were not adequate to meet the team's needs. Their choices came down to the finger and dovetail joints, with the latter having a small edge in the scoring. After the team had had a chance to digest the results, Norm was ready to ask a critical question.

Goals
To identify and implement a drawer joint that can handle a 100 lb. fill load and a 50 lb. racking load, while being aesthetically pleasing to customers.

Alternative Evaluation

	Different Glue	Rabbet Joint	Finger Joint	Dovetail Joint	
100 lb. Load Strength	S	+	++	+++	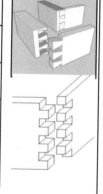
100 lb. Rack Strength	S	+	+++	+++	
Aesthetically Pleasing	S	S	++	+++	
+	0	2	7	9	
-	0	0	0	0	

FIGURE 7.15: The next section of the Woodchuck team's knowledge brief, showing the goals they had established for an effective solution to their joint-reliability problem, and the Pugh matrix they used to identify the best of several alternatives. Pictures of the dovetail and finger-joint alternatives are provided at the right of the matrix.

"Now we have to make a decision," he said. "It seems obvious that we are down to just two viable alternatives. One factor we have not considered is the cost to implement either of these options. Do you guys think we need another learning cycle to compare the costs of the finger and dovetail joints?" Verner was ready with a response.

"I don't think so, boss," he said. "I kept track of my time as I was making up the samples. Admittedly, the commercial jig we were using was finicky to set up, but once it was dialed in, things went pretty fast. Based on the higher margins we should get for this new cabinet line, I think either joint is well within our budget."

"Great," said Norm. "So unless someone disagrees, I'm ready to go forward with the dovetail joint. I think the aesthetics are worth any extra time it might take." He scanned the group to see if there was any dissent. "Okay, so our learning cycles are over, and it's time to make some money. On that end, I have some good news. While I was getting feedback on our drawer samples, I had an opportunity to do some selling. It turns out that one of the prospective customers I visited is about to order closet cabinetry for a new high-rise condominium being built just east of The Strip. We're talking two-hundred closets! The only problem is that we need to ramp up to production rates within the next month, and we better not screw this up or we'll be out of this business before we even get started."

"Raycine," he continued, "I want you to document the reasons for our choice in the "countermeasure selection" section of our knowledge brief, along with how the design change will be integrated into our production system. I also want a schedule for implementation, and even more important, for follow-up. We should test every drawer in the first five production units we build, based on the verification methods we have been using. But I also want you to pull unit number fifty from the line and perform the same tests. This way we can be sure that nothing has drifted in our production process, and that our selected countermeasure is really a solution. Assuming that the follow-up tests go according to plan, I think we can call this problem solved!"

■ ■ ■

The final result of the Woodchuck team's learning efforts is shown in Figure 7.16. Fortunately, the condominium deal was signed, and with their quality verification measures in place, the customer was delighted with the results. By using systematic problem-solving, Raycine, Verner, and the production team were able to advance their knowledge to a new level. It seems that through rapid learning cycles, the team had proven once and for all that Woodchuck Custom Cabinets could indeed chuck wood.

Advanced Topic: Achieving Knowledge-Based Development

Within the animal kingdom, there are a number of species that display exceptional problem-solving abilities: primates, dolphins, elephants, and even parrots. However, to find the animal with the most adaptable and innovative mind, you must look in an entirely different phylum. According to many animal behaviorists, the giant Pacific octopus is the most effective and adaptable problem-solver in the natural world (other than some humans, of course). Yet, due to a fluke of evolution, the octopus has never reached its full potential as the dominant predator in the world's oceans; the female octopus lives a tragically short life. After only a few short years, the female will mate for the first and last time, and then hide herself away in a secluded niche to lay tens of thousands of eggs. She will spend the next six months tending and protecting her eggs, without ever leaving the niche for food. Once the eggs hatch, she crawls from her lair and dies of starvation within just a few days. As a result of this sad anomaly, she never has a chance to nurture her young, and therefore fails to pass along lessons that have accumulated in her species' subconscious over many centuries. Each new generation of octopi begins with a blank slate, and must learn every lesson of survival for themselves.

Well, it doesn't take a giant Pacific octopus to see where I am going with this. Assuming that a product development team employs the methods in this chapter, they will gain new and valuable knowledge that will be critical to their firm's survival. Yet once the project is complete, that knowledge will likely scatter to the four winds, due to entropy, reassignment of team members, and employee turnover. As a result, the next project team, much like those naïve little octopi, must forge their own way, without the benefit of past learning. Learning-Cycle Events and rapid learning cycles represent tactical means to a product-specific end. However there is a critical strategic aspect to team learning that must be considered. Firms that build upon their past experience will thrive, while those that allow that vital essence to slip away will likely find themselves on the endangered-species list.

Self-documenting tools such as the Pugh matrix are an excellent starting point toward achieving true knowledge-based development. However, the real opportunity lies in the knowledge brief. By creating a searchable archive of knowledge briefs, each future development team will have easy access to the learnings of their predecessors. The software tool that you use to create such an archive is not important; any good Product Data Management (PDM) application will do. I suggest, however, that you avoid the temptation to create a "directory of knowledge." Knowledge can be organized in many ways; by choosing one taxonomy you are potentially creating a barrier to those users who see things differently. However, by simply embedding a comprehensive list of keywords in the theme statement of each knowledge brief, users can employ a search engine to find the knowledge that they seek in a far more efficient way.

While knowledge briefs are a critical enabler of knowledge-based development, the true power of this methodology lies in the integration of knowledge briefs into trade-off tools such as the performance curve shown in Figure 7.17. Toyota has famously harnessed these graphs to perform real-time trade studies for next-generation vehicles. Their inherent simplicity is their strength: It takes very little time to explore different design scenarios and identify promising avenues for further investigation. It is important to note that performance curves are based on empirical data, not theoretical calculations. With this solid basis in experiment, performance curves have a higher degree of accuracy than could ever be achieved through mathematical models or simulations. Over time, each new project will contribute additional knowledge to an ever-expanding suite of performance curves, as shown in Figure 7.18.

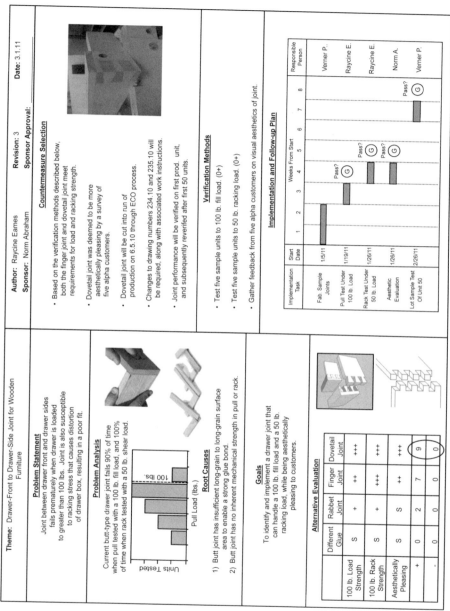

FIGURE 7.16: The completed knowledge brief, showing in storyboard form the process used to solve joint-failure problems on Woodchuck's new line of closet cabinetry.

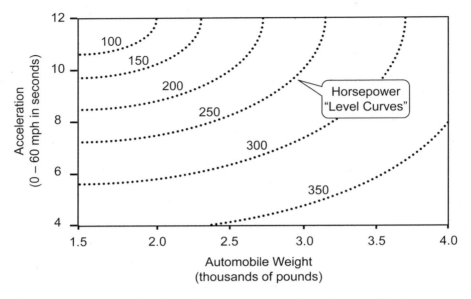

FIGURE 7.17: An example of a performance curve, such as those used by Toyota in early design trade-off studies. This empirical graph displays three interdependent variables on a two-dimensional plot, thereby allowing rapid investigation of alternative design scenarios.

All of this sounds like a fine ideal, except for one minor problem. Capturing, archiving, and organizing knowledge takes time. It is therefore critical that your firm distinguishes between *persistent knowledge* and *transient knowledge*. Persistent knowledge retains its value over extended periods of time, whereas the value of transient knowledge diminishes rapidly. I spent the early part of my career in the semiconductor industry. My firm invested massive amounts of time and money learning how to optimize a given silicon-wafer technology, only to find that this knowledge was rendered all but useless the very next year due to the arrival of the next generation of fabrication processes. Industries that exhibit rapid change, or those that are susceptible to disruptive

FIGURE 7.18: Each development project contributes new knowledge to an ever-expanding knowledge base for future design teams. It is vital, however, that firms focus on capturing and integrating persistent knowledge, and avoid wasting time on transient knowledge that will rapidly lose its future value.

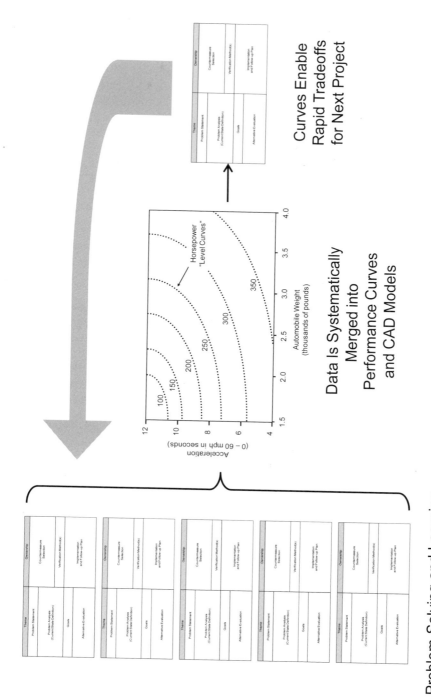

Curves Enable
Rapid Tradeoffs
for Next Project

Data Is Systematically
Merged into
Performance Curves
and CAD Models

Problem-Solving and Learning
over Multiple Development Projects

227

technologies (see Christenson (1997)), will have a greater percentage of transient knowledge. Likewise, knowledge that is highly application-specific will likely have little or no value on future projects. Given the limited time available to perform knowledge capture, it is vital that your firm identifies persistent knowledge for your type of products, and avoids wasting time on archiving transient knowledge. Indeed, understanding this distinction is the key to implementing a practical form of knowledge-based development.

Chapter References

Christensen, C. M., 1997, *The Innovator's Dilemma*, Harvard Business School Press.

Davenport, T. H., and L. Prusak, 1998, *Working Knowledge*, Harvard Business School Press.

Harvard Business Review, 1998, *Harvard Business Review on Knowledge Management*, Harvard Business School Press.

Imai, M., 1997, *Gemba Kaizen*, McGraw-Hill.

Kennedy, M. N., 2003, *Product Development for the Lean Enterprise*, Oaklea Press.

Kennedy, M. N., Harmon, K., and E. Minnock, 2008, *Ready, Set, Dominate*, Oaklea Press.

Mascitelli, R., 2004, *The Lean Design Guidebook*, Technology Perspectives.

Nonaka, I., and H. Takeuchi, 1995, *The Knowledge Creating Company*, Oxford University Press.

Pugh, S., 1991, *Total Design*, Addison-Wesley.

Schipper, T., and M. Swets, 2010, *Innovative Lean Development*, CRC Press.

Senge, P. M., 1990, *The Fifth Discipline*, Currency Doubleday.

Senge, P. M., et al, 1994, *The Fifth Discipline Fieldbook*, Currency Doubleday.

Shook, J., 2008, *Managing to Learn*, Lean Enterprise Institute.

Sobek, D. K. II, et al, 1998, "Another look at how Toyota integrates product development," *Harvard Business Review*, July-August Issue.

Sobek, D. K. II, et al, 1999, "Toyota's principles of set-based concurrent engineering," *Sloan Management Review*, Vol. 40, No. 2.

Sobek, D. K., and A. Smalley, 2008, *Understanding A3 Thinking*, CRC Press.

Spear, S. J., 2009, *Chasing the Rabbit*, McGraw-Hill.

Ward, A., 2007, *Lean Product and Process Development*, Lean Enterprise Institute.

8

The Lean 3P / Cost-Optimization Event(s)

Background and Overview

Once upon a time, there were four blind engineers and a product. Each engineer was asked to examine the product as best they could, and then describe the nature of the product from their perspective. The first, who had a strong background in concurrent engineering (see Anderson (2003)), completed his investigation and reported his results.

"The product has obviously been designed with an over-the-wall mentality," he announced. "Many of the internal parts are complex, and there appears to be a number of high-cost components that could have been better optimized. In addition, there are several unproducible features that will give the factory no end of headaches. Clearly the developers didn't involve manufacturing engineers and production specialists in the design of this product."

The second blind designer, who was very knowledgeable in the methods of value engineering (see Brown (1992), Mudge (1989), and Park (1999)), took her turn next.

"I agree with those conclusions," she said, "but the real problem with this product is that the development team didn't question their fundamental design assumptions. Designers are often trapped by their assumptions to such a degree that they overlook innovative solutions that can reduce cost, improve quality, and in many cases, actually improve performance. The product should have been decomposed into 'functions' and then systematically analyzed for improvement opportunities."

"All well and good," said the third engineer after completing his investigation. He was a Six Sigma Master Blackbelt (see George (2002)), and oozed statistics from every pore. "But the real problem is variability. Many of the parts appear to require very tight production tolerances. If the production process cannot achieve the precision and accuracy required to make these parts, then the product will suffer from unacceptable yield losses and high rework costs. The problem with this product is that the designers didn't consider production process capability."

Finally, the fourth engineer, a specialist in Design for Manufacture and Assembly (see Boothroyd, et al (2002), Bralla (1999), and Huthwaite (2004)), announced his conclusions.

"You are all correct, as far as you went," he said, "but you missed the obvious. The product uses materials that are difficult to machine and cause high wear on tools. Furthermore, the assembly of this product will be a nightmare. Lots of small parts that can be misoriented, and the order of assembly seems to be all wrong. Unquestionably, the biggest problem is that the product design was not optimized for easy machinability and error-proof assembly."

This story, of course, has much in common with the old Sufi tale (*sans* engineers and substituting an elephant), and indeed the conclusion is the same: If you take a narrow perspective when considering a problem, you will likely miss the big picture. The irony in the above story is that all four of our narrowly focused engineers were correct, and yet their understanding of the problem was incomplete. Each of the methodologies that they represented is necessary to the design of an optimized product, but none is sufficient on its own. At the highest level, there are two overarching truths about product cost and quality optimization:

1. The highest leverage for design optimization occurs in the earliest stages of development. It becomes increasingly difficult

and expensive to address cost and quality issues as the product design approaches production launch, as shown in Figure 8.1.

2. The knowledge required to develop a cost-effective, high-quality product resides in many heads, and without intensive collaboration among designers and manufacturing / quality specialists, a product design will inevitably be suboptimal.

Many of the great improvement methodologies of the past three decades (e.g., Total Quality Management (TQM), Design for Six Sigma (DFSS), Design for Manufacture and Assembly (DFMA), and others) have attempted to address these truths. Unfortunately, all fall short of a truly comprehensive system for product and process co-design. In more recent years, an effort has been made to gain a more holistic perspective.

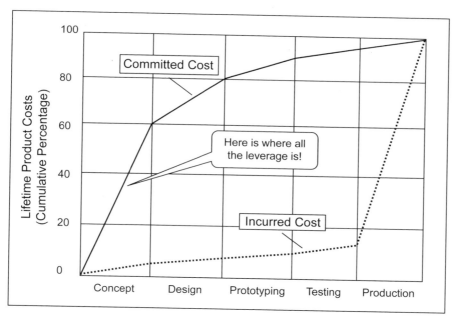

FIGURE 8.1: The greatest leverage for optimizing the cost and quality of a new product occurs in the earliest stages of development, prior to the finalization of a design concept. While the incurred cost of development (i.e., the non-recurring development cost) is relatively linear, the committed manufacturing cost of a product design follows a very different trajectory.

The relatively narrow focus of DFMA, for example, has expanded into Design for Excellence (DfX, see Bralla (1995)), which encompasses all of the "ilities" of new product development: manufacturability, reliability, usability, maintainability, and so on. Likewise, the powerful tools of DFSS have been merged of late with the highly efficient techniques of lean thinking to yield an integrated Lean Six Sigma approach. Yet all these attempts still miss the point: It's not just about the tools you use. The entire system that your firm employs to commercialize a new product must be infused with considerations of cost and quality. This ideal is best embodied in the process that Toyota uses to achieve product and process co-development; their so-called 3P methodology (note that 3P stands for either Production Preparation Process or Production Process Preparation, depending on who you ask, see Womack (1990), Liker (2004), Locher (2008)).

At Toyota, cross-functional collaboration begins at the onset of a development project, and continues seamlessly through to product launch; two parallel design teams, one for the product and the other for the production process, work together as one to deliver a successful commercial product. Although the interaction among designers and production specialists is continuous, the 3P process is loosely organized into four "phases":

- **Information Phase** – Past production and process history is investigated and these previous learnings are adapted to the forecasted needs of the product under development.

- **Innovation Phase** – Multiple alternatives are considered for each critical process step, emphasizing those that require significant capital investment. Knowledge gaps for new processes are closed through the creation of knowledge briefs. Risks are identified, on both the design and process side, and systematically mitigated.

- **Redesign Phase** – Based on the learnings gained during the first two phases, a conceptual production line is designed, simulated, tested, and refined. Extensive interaction with the product designers enables minor production-launch issues to be identified.

- **Optimization Phase** – The production line is finalized in parallel with the product design itself. Minor adjustments to both the product and process design are implemented to smooth the transition to production. A finalized production launch plan is generated.

The tools that Toyota's developers use during each phase are selected based on what is needed at the time, rather than being treated as an end in themselves. For example, Toyota employs an aggressive form of value engineering, with each phase utilizing a different level of value analysis. Likewise, there are no separate Lean Six Sigma specialists that hover over the new product design and perform "blackbelt projects" to improve it. Instead, each developer has been trained in the appropriate statistical tools necessary to perform their job, and understands when to use which tool to accomplish their design goals. Underlying the 3P methodology is the recognition that product designers and developers have almost complete control over the ultimate cost and quality of a new product (see Mascitelli (2004)). There are five "cost knobs" that designers can adjust during development to impact production cost and delivered quality, as shown in Figure 8.2. Each of these cost categories should be considered as tradeoffs are performed and design decisions are made. In fact, it would not be an exaggeration to state that the scope of a product development project should actually encompass both the design of the new product *and* the design of the factory in which it will be manufactured.

The Toyota 3P process represents a finely honed future state for product and process co-development, but it has a fundamental limitation; it is not easy to scale. Toyota has massive budgets and enormous dedicated teams available to execute a new vehicle project. With these vast resources at their disposal, they don't suffer from the pragmatic realities of the typical firm: many small projects, precious few manufacturing engineers, time-sharing of developers between design projects and sustaining factory support, limited budgets, and aggressive schedules. So how can the best elements of the Toyota 3P methodology be adapted to this far more constrained environment? The answer, not surprisingly, is through the use of events.

233

"Cost Knob"	Possible Opportunities for Design Team
Direct Labor	• Simplify product assembly • Automate manual operations • Reduce test and inspection requirements
Direct Material	• Use lower-cost materials • Use higher-volume materials • Reduce scrap and wastage
Indirect Overhead	• Simplify initial factory setup • Reduce the number and variety of parts used • Reduce material-handling and storage
Design Costs	• Reuse existing design elements • Purchase commercial-off-the-shelf components • Accelerate the design process
Capital Equipment	• Design product for existing processes / equipment • Select processes with low tooling costs • Reduce product tolerances

FIGURE 8.2: There are five "cost knobs" (aka, cost categories) that designers can adjust when performing design tradeoffs. These knobs are interdependent, meaning that adjusting one cost knob will often have an effect on other costs. Hence, all five of these categories must be considered to maximize profitability.

Three Discrete Events Enable a Continuum of Collaboration

Although continuous collaboration is a fine ideal, the practical realities of new product development in most firms make this goal virtually unattainable. Fortunately, I have had the opportunity to work with several leading manufacturing firms to develop a discrete version of the 3P process that is both pragmatic and highly effective. This approach is based on three consecutive events, as shown in Figure 8.3. The first event, titled the Design 3P Event, is basically an innovation session, with a focus on identifying design improvement opportunities to achieve higher quality, lower cost, and improved manufacturability. Although preliminary discussions should occur during this event with respect to production planning and process selection, the primary objective is to identify product improvements prior to freezing a conceptual design. Hence, the timing of this event is crucial: If the Design 3P Event is held too late in the process, its effectiveness will be substantially diminished. I suggest that the ideal timing would be at roughly the 80-percent completion point of a new product's conceptual design. Note that in the figure, a linkage is shown between the Design 3P Event and the Concept Review and Freeze Event (see Chapter 9). There should be similar linkages between the other 3P and Design Review Events as well. I recommend that a fixed time-period be established between 3P Events and Design Review Events, such that once the appropriate 3P Event is held, there is a clock ticking to get design changes rapidly integrated before holding the associated Design Review and Freeze Event.

Once a design concept for a new product has been reviewed and frozen, the detailed design process begins. As the product's detailed design approaches the 80-percent completion point, the Process 3P Event is held. This Event shifts the focus from design innovations to a combination of product design and manufacturing process optimization. Typically the proportion of effort is roughly 50 / 50 between product and process improvements, whereas the proportion for the Design 3P Event would be closer to 90-percent design innovation and 10-percent process considerations. The last of the three-event sequence that makes up this discrete approach to 3P implementation is titled the Production 3P Event. This is a serious production-readiness and line-*kaizen* event, and may well be similar to events that you are already holding in your firm. The goal is to validate the production system design, and to ensure that there are no incompatibilities between the product and the process. In this final 3P event, the ratio of attention shifts once again, with 90 percent of the effort expended on production issues, and only 10 percent on identifying minor tweaks to the product design prior to launch. An overview of the three proposed 3P Events is provided in Figure 8.4.

In this chapter, I will describe each of the three 3P Events in some detail. However, the degree of specifics that I can provide will, of necessity, be somewhat different for each event. It is possible, for example, to generically describe the proceedings of the Design 3P Event, since the tools and methods used in that meeting are common to virtually every type of product (including hardware, software, and even service products). Once we reach the Process 3P Event, however, the specifics of the meeting become heavily dependent on the nature of the product, the types of manufacturing processes that are required, and the production volumes involved. Hence, my description of this second event will be at a somewhat higher level, although there are still several tools and techniques that are almost always applicable. The Production 3P Event is the most difficult to describe generically, and for this case I must depend on the reader to fill in the blanks, based on a broad overview of the goals and typical proceedings. For these reasons, I will only provide a simulated case example for the Design 3P Event: You will have to create your own product-specific narratives for the remaining two events.

One final note before we begin our 3P journey. The Event-Driven Lean Product Development process is highly flexible, and a successful implementation of 3P takes advantage of this adaptability. Depending upon the complexity of your products, for example, you may need to hold a series of Design 3P Events, the first addressing the system-level product, and then subsequent events focusing on major subsystems. Likewise, if your firm must seek regulatory agency approval for your products, you may have to modify the 3P process to meet those externally-driven milestones. Finally, your firm may have already adopted production-preparation tools such as Failure Mode and Effect Analysis (FMEA) as part of your standard development process. The good news is that if you have a tool or method that is working for you, then just embed it into the Event-Driven LPD framework and you're good to go. In the case of FMEA, for example, you can schedule your series of FMEA events in sequence with the appropriate 3P Events. A Design FMEA would be a natural predecessor to the Design 3P Event, and would provide a beneficial feed of design improvement opportunities to that event. Similarly, you can pair the Process FMEA with the Process 3P Event, and so forth. Never give up something that is working for you: Just find a logical place for it in the Event-Driven Lean Product Development process.

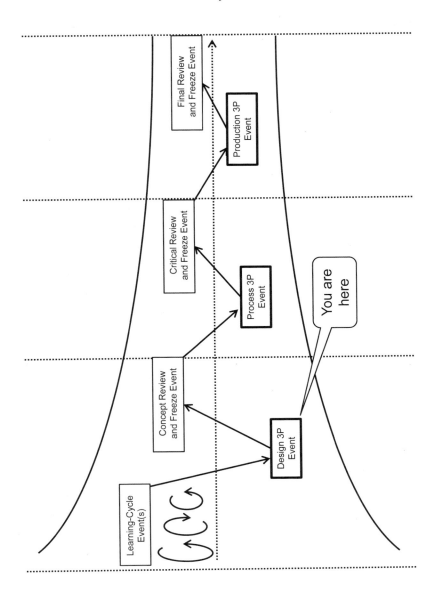

FIGURE 8.3: An expanded view of the Event-Driven Lean Product Development process, showing the approximate timing and linkages between the three 3P Events discussed in this chapter and their associated Design Review and Freeze Events.

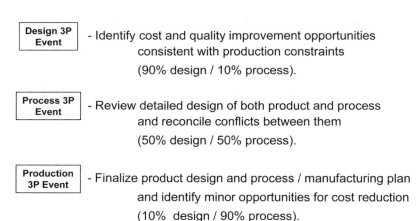

FIGURE 8.4: The Design 3P Event is primarily focused on indentifying innovative improvements to the new product design, and includes only a high-level discussion of process-related issues. The Process 3P Event is equally balanced between product and process design enhancements, while the Production 3P Event is almost entirely dedicated to ensuring production readiness and finalizing the line design.

General Description of the Design 3P Event

The most powerful of the three 3P Events is unquestionably the Design 3P. Indeed, this event answers the question, "How can we get manufacturing involved early in development?" But the benefits of this first event go far beyond enforcing concurrent engineering. This is, at its core, an *innovation* event. Rather than attempting to reduce unit production cost by cheapening the product, or trying to improve quality through costly overdesign, the value-engineering tools embedded in the Design 3P Event enable true optimization: the desired performance, at the lowest possible cost, delivered with superior quality. This is achieved through intensive collaboration and structured brainstorming, along with a trick or two to help teams break through barriers to innovation.

An overview of a typical Design 3P Event is provided in Figure 8.5. As with all of the 3P Events, the primary focus is on the interface and interdependencies between design / engineering and manufacturing / quality. That being said, the involvement of several other functions is vital to executing a successful event. Strategic suppliers and internal

The Design 3P Event

Objective: To utilize innovative cost-reduction and quality-enhancement tools early in the development process to reduce product manufacturing cost and improve manufacturability and delivered quality.

Inputs:
- Market Requirements Brief (updated)
- Engineering requirements (updated)
- Completed knowledge briefs
- Design concepts, drawings, prototypes, models, etc.
- Past history: quality issues, customer satisfaction issues, etc.

Outputs:
- Preliminary manufacturing plan
- Prioritized list of critical-to-cost / critical-to-quality opportunities
- Innovative alternatives to address highest-ranking opportunities
- Action items to Implement the above

Attendees (typical):
- Team leader
- Team members (cross-functional development team)
- Operations / manufacturing / process subject-matter experts
- Others (strategic suppliers, supply chain, quality, etc.)

Agenda (typical):

8:00 – 9:00	Overview of preliminary design concept(s) and mfg. plan
9:00 – 11:00	Brainstorming on critical cost and quality opportunities
11:00 – 12:00	Ranking of cost / quality improvement opportunities
12:00 – 4:00	Rapid innovation cycles using Quick-Look Value Engineering (focused on highest-ranking opportunities)
4:00 – 4:30	Identify actions to close out event
4:30 – 5:00	Management outbriefing / learning opportunities

FIGURE 8.5: An overview of a typical Design 3P Event. The primary focus of this event is on gathering early design input from manufacturing and quality engineering, with the goal of identifying innovative design improvements that will optimize unit production cost and delivered quality.

procurement specialists can have considerable impact by helping to determine what can and cannot be done to improve the product. Similarly, the development team's marketing and sales representatives can play a pivotzal role as surrogates for the customer, offering feedback to the team on how a proposed design improvement might affect customer acceptance of the new product.

The most valuable inputs to the Design 3P Event come from past history: What are the most common cost and quality problems that were experienced on previous products? The sources of this data are manifold. If your firm captures "external" quality data from the field (in the form of customer returns, complaints, installation problems, etc.), for example, then this information will represent an excellent starting point for improvement brainstorming. Likewise, "internal" quality data, including manufacturing yield loss, rework, repairs, scrap, and other wastage, will enable a more effective innovation session. Additional inputs to the event should include any conceptual design documentation, and in particular, any physical artifacts, models, or prototypes that have been created. Brainstorming is greatly facilitated by the availability of physical objects that can be passed around and referred to during idea generation. Finally, as with all events, the Design 3P Event team should have at their fingertips updated versions of the project's guiding documents, including the Market Requirements Brief, engineering specifications, and so on.

The sample agenda that I have provided begins with an overview of preliminary production plans and assumptions for the new product. Naturally, at this early stage of development, this material will be sketchy. However, it is important that any initial thoughts on production be voiced and discussed by the team. This is particularly crucial if there are any fundamental assumptions about where and how the product will be manufactured. For example, it is common for a proposed new product to be assigned to a specific factory location, or even a specific line, as a means to optimize a firm's production capacity utilization. If this represents an unshakable mandate from management (e.g., the whole purpose of the new product is to fill an underutilized line), then this needs to be made clear to the event participants before brainstorming begins. Similarly, if the product is intended for contract manufacture or overseas production, these assumptions must be identified up front. An overview of the preliminary manufacturing plan should include:

- General assumptions regarding where and how the new product would be manufactured.
- Overview of the capital equipment budget, along with any underlying assumptions.
- Requirements for commonality with existing products, part sharing, backward compatibility, etc.

- A high-level description of the logistics and supply-chain structure, along with identification of strategic suppliers.

- Capacity estimates, *takt*-time goals, and other specifics that can be derived from the projected sales volumes for the new product.

Once the discussion of the preliminary manufacturing plan is complete, the remainder of the Design 3P Event is dedicated to innovative problem-solving. The first step in this process is to identify fruit that is ripe for the picking; the highest-leverage opportunities for improvement to cost or quality. To accomplish this, I use two straightforward definitions to communicate what the event team should be looking for:

Critical-to-Cost (CTC):

Any design- or process-related factor that has a high potential impact on the new product's unit production cost.

Critical-to-Quality (CTQ):

Any design- or process-related factor that has a high potential impact on yield, defects, rework, customer returns, assembly time, installation time, etc.

The identification of CTC and CTQ opportunities should always be based on past experience. Although raw data is useful, a far better way to harvest your historical knowledge and apply it to each new product development project is through the use of *trigger lists*. You may recall that I introduced the concept of the trigger list in Chapter 6, as a means of stimulating the brainstorming of project risks. The same approach can be used during the Design 3P Event to help the team generate a comprehensive list of CTC and CTQ issues. Generic examples of trigger lists for these two categories are shown in Figures 8.6 and 8.7. You should note that there is a significant overlap between these two areas of opportunity. It is often the case that a quality issue will manifest itself as a cost issue as well, and vice versa. Fortunately, there is no harm in discussing a similar issue under both headings, and it might be beneficial to look at a given situation from both a quality and cost perspective.

Examples of Critical-to-Cost Considerations
• Reduce parts count
• Simplify assembly
• Reduce use of screws / small fasteners
• Reduce cost of testing
• Reduce or eliminate unique / once-used parts
• Foolproof assembly of parts that can be misoriented
• Simplify supply chain
• Eliminate tight-tolerance parts
• Eliminate exotic raw materials
• Reduce assembly steps requiring a high skill level
• Reduce capital-intensive process steps
• Resolve low-yielding process steps
• Eliminate excessive complexity
• Incompatibility with existing flow lines or work cells
• Optimize cost of packaging and shipping

FIGURE 8.6: Generic example of a trigger list for critical-to-cost issues. Of course, your firm should generate its own product-specific list for use during brainstorming.

Examples of Critical-to-Quality Considerations
• Minimize number of connection points
• Drive possible connection points outward
• Simplify customer connections / installation
• Quality of surface finish
• Design meets test requirements
• Design meets code / regulatory requirements
• Reduce / eliminate once-used parts and materials
• Parts that can come loose during shipping
• Parts that can be misoriented during assembly
• Parts that are not properly labeled
• Tolerance stack-up issues
• Ratio of product tolerances to process accuracy / precision (C_p)
• Reduce delicate assembly steps
• Raw-material variability
• Extremes of use environment
• Reliability issues
• Design of packaging to avoid shipping damage

FIGURE 8.7: Generic example of a trigger list for critical-to-quality opportunities.

The trigger lists provide fodder for brainstorming by the group, with the goal of generating a comprehensive list of critical factors. However, as always in a brainstorming session, we must have a method for prioritizing these opportunities. There is typically little time available in a project schedule for integrating new ideas and improvements to a design. It is therefore vital that the most promising opportunities be addressed first. To accomplish this, I recommend using two 1-to-5 scores (not surprising, if you have been paying attention), as shown in Figure 8.8. This ranking system is similar to the one used to prioritize project risks in Chapter 6, and indeed one of the two metrics is identical: the impact on the product if a given opportunity is successfully addressed. A high score for impact implies that an improvement to a CTC / CTQ issue would have a substantial impact on either cost or quality, whereas a low score indicates a negligible impact on those factors. The second 1-to-5 score is an indication of how "easy" it would be to improve a given cost or quality issue. This metric is important, since it would be futile to waste precious time and resources on intractable improvement opportunities. A 1-score for "ease" implies that improvement would be very difficult (i.e., there are significant roadblocks preventing the team from identifying a better alternative). This might be the case, for example, if a given component is vital to meeting performance goals, and cannot be altered without negatively impacting product performance. Another example would be parts that must be common across multiple products within your product line; any change would cause the new product to be incompatible with this part-sharing strategy. On the other hand, a 5-score would indicate that an opportunity would be straightforward to improve. This is often the case when a CTC or CTQ issue has been on the minds of designers for some time, and there are already several proposed ideas as to how improvement can be achieved.

As with previous scoring activities, once the brainstormed list of CTC and CTQ issues is finalized, the entire group votes on these two 1-to-5 scores, with the facilitator averaging the responses from the attendees. The scores for each improvement opportunity are then multiplied together to create an Action Priority Number – a prioritized ranking that will be used to guide activities throughout the remainder of the event. A template is provided in Figure 8.9 for capturing and ranking the CTC and

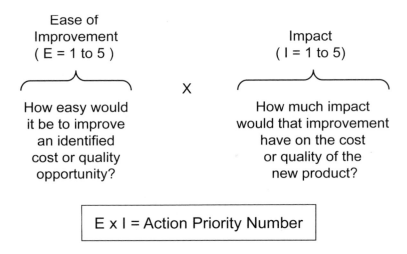

Ease of Improvement (E = 1 to 5)		Impact (I = 1 to 5)
How easy would it be to improve an identified cost or quality opportunity?	X	How much impact would that improvement have on the cost or quality of the new product?

E x I = Action Priority Number

FIGURE 8.8: A familiar ranking system is used to prioritize critical-to-cost (CTC) and critical-to-quality (CTQ) improvement opportunities. Note that while the impact score is similar to the one previously used for the ranking of project risks, an ease-of-improvement score is utilized here in place of "probability of occurrence" to help identify opportunities that can be quickly and effectively addressed.

CTQ improvement opportunities. Once priorities have been established, the highest-ranking items will be systematically investigated through the use of what I call the Quick-Look Value Engineering methodology. This innovation technique will be described later in the chapter.

It is time for another fictional case example to illustrate how a ranked list of CTC and CTQ opportunities can be effectively generated. First, however, I should mention that the agenda that I've proposed is just a starting point for your own improvisation. The core steps should always be performed, however you have considerable latitude to include additional tools or activities that you feel will benefit the cost and quality of the new product. For example, you might tie several methods from the DFSS toolbox to this event, including Design Failure Mode and Effect Analysis (Design FMEA) and potentially one or more Design of Experiments (DOEs). You could also incorporate DFMA tools, such as design efficiency analysis or a review of material and process alternatives for key components. You might even decide to include a conceptual trade-off tool such as my Twenty-Cost-Levers

Critical-to-Quality or Critical-to-Cost Opportunity	C / Q	Subjective Rating		Action Priority No.
		(E)	(I)	

FIGURE 8.9: A template for capturing brainstormed CTC and CTQ opportunities. The Action Priority Number on the right represents the product of the "ease" and "impact" scores for a given improvement opportunity.

matrix (see Mascitelli (2004)), to provide the team with some early direction as to which product architecture might yield the lowest overall cost. The sky's the limit, provided that you are mindful of available time and short attention spans.

Event Simulation: Bimford Tools and the EcoDrill (Part I)

It had taken fifty years, but Bimford Tools was finally going green. A new CEO had recently joined the company, and had brought with him an updated vision for the brand that was fresh, current, and politically correct. Every tool in Bimford's extensive lineup was to undergo an environmentally-friendly makeover, beginning with their flagship product, the HoleHog power drill. Along with a substantial redesign would come a new name, the EcoDrill, that would advertise to the world the new tool's sustainable pedigree. Of course, at the onset of this development project no one within the design engineering group had a clue what it meant for a product to be "green," beyond the lurid chartreuse color that

245

had been chosen by marketing for the entire EcoTool product line. It had taken several iterations of the Market Requirements Event for a clear set of engineering requirements to emerge, and several learning cycles to reduce knowledge gaps. Finally, however, Al Borman and his project team began developing a conceptual design.

Three months of effort later, the team had arrived at a neat little design, with an excellent mix of performance and features. Environmentally-friendly materials were to be used throughout, and even the insulation on the wiring would be made from post-consumer plastic. Now, with only a month left before the scheduled Concept Design Review and Freeze Event, the team discovered that in the interest of pursuing performance and sustainability, they had neglected cost and quality. Initial production cost estimates exceeded their target cost by over 20 percent, and there were a number of critical quality issues that had not yet been addressed. With these shortfalls on their minds, the team had gathered for what they hoped would be their salvation: The Design 3P Event.

The preliminaries had gone well thus far. The event attendees discussed various manufacturing constraints, including a mandate from the CEO that the new drill would be produced in the U.S. on an entirely new, energy-efficient production line. Once preliminary manufacturing plans were understood and agreed upon by the group, it was time to attack their cost and quality challenges. After having participated in several brainstorming activities thus far (as part of both the Market Requirements Event and the Project Planning / Risk-Mitigation Event), the team was well-prepared for yet another idea-generation session. Al brought a flip-chart easel to the front of the conference room, and with marker in hand, kicked off the process.

"Each of you should have been thinking about the most critical cost, quality, and manufacturability issues that need to be addressed on the EcoDrill," he began. "First we are going to consider critical-to-quality challenges, starting with field failures and customer satisfaction issues, and work backwards to our own internal manufacturing processes. The easiest way to generate a list of quality improvement opportunities is to use our past experience as a guide. Can someone pull up our customer satisfaction data from the venerable HoleHog line?" A representative of the sales department quickly responded.

"I've got the list of customer complaints here in front of me," said the sales rep. "If I sort these by frequency of occurrence, the most common cause of customer dissatisfaction is excessive noise – our current product sounds like a garbage disposal when running under full load. Even though we have a reputation for high-reliability tools, the noise these things make gives the impression that they're about to fall apart."

"Okay, so our first improvement opportunity is to reduce operating noise," said Al. "What's next on the list?" The sales rep went on to enumerate other frequent complaints, including power cords that cracked after extensive exposure to sunlight, an abrupt jerking motion when the drill is first started, and a clumsy chuck that allows the bit to come loose during aggressive use. Each of these improvement opportunities represented external quality issues; problems that had occurred after the product had been shipped from the factory. With the above items as a starting point, Al asked the team to consider their own experiences and come up with additional prospects for improvement.

"Well, we do have a new challenge regarding the reliability of the EcoDrill," suggested one of the mechanical engineers. "The 100-percent-recycled plastic material that we have selected for the motor housing is probably not as robust as our previous compression-molded polymer. I think it will need some additional reinforcement to meet our long-term reliability standards."

This and other external quality issues were added to the list, and after several more minutes of discussion, Al gave the team some new direction.

"Okay, so we have a pretty thorough list of quality issues from the customer's perspective. What about internal quality problems? Aren't we tracking factory rejects, rework, and test-failure data?"

"You bet we are," said the development team's manufacturing engineer. "I have a whole list of manufacturability issues that are costing us a ton of money. The biggest hitter on the list is the insertion of the motor into the gearbox housing. We are damaging the coils on the motor more than 10 percent of the time, resulting in very disruptive line stoppages to retest, and often reject, the motor." The manufacturing engineer went on to describe several other problems, including burrs on castings, poor alignment of injection-molded parts, and difficult assembly steps. The team's list of quality improvement opportunities soon grew to fill several flip-chart sheets.

"Well, we certainly have our work cut out for us," said Al, after the first round of brainstorming was complete. "What makes matters worse is that we can't just throw money at these critical-to-quality issues. Our current design concept appears to be at least 20-percent over our target manufacturing cost, so any solutions we come up with for quality problems cannot increase our cost one penny. And while we're on the subject of cost, our next activity will be to identify critical-to-cost items. We will need to be pretty aggressive here, if we are to avoid a management intervention on our project. The bottom line is that our current design has an unacceptable bottom line." Al turned on the overhead projector and brought up the preliminary bill-of-materials that the team had generated over the past several months.

"I'm a logical kind of guy," he continued, "so it seems reasonable to me that if we are going to reduce the recurring cost of this product, we should start with the most expensive components. Given the magnitude of our cost problem, it would be a waste of time to worry about penny parts. If I rank-order this BOM based on our current cost estimates, there are three obvious killers. First, the new chuck design that we've proposed is by far the most expensive component in the entire drill." The team had envisioned a breakthrough design for the bit chuck that was keyless, torque-adjustable, and had a magnetized head to hold bits securely during insertion and removal. Unfortunately, the cost estimates for this advanced concept were sky high. It was therefore noted on the flip chart under critical-to-cost issues. "Looking farther down the list, there are two other high-leverage opportunities," Al said. "The fancy molded grip for the EcoDrill is a cost driver, as well as the control electronics board. In the latter case, we are running up against environmental challenges. If we want to meet the most recent standards for sustainable design, we have to use an entirely new manufacturing process to fabricate our circuit board, including different components and lead-free soldering." These additional high-cost items were added to the brainstorming list, along with several other opportunities that the team believed could help reduce material cost.

"We have one more place we can look for cost savings," Al continued. "Our labor cost estimates are almost double what we have experienced on our current line of power drills. Where is all of this additional labor cost coming from?" This time, a production-line supervisor offered some insight.

"Well, the truth is that this green stuff is a pain in the neck from a manufacturing standpoint. The new line we are planning to build will use recycled cutting fluids, low-energy-consumption heat treatments, and a low VOC (volatile organic compound) painting process. Each of these new technologies requires either higher maintenance, more operator interaction, or runs at a slower rate. And then, of course, there is your magic bit chuck that will be a bear to assemble and very finicky to align and adjust. Anything we can come up with to error-proof that design would be money in the bank."

■ ■ ■

With these opportunities as a starting point, the team went on to fill several more flip-chart sheets with ideas for cost improvements. At last, it was time to prioritize their opportunities. Beginning with the first item on the list, the attendees began holding up fingers; one finger through five fingers indicating a 1-to-5 scoring range for both "impact" and "ease of improvement." The results of the EcoDrill team's ranking of CTQ and CTC issues is shown in Figure 8.10. The team rightly combined both categories of improvement opportunity for prioritization purposes: The highest-ranking issues would be addressed based on their Action Priority Number, regardless of whether they were primarily a cost or a quality challenge. It is evident from the team's output that several iterations of the Quick-Look Value Engineering technique would be required to make a dent in their extensive list.

Critical-to-Quality or Critical-to-Cost Opportunity	C / Q	Subjective Rating		Action Priority No.
		(E)	(I)	
Excessive noise under full load	Q	3	5	15
Power cords crack when exposed to the sun	Q	5	3	15
Jerking motion upon startup of drill	Q	2	4	8
Bit comes loose during aggressive use	Q	4	5	20
Need to reinforce plastic motor housing	Q	4	3	12
Rework due to motor insertion into gearbox	Q	3	3	9
Poor alignment of housing parts	Q	3	2	6
Material cost of new chuck design	C	2	5	10
Material cost of plastic-molded grip	C	4	4	16
Material cost of "green" electronics board	C	2	4	8
Labor cost of bit-chuck assembly	C	5	4	20

FIGURE 8.10: The results of the EcoDrill product development team's brainstorming on CTQ and CTC improvement opportunities. Issues that received an Action Priority Number of 20 in the above example would be the first to be addressed using the Quick-Look Value Engineering technique.

Intermission: Collaborative Innovation through Quick-Look Value Engineering

Generating a prioritized list of cost and quality improvement opportunities is straightforward, but how can a development team rapidly convert these opportunities into specific design changes that will yield a higher-value product? To answer this question, I will revive an old methodology, but with a lean makeover. In the 1950's and 1960's, many large industrial firms began to adopt a methodology that was pioneered by teams at General Electric and RCA. This approach, known as *value engineering,* was intended as a means of democratizing manufactured products for a newly globalized market: Lower-cost goods could be sold to a substantially larger market segment, particularly in countries that were still recovering from the devastation of World War II. Basically, value engineering is an innovation process in which a given design element is decomposed into its bare essence, reconsidered from the standpoint of cost and quality, and ultimately improved to yield higher customer value.

Sounds like just what we are looking for. In fact, during the 1970's many Japanese companies were so inspired by this value-focused philosophy that they adopted it as a core process. To this day, Toyota, Panasonic, Sharp, and others still use an adapted form of value engineering as part of their product commercialization process.

Unfortunately, as with many great improvement methodologies, value engineering began to gain weight – what had been an efficient team-based tool grew into whole departments of value engineers. Likewise, the method itself became increasingly arcane and time-consuming. Rather than being applied as a surgical tool, it grew into a cumbersome front-to-back process, using phased activities referred to as "first-look," "second-look," and so on. Soon firms began to question the return on investment of value engineering, and over the past several decades it has fallen somewhat out of favor. Well, my goal is to resurrect this powerful approach and place it at center stage in the 3P process. To accomplish this, however, I have filtered out the most vital principles to yield a quick-turn process for innovative problem-solving. Indeed, you could think of Quick-Look Value Engineering as a "shorthand" version of the full-blown, A3-based knowledge brief.

The Quick-Look Value Engineering tool is illustrated in Figure 8.11. The process begins by identifying a promising cost or quality improvement opportunity (shown in the upper left-hand corner of the figure). This first step is easy if you have performed the CTQ / CTC prioritization described in the previous section. Simply pick a high-ranking opportunity from your brainstormed list and you are ready for the next step. Once a prime candidate has been chosen, the design element involved is decomposed into its essential *functions*. This step is critical to the value-engineering methodology: The "functional-definition" technique (described later in this section) strips away all underlying assumptions about how the required functions must be performed. Assumptions are like blind spots for developers. Once a design concept has been selected, it is difficult for the development team to take a step backward and question whether they have chosen the best approach. As a result, cost and quality improvements will tend to be narrow in focus; little more than minor adjustments to what might be a fundamentally flawed design. Stripping away any underlying assumptions allows the team to

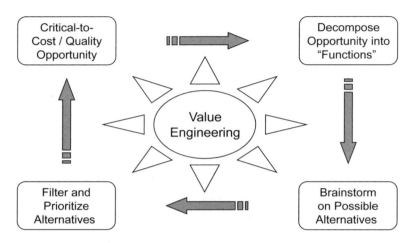

FIGURE 8.11: The Quick-Look Value Engineering process begins with the selection of a cost or quality improvement opportunity, as shown in the upper left-hand corner. The opportunity selected for improvement is then decomposed into its essential function(s), and brainstorming is performed to identify alternative ways in which the function(s) can be performed. These alternatives are then filtered for viability, action items are assigned to further investigate promising alternatives, and the cycle begins again with the next improvement opportunity.

objectively consider alternative ways in which the required function(s) can be performed. In value engineering, the fundamental question that is being asked is: "If we can't do it the way we have currently proposed, how else might the same function(s) be performed, and are those alternative approaches lower cost and/or higher quality?"

Once all assumptions have been set aside, it is time for innovative brainstorming by a cross-functional team. If your Design 3P Event involves a relatively small group, then you may decide to use the entire team to perform this idea-generation activity. On the other hand, if you have a relatively large number of participants (say eight or more) at your disposal, it would make sense to divide the group into several smaller sub-teams, and have multiple Quick-Look Value Engineering activities running in parallel. In this situation, the membership of each sub-team should be carefully considered to ensure that the functional disciplines involved are matched with the nature of the improvement opportunity they will be addressing. The brainstorming process is focused on how to best perform the required function(s), not on how to fix an existing design element. Once several alternatives have been generated, a familiar tool is used (provided that you have read Chapter 7) to filter them: the Pugh matrix (aka, the concept-selection matrix). The desired output of this four-step cycle is a set of alternatives that appear to be viable (i.e., they have a high potential to perform all required functions at a lower cost and/or a higher quality level). Of course, it is possible that the current design will prove to be the best of the bunch. If this is the case, the Design 3P team simply repeats the Quick-Look Value Engineering process for the next ripe prospect on their prioritized list.

With the above overview in mind, I'll describe some of the key activities within the process in more detail. The most unique aspect of Quick-Look Value Engineering is the decomposition of an improvement opportunity into one or more functions. To accomplish this, we will use a trick referred to as "verb / noun naming," as shown in Figure 8.12. The goal is to strip away all modifying words, and use only a verb and a noun to describe a given function. In the figure, for example, the function of the lead in a pencil is described as "make marks." It does not have to be made of graphite, be black or cylindrical, or housed within a wooden shaft. In principle, there are a multitude of ways in which marks can be made that are different, and potentially better, than the way it is currently done. Admittedly, it would be hard to argue that the design of a pencil is not already fully optimized. Nonetheless, the technique of verb / noun naming can have powerful consequences once idea-generation begins: It increases the probability that design alternatives will be proposed which might never have been considered had the starting point been "graphite cylinder embedded in a wooden shaft that makes black marks." A given design element may have several basic functions, but you should avoid including every attribute that an improvement opportunity might possess. The distinction between functions and attributes is subtle, but basically you are looking for the key contributions that a given design element provides to the product. The fewer the functions that you identify, the easier it will be to find a better alternative.

Once a given improvement opportunity has been decomposed into its functions, it is time for the team to propose alternative ways in which those functions might be performed. There are several ways in which this can proceed. The team might propose a redesign of a design element

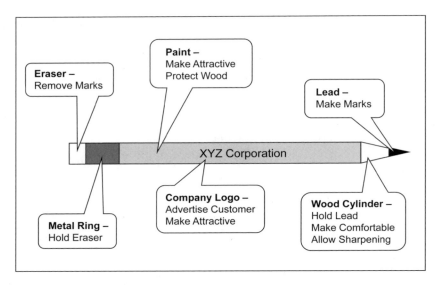

FIGURE 8.12: The Quick-Look Value Engineering process utilizes a verbal trick referred to as "verb / noun naming," in which a two-word functional description is used to strip away assumptions about a given design element. The resulting functional definitions can then be used to generate alternative approaches that might be lower cost and/or higher quality.

that can perform all of the identified functions better and cheaper. They might also find ways in which the required functions could be performed by other elements of the product design. It may even be possible to completely eliminate some design elements by recombining functions in an innovative way, as shown in Figure 8.13. This mixing and matching of functions can lead to breakthroughs in product design, so it is worth taking the time to consider options beyond simple "drop-in" replacements for an existing design element. As always, brainstorming should be free and unencumbered by preconceptions and narrow thinking: Any and all ideas should be given equal weight, since they will be filtered for viability in the next step in the process. To encourage divergent thinking, it is worthwhile to bring external (i.e., outside of the firm) knowledge into the discussion. As I mentioned previously, including strategic suppliers or external technical consultants in the exercise can be very valuable. You could also consider how your competition performs similar functions in their products, or how these functions are performed by

Functions   Function   Design
                   Alternatives   Alternatives

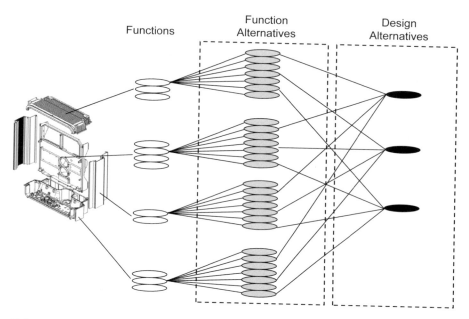

FIGURE 8.13: Once an improvement opportunity has been decomposed into its essential functions, the Design 3P team is free to consider multiple alternatives that might be lower cost and / or higher quality. Often, the best alternatives involve recombining or reallocating functions among other design elements in the product in a clever way.

products from other industries. You might even ponder how nature performs similar functions (often referred to as "biomimicry"). I've found that some firms have benefited from the use of TRIZ innovation tools (see Fey, et al (2005)), which provide a rich database of useful solutions to generic design problems.

The last step in the Quick-Look Value Engineering process is to filter the brainstormed alternatives using the Pugh matrix previously described in Chapter 7. The default approach used in the matrix should be the current design element that you've identified for possible improvement. Alternatives are listed, as before, along the top row of the matrix. The "must-have" criteria used for filtering can be any attribute or factor that can separate the viable alternatives from the non-starters. Be sure, however, to always include "lower cost" and "higher quality" as filtering criteria, since these are, after all, the reasons for using this tool in the first place. Scoring is performed as before, with pluses and minuses indicating the relative benefits and disbenefits of your alternatives. I typically don't use weighting factors for this application of the Pugh matrix, since the goal is to perform this activity quickly, and then move on to the next improvement opportunity on your prioritized list. Use your own judgment, but my preference is to harness the cross-functional event team in the most efficient manner possible. With limited time and a number of improvement opportunities to deal with, I am willing to accept a quick filtering of alternatives, and then allow the design team to make the final selections after the event is concluded. In principle, each application of Quick-Look Value Engineering can be completed in one to two hours, allowing time for several iterations in a one-day event. Naturally, if your product is complex and improvement opportunities abound, you might extend the event to a second or even a third day to capture the maximum benefit.

It is time to return to our fictional case example, in which a challenging quality issue will be addressed by the EcoDrill design team using the powerful innovation methodology described above.

Event Simulation: Bimford Tools and the EcoDrill (Part II)

After generating a prioritized list of cost and quality improvement possibilities, the EcoDrill team was ready to begin attacking the highest-ranking opportunities using Quick-Look Value Engineering. Al Borman began the session by proposing the first candidate for improvement.

"Well, based on our scores," Al began, "we have two prospects that have bubbled to the top: bits coming loose during aggressive use, and the labor cost of assembling our new bit-chuck design. I'm going to suggest that we begin with the cost of assembling the bit chuck, since the changes we might make to that subassembly could affect other aspects of the product's performance." He went to the conference room's whiteboard and drew a Pugh-matrix template. "Now keep in mind that we must begin our process by identifying the critical functions that this assembly performs. This should help us think differently about how the chuck should be designed and assembled. Remember, there are no rules here – you can propose anything that comes to mind, as long as it can perform the required functions."

After some discussion, the team agreed that the bit-chuck assembly must perform several key functions. Using the verb / noun naming technique, they identified the following functions:

- Hold bit
- Adjust torque
- Transfer power

Based on these three functions, and with no other restrictions, the team began generating alternatives to the current (i.e., the default) design.

"You know, we have been assuming that the only way to go is a four-jaw chuck assembly," said one of the team's mechanical engineers. "Why not go with a three-jaw configuration? It would certainly be easier to assemble and would probably be lower cost as well." Al added this suggestion to the top of the Pugh matrix without comment: He was careful not to bias the group by showing either enthusiasm or distain for any proposed idea. Another hand went up from the group.

"One of the big problems with the assembly of this thing is that in the current design, each of the four jaws is slightly different," suggested a manufacturing engineer. "If we made the jaws identical, there would be no confusion over how to assemble the components, and no chance of mistakes that would require rework later." Again, the idea was added to the matrix. Additional ideas were proposed and captured: the use of a planetary gear system instead of the current rack-and-pinion design, using index pins on the gear housing to error-proof the assembly process, and creating a self-aligning torque-adjustment mechanism. Some of these ideas involved significant design changes, while others represented relatively minor modifications to the existing design. All of the proposed concepts, however, delivered the three functions that were required to meet the product's design requirements.

"I think we have a pretty good list of alternatives," Al said. "Any other ideas before we begin discussing the benefits and disbenefits of these options?" He looked around the room, and saw no more raised hands. "Okay, so let's walk through each of these ideas and discuss how they might work, what would be the advantages, and what could go wrong."

A half-hour discussion ensued, during which there was much debate about the relative cost of each alternative, and whether it would solve the labor problem without sacrificing functionality. Once the debate began to ebb, it was time to use the power of the Pugh matrix to capture the thoughts that had been voiced, and reach a consensus regarding which design alternatives would merit further investigation.

"We need to establish some filtering criteria to help us sort out this list of ideas," Al said. "Clearly there are two criteria that have to be up here: lower material cost and lower labor cost. After all, our goal is to reduce the overall cost of the product so we can solve our profit-margin problem. It would be useless to just trade one source of cost for another." He proceeded to add these two filtering criteria to the left column of the Pugh matrix. Others in the group proposed additional filters: high reliability, a solid bit grip, low noise (since this had been highlighted as a separate quality issue), and reduced rework. With both the alternatives and the filtering criteria in place, it was time for the team to score the various ideas.

"Remember that we have a range of from three pluses to three minuses to work with," said Al. "I suggest that we go through each alternative from top to bottom. Someone can suggest a score for each box, and we'll discuss that proposal and see if we agree. Don't worry about getting it right the first time. Once we have the matrix filled out, we will go through it again as a sanity check. We can change anything we want, but eventually we'll have to converge on a final version." With that, the scoring process began. After several iterations of scoring and discussion, followed by rescoring and more discussion, the team arrived at the finalized matrix shown in Figure 8.14.

"Well, this is interesting," said Al. "It seems we have several viable design improvements, and at least one marginal prospect. The interchangeable jaws and the index pins seem like no-brainers. They are easy to implement, don't affect performance at all, and won't add any material cost. If anything, the interchangeable jaws should reduce material cost somewhat. On the other hand, it's pretty clear that the self-aligning torque adjustment and the three-jaw idea are just not worth pursuing. They both have some significant negatives, and no real solid advantages. Moreover, during our discussion, it was obvious that from a performance

Filtering Criteria \ Design Alternatives	Default design	Three-jaw chuck	Interchangeable jaws	Planetary gear system	Index pins on gear housing	Self-aligning torque adjust.
Lower material cost	S	++	S	- -	S	- -
Lower labor cost	S	++	+	++	+	+
High reliability	S	-	S	+	S	S
Solid bit grip	S	- -	S	S	S	S
Low noise	S	S	S	++	S	S
Less rework	S	+	+	++	+	+
Totals +	0	5	2	7	2	2
−	0	3	0	2	0	2

FIGURE 8.14: The results of the EcoDrill team's first iteration of Quick-Look Value Engineering. In this case, the "interchangeable jaws" and "index pins on gear housing" design improvements would be selected for implementation, while some additional investigation might be warranted for the "planetary gear system" alternative.

standpoint, these options would probably not meet our requirements. We do have a marginal candidate, however. Even though the planetary gear assembly has two negatives on cost, we really don't have any pricing information to back this up. Moreover, look at all of the advantages this option has. Even though I am personally skeptical, I think we would be foolish not to at least go out and get some quotes. If the cost of this new approach is even close to the current design, I think the advantages would far outweigh the disadvantages."

The EcoDrill team went on to perform several more iterations of the Quick-Look Value Engineering method, attacking critical cost and quality issues in order of priority. The result of the one-day session was a significant reduction in manufacturing cost, and some excellent ideas for improving product quality. The event closed, as always, with the assignment of action items to implement the improvements that had been clear winners. Al Borman assigned himself a final action item: His challenge would be to convince the marketing director to change the color of the EcoDrill from chartreuse to a nice, environmentally-friendly forest green.

General Description of the Process 3P Event

Unlike the Design 3P Event, the final two events in the 3P process are strongly influenced by the specifics of the product and manufacturing processes involved. Hence, my descriptions of these events will be more general in nature. The reader will have to fill in the blanks, based on your own unique circumstances. Once the Design 3P Event has been successfully concluded, and the appropriate design improvements have been implemented, the product development team can move on to finalize the conceptual design of the product. (Note that this is accomplished by holding the Concept Design Review and Freeze Event covered in Chapter 9.) Subsequently, a period of detailed design work would begin. At some point prior to freezing the detailed product design, the Process 3P Event is scheduled, as described in Figure 8.15. The exact timing of this event, however, is determined by several factors. From the standpoint of design maturity, it is important that this second 3P event be held prior to the detailed design becoming etched in stone. Again, we need to allow time in the project schedule for the incorporation of design improvements. For this event, however, the range of possible design modifications is significantly narrower. The Process 3P Event occurs at a point in the development process where any major design change would likely cause a slip to the product's launch date, so only relatively minor adjustments are considered. The primary emphasis of this intermediate event is on establishing a clear vision of the production flow for the new product, and on reducing the capital investment and recurring labor costs involved. Hence, several production-related factors should be considered when determining the best time to schedule the Process 3P Event.

The first of these factors is the lead-time associated with production preparation. If the manufacture of your new product will require the acquisition of tooling, fixturing, automation equipment, or other long-lead items, the Process 3P Event must be held sufficiently in advance of

---

The Process 3P Event

Objective: To plan the value streams for both external (supply chain) and internal (factory) processes, and identify both design- and capital-optimization opportunities to achieve optimal lean manufacturability.

Inputs:

- Market Requirements Brief (updated)
- Engineering requirements (updated)
- Detailed design drawings, prototypes and test results
- Outputs from previous 3P Event (updated)

Outputs:

- Revised manufacturing plan
- Preliminary internal / external value-stream maps
- Cost-reduction opportunities for capital-intensive processes
- Cost-reduction opportunities for labor-intensive processes
- Action assignments to implement the above

Attendees (typical):

- Team leader
- Team members (cross-functional development team)
- Operations / manufacturing / process subject-matter experts
- Others (strategic suppliers, supply chain, quality, etc.)

FIGURE 8.15: Overview of the Process 3P Event. The timing of this event is determined by several factors, but the most critical consideration is allowing enough time in the project schedule to incorporate design improvements without adversely affecting the product's launch date.

these schedule constraints to allow time to incorporate improvements prior to placing orders. Likewise, if the new product must undergo regulatory review and approval, the timing of the event might be affected by when specific information or physical artifacts must be provided to the involved agencies. Other considerations might include the time required for facility modifications, lead-times on prototype and production parts, and the scheduling of critical trade shows or other externally-driven milestones. In summary, you may need to move the Process 3P Event to a point somewhat earlier in the development process than might otherwise be necessary from just a design perspective.

The primary goal of the Process 3P Event is to create an optimized plan for production. To this end, a considerable amount of time should be invested in mapping out the flow of both the internal and external value streams for the new product, as shown in Figure 8.16. (Note that value-stream-mapping techniques for recurring processes are not discussed in this book, since there are a number of excellent references available, see for example, Rother, et al (1999).) The external value stream is just another term for the supply chain. How will materials flow amongst critical suppliers, and ultimately to your factory for fabrication, assembly and test? What will be your strategy for just-in-time (JIT) delivery of materials? Will a supply-chain *kanban* (i.e, pull or signaling) system be used? Will suppliers perform quality testing or pre-assembly of components? Who will kit the parts for production? The level of detail required is determined by the partitioning of work between internal and external "factories" for the new product. If your firm plans to vertically integrate production (i.e., most of the value-added work is performed in your own factory), then the supply-chain value-stream map may be nothing more than a supplier list. On the other hand, if you are depending on value-added suppliers or contract manufacturers for a large portion of fabrication and assembly, then the supply-chain mapping exercise must be performed in great detail. The internal production value stream should be addressed with the same factors in mind. Obviously, both the external and internal value streams must flow together seamlessly to yield a high-quality product, so you cannot optimize one without careful consideration of the other.

The other critical activity that should take place during the Process 3P Event is the optimization of any production process steps that require either a large capital investment or a considerable amount of recurring labor. The technique that I recommend for this optimization process is one that Toyota has made somewhat famous: the Seven-Alternatives method. The underlying philosophy of this technique is, yet again, set-based design; the consideration of multiple alternative approaches which are then systematically down-selected to a best choice. The general idea is to select a high-impact opportunity for improvement, from either a capital-investment or labor-cost perspective, and then to identify seven

FIGURE 8.16: An illustration of the knowledge flows for the Process 3P Event. The two major activities in this event are the value-stream mapping of internal and external production flows, and the optimization of capital- and labor-intensive manufacturing operations.

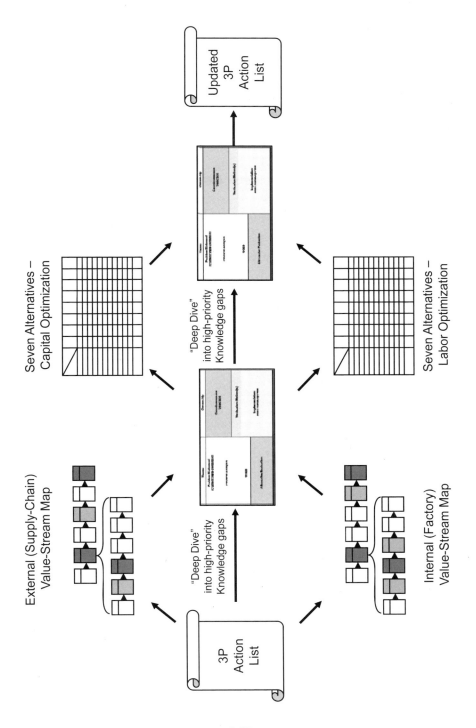

possible ways in which that process might be performed. These options can include design changes, process changes, or a combination thereof. Why seven alternatives? No good reason, other than the fact that Toyota does it that way. The number of alternatives is arbitrary, of course, but the goal is to generate a comprehensive list of options that span the space of possibilities. If you question whether there can be seven different ways to accomplish the same production process step, then consider the examples shown in Figure 8.17. Note that these examples include different fabrication processes, alternative part choices, and various design options as well. Any and all of these improvement possibilities are acceptable, provided that the project schedule permits their implementation.

In reality, the Seven-Alternatives method is just another application of the Pugh matrix described earlier in this chapter. In this case, however, I recommend using the matrix as more of a decision tool than just a discussion tool. Hence, I typically include weighting factors for each "must-have" selection criterion, as shown in Figure 8.18. In this figure, I've provided some recommended criteria that you might use as

Design Element	Process Alternative						
	1	2	3	4	5	6	7
Metal Cylinder with Bottom	Deep-Drawn	Cut from Tube Stock & Welded	Milled from Solid Bar Stock	Rolled from Sheet Stock & Welded	Liquid Metal Injection Molded	Sand Cast	Die Cast
Plastic Enclosure	Injection Molded	Com-pression Molded	Vacuum Formed	Structural-Foam Molded	Welded from Sheet Stock	Milled from Solid Stock	Extruded and Machined
Electronic Circuit	Single-Layer Printed Circuit Board (PCB)	Multilayer PCB	Flexible PCB	Wirewrap Circuit Board	Multi-chip Module	Surface Mount vs. Through-Hole	Application-Specific Integrated Circuit (ASIC)
Mechanical Fastener for Final Assembly	Screws	Pins	Clips	Barbs	Captive-Nut Fasteners	Rivets	Velcro

FIGURE 8.17: Some examples of seven different ways in which some common design elements can be manufactured. Note that the alternatives include design changes, process options, and in most cases a combination of the two.

Must-Have Criteria \ Process Alternatives	Weighting Factor	Alternative #1	Alternative #2	Alternative #3	Alternative #4	Alternative #5	Alternative #6	Alternative #7
Lower Capital Cost								
Lower Labor Cost								
Lower Part Cost								
Meets Customer Rqmts.								
Low Technical Risk								
Reduces Defects								
Allows One-Piece Flow								
Low Maintenance								
Easy to Train								
Safe / Ergonomic								
Flexible Capacity								
Meets TAKT Time								
Minimal Develop. Time								
Other?								
Totals	+ / −							

FIGURE 8.18: An example of a weighted Pugh matrix that can be used to determine the best choice among seven design / process alternatives. The generic "must-have" criteria that are provided in this template will apply to almost any lean manufacturing environment.

a starting point. These filters ensure compatibility with a lean production environment, and can be used for virtually any situation involving production processes. Of course, you should adapt my generic list to reflect the most important considerations for your firm. Otherwise, the scoring of alternatives proceeds in the same manner as was previously described. An initial scoring should be performed during the Process 3P Event itself, but it is common for there to be a number of open issues or questions that cannot be resolved in real time. The first iteration of the Seven-Alternatives method should be thought of as a baseline for further investigation, and should not be finalized until all unknowns are bedded down by the team. In this way, the Seven-Alternatives matrix acts as a decision tool rather than just a filter, with the logic behind your choice among alternatives being automatically documented for future use.

As the Process 3P Event progresses, it is likely that knowledge gaps will be identified during both the value-stream-mapping activities and the Seven-Alternatives discussions. If these knowledge gaps are significant, and represent issues that would be relevant to future products, it is sensible to use the A3-based problem-solving methodology described in Chapter 7. If the open issues are straightforward, however, an assignment of action items is all that is necessary. The desired output of the Process 3P Event is an optimized list of capital investments, ideas for improvement to labor-intensive process steps, and preliminary value-stream maps for both the internal and external production activities. As mentioned before, there are other possible tools and methods that could be included in this event as well. A Process FMEA could be performed just prior to the event, for example, as a source of critical issues for resolution by the event team. Tools from DFSS, such as process capability analysis and reviews of design-for-manufacturability checklists, could also be incorporated. Be sure to limit the scope of the event to a reasonable timeframe, and always consider whether a tool or method demands a large, cross-functional group to be effective, or could be used successfully by the development team outside of the formal event.

Finally, it is worth re-emphasizing that although the 3P Events described in this chapter offer a framework for product and process co-development, they are not a substitute for constant communication and collaboration between design / engineering and production operations. There should be a rich and continuous dialog occurring between these functions throughout conceptual and detailed design, with the formal 3P Events occurring at critical junctures in the evolution of the product. Any changes to the product design should be immediately shared and explained to the production representatives on the development team, and likewise any decisions made regarding production methods should be vetted by the product designers. This continuous communication and collaborative resolution of conflicts is the ultimate goal of the Production Preparation Process.

General Description of the Production 3P Event

The successful completion of the Process 3P Event should trigger an immediate rampup of activity within your operations group. With value-stream maps established for both internal and external production flows, the implementation process can begin. From this point forward, it becomes difficult for me to describe the specifics of the 3P process, other than providing some broad recommendations and generalities. This is because the nature of your products will drive both the order and type of activities required to complete your production preparation. If your firm manufactures apparel, for example, the path you must follow to a successful product launch will be dramatically different from that of a firm that produces chemical fertilizer or machine tools. Regardless of your industry sector, however, there is a final event that should be part of your pre-launch efforts: the Production 3P Event.

Actually, the Production 3P Event that is described in Figure 8.19 is probably best implemented as a series of mini-events rather than a single large event at a particular point in time. There are a number of critical activities that must be performed during the latter portion of the product development process, and in most cases they are serially dependant. Holding a series of relatively short-duration meetings to address each of these activities in sequence may better suit this reality. The following is a typical list of milestones that must be completed prior to a successful product launch:

- Creation of physical models or virtual simulations of the production lines or cells that will be required. This activity should include consideration of *takt* time, overall line capacity and constraints, layout for optimal flow, material-handling strategy, flexibility to adapt to variable demand, test and inspection plans, and so on.

- Procurement of long-lead capital equipment and production materials.

- Establishment of supply-chain and logistics systems for recurring production.

- Fabrication of qualification (i.e., preproduction) units and the testing thereof.

- Finalization of production documentation, including BOMs, drawings, routings, work instructions, test procedures, etc.

- Placement of product design documentation under formal configuration control.

- Validation of new production processes and equipment.

- Successful completion of a "line *kaizen*" (i.e., a pilot production run) that allows for real-time corrections and improvements to the production line.

- Finalization of a production launch plan and a first shipment date.

- Successful completion of the new product's Production Readiness Checklist.

The order and scale of the above activities is highly variable, but in each case, representatives of design / engineering should be involved to ensure continued alignment of the entire cross-functional team at every step prior to launch. The guiding document for all activities included in the Production 3P Event is the Production Readiness Checklist; something that no firm should be without. This checklist should be used throughout the product development process as both a beacon and a sanity check. For example, it should be reviewed early in development during the Project Planning / Risk-Mitigation Event to ensure that no critical deliverable is inadvertently omitted from the project plan. During the 3P process, it is continuously referred to as an indicator of what activities should be initiated and when. Finally, it is the last "gate" that the co-developed product and process must pass through prior to the first shipment of the product. A generic (and very high-level) example of a Production Readiness Checklist is provided in Figure 8.20.

At some point during the final stages of production preparation, the product design must be finalized, frozen, and placed under formal configuration control. A method for performing this critical step is provided in the Final Design Review and Freeze Event described in

The Lean 3P / Cost-Optimization Event(s)

The Production 3P Event

Objective: To create a detailed plan for process implementation and supply-chain configuration that will ensure production readiness and allow smooth and immediate transfer of the new product design to rate production.

Inputs:
- Market Requirements Brief (updated)
- Engineering requirements (updated)
- Finalized design drawings, preproduction prototypes, and test results
- Outputs from previous 3P Events (updated)

Outputs:
- Finalized manufacturing plan
- Finalized internal / external value-stream maps
- Finalized capital plan
- Process capability analysis
- Finalized factory layout
- Action assignments to implement the above
- Successful completion of the Production Readiness Checklist

Attendees (typical):
- Team leader
- Team members (cross-functional development team)
- Operations / manufacturing / process subject-matter experts
- Others (strategic suppliers, supply chain, quality, etc.)

FIGURE 8.19: Overview of the Production 3P Event. In many cases, this event is best implemented as a series of mini-events that focus on specific deliverables and milestones required to achieve production readiness.

Chapter 9. Exactly when this final freeze should occur will depend on the specifics of your product, but in general it should take place as late in the process as possible. This is not to say that your product design should not be under *informal* configuration control beginning in the early stages of development. Most Enterprise Resource Planning (ERP) software packages include provisions for informal and formal control of product documentation. I strongly recommend using the informal system for as long as possible, to allow the team to make last minute design adjustments without having to go through a formal Engineering Change Notice (ECN) process. While this delay in formal control is convenient, it may be mitigated by practical considerations, such as the need to provide fully-documented prototypes to regulatory agencies.

269

1) *Qualification Test Data –*
- ☐ Has a statistically-valid sampling of prototypes been tested?
- ☐ Have all critical environmental conditions been tested?
- ☐ Were prototypes fabricated using production tools / methods?

2) *Final Production Launch Plan –*
- ☐ Are volume forecasts up-to-date and documented?
- ☐ Is procurement prepared to meet the ramp-up plan?
- ☐ Are operators trained in all required processes?
- ☐ Have distributors, transportation logistics, warehouses, etc., been notified and are they prepared?
- ☐ Can the first shipment date be finalized?
- ☐ Have all BOM(s), drawings, etc. been released to production and are they under formal configuration control?

3) *Final Layout for Lines and Cells –*
- ☐ Are all lines and cells laid out and tested for flow?
- ☐ Is material-handling equipment in place and tested?
- ☐ Are material bins and *kanbans* in place and tested?
- ☐ Are all poke-yoke fixtures in place and tested?
- ☐ Have production tools been calibrated and validated?
- ☐ Is all manufacturing documentation in place?

4) *Manufacturing Test / Inspection –*
- ☐ Are all test equipment and fixtures in place and validated?
- ☐ Is all test equipment calibrated?
- ☐ Are test procedures documented and validated?
- ☐ Are test technicians trained and are pass / fail criteria clear?

5) *Sourcing / Supply Chain –*
- ☐ Are all suppliers certified and under contract / purchase order?
- ☐ Is supplier test equipment in place and validated?
- ☐ Is all supplier documentation in place?
- ☐ Have contingencies been made for supplier outages?
- ☐ Is a JIT delivery schedule in place for key suppliers?

FIGURE 8.20: A generic example of a Production Readiness Checklist (continued on facing page). Every firm should use a checklist of this type to guide the activities associated with the Production 3P Event.

Distribution / Logistics –
- ☐ Have distributors and transportation logistics been informed of launch date and ramp-up schedule?
- ☐ Is packaging complete and tested?
- ☐ Has warehouse space been allocated?

Sustaining Manufacturing Support –
- ☐ Are plans in place for Total Preventative Maintenance (TPM)?
- ☐ Are tracking systems in place for defects, scrap, rework, customer returns, and warrantee / repair?
- ☐ Has all product / process documentation been entered into the ERP system?
- ☐ Has an engineering-change system been established?
- ☐ Has an approach been defined for engineering support of production?

Finance / IT –
- ☐ Have financial systems been updated to handle the new product?
- ☐ Are accounts receivable and payable set up for suppliers, distributors, field support, warrantee repair, etc.?

Marketing and Sales –
- ☐ Are all marketing communications / sales materials complete?
- ☐ Have systems been put in place to track sales channels, customer satisfaction, returns, etc.?
- ☐ Has the sales staff been trained regarding the new product?
- ☐ Have field support / applications engineers been trained?
- ☐ Has an advertising and promotions plan been established?

Other Topics –
- ☐ This is not a complete list! You need to develop your own checklist over time that covers all aspects of production readiness for your firm.

Those readers who live on the design /engineering side of the tracks might be wondering, "Once the Production 3P Event is complete, is the cross-functional team done?" In other words, when can the developers of a new product move on to the next fun and challenging project. Sorry, but you will have to stay engaged for a much longer period than you were probably hoping. From a standpoint of risk reduction and team learning, it is vital that the development team stay committed to a new product well beyond the shipment of the first production unit. This doesn't mean that designers can't begin work on new projects, but they must make themselves available to the manufacturing team at a moment's notice to solve problems and facilitate a smooth rampup to rate production. This "cradle-to-rate" philosophy is important from a strategic perspective as well. If engineers and designers lose interest in a product once the fun part is over, then they miss the opportunity to learn how their new product fares in the demanding world of production. Without this knowledge, they are destined to repeat mistakes that can be costly and time-consuming once the product is transitioned to the factory. If these individuals are required to live with the ramifications of their design efforts, they will be far more likely to pay attention to details, listen to inputs from operations, and deliver a truly production-ready product.

Advanced Topic: Integrating Agile Software with Less-than-Agile Hardware

One of the most obvious goals of the 3P process is to synchronize the development of a product design with the manufacturing processes required to produce it. You might think it strange, therefore, that the final section of this chapter would be dedicated to the inclusion and integration of software development into this picture. If your products do not involve software, you can skip this section without concern. However, for those readers whose products involve both software and hardware elements, understanding how to synchronize these interdependent activities can be vital to successful project execution. Hence, I will share some thoughts on how these diverse environments can be aligned in an efficient and noninvasive manner.

Even if you have a hardware bent, the need for continuous communication and exchange of deliverables between hardware and software teams should be evident. In many cases, for example, the software team cannot proceed beyond conceptual design without having hardware artifacts available for code testing (e.g., a sample motherboard or control board, along with appropriate kernels or drivers). Likewise, it would be difficult to fully verify the performance of a hardware prototype without having test versions of the software and operating system available to drive it. Hence, there is a compelling need on both sides of the HW / SW interface to agree upon the exchange of required deliverables. Moreover, most of the events described in this book cannot be executed successfully without considering the interactions between hardware and software. It is with these practical concerns in mind that I propose a flexible approach to communication across the physical / virtual boundary.

The challenges associated with managing the HW / SW interface are largely determined by the approach used for software development. If your software gurus employ a traditional waterfall philosophy (i.e., sequential tasks, usually guided by a Gantt chart), then effective communication can be achieved using the same lean methods as would be used for a hardware-only product. The needs and feeds of both the hardware and software teams can be captured on the project master schedule, and progress can be tracked using a shared visual project board and HW / SW stand-up meetings (see Chapter 4). Although this might seem to be an ideal situation, as the complexity of the software portion of a product increases, the effectiveness of waterfall development diminishes significantly. For software-intensive products, many firms have adopted an agile programming methodology (or the similar methods of lean software development or extreme programming). Here is where things get complicated. Agile Software Development rejects the constraints of waterfall development in favor of a layered and iterative approach, wherein "issues" are systematically addressed in short-duration learning cycles (see Schwaber (2002)). Even the language of agile development can be off-putting to hardware designers: burn-down charts, scrums, MUSCOWs (i.e., must-haves, should-haves, could-haves, and won't dos), and so on. In fact, once software developers have drank the agile kool-aid, they may begin to resent the constraint of having to deliver intermediate test code to the hardware team. Can this marriage be saved?

The answer is yes, but with some compromises on both sides. The communication diagram shown in Figure 8.21 can be helpful in connecting the disparate worlds of agile software and not-so-agile hardware. Even if your hardware developers use rapid learning cycles in the early stages of a project, these cycles will likely be of varying durations and asynchronous with software learning cycles. Once risks are mitigated and knowledge gaps are closed, the hardware team is forced to adopt a more traditional waterfall execution plan, due to the practical constraints of material procurement and prototype fabrication / testing. How can efficient communication and handoffs between these two environments be achieved? Coordination and integration meetings are the key, but the timing of these exchanges is critical. Since the typical implementation of Agile Software Development involves learning cycles of two weeks, it makes sense to schedule informal coordination meetings that are synchronized with these cycles. Ideally, these informal coordination meetings would occur just prior to the software "scrum-of-scrums" meeting, wherein the programming team consolidates their achievements from the previous learning cycle and plans the next cycle of activities. In this way, both sides of the HW / SW interface can share status, progress, and issues, and highlight upcoming handoffs between the groups. A deliverables map such as the one shown in the figure can help to clearly identify these interdependencies. Upcoming events can be shown on the same timeline to drive additional synchronization of the two development environments.

Although bi-weekly informal coordination meetings may be sufficient for some projects, more aggressive integration meetings will likely be necessary at somewhat longer intervals. These meetings are more structured, and focus on sharing the collective learning of both the hardware and software developers, along with discussion of shared risks and upcoming critical-path milestones. A monthly frequency for these meetings would make sense on most projects, with the duration of the meetings being determined by the complexity of the product and the degree of interdependency between hardware and software. In this way,

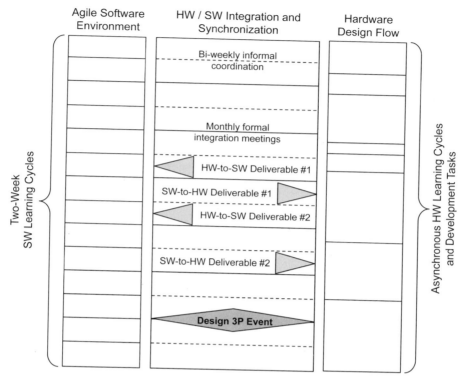

FIGURE 8.21: A schematic diagram of how agile software developers and more traditional hardware developers can synchronize their work, coordinate status and progress, and establish collaborative plans for various Lean Product Development Events. Note that in this figure, calendar-time runs from the top to the bottom.

the teams would alternate between informal coordination meetings and more detailed integration meetings on a bi-weekly basis.

Beyond these informal and formal meetings, and the occasional exchange of deliverables, agile programmers and hardware developers can be left to pursue their goals in the manner of their choice. As with any relationship, however, some empathy and understanding is essential. If you are an agile software developer, you must tolerate the often plodding and serially-dependant nature of hardware execution. Keep in mind that those hardware folks must wear the albatross of the physical world around their necks, so be patient with them. Likewise, those of you on the hardware side must put up with the weird jargon and barely concealed self-satisfaction of the agile programmers on your team. With a little giving on both sides, your relationship can succeed. You might even find that you like each other, or at least that you can learn from each other. After all, it is often said that opposites attract.

Chapter References

Anderson, D. M., 1997, *Agile Product Development for Mass Customization*, Irwin Professional Publishing.

Anderson, D. M., 2003, *Design for Manufacturability and Concurrent Engineering*, CIM Press.

Boothroyd, G., Dewhurst, P., and W. Knight, 2002, *Product Design for Manufacture and Assembly, 2nd Edition*, Marcel Dekker.

Bralla, J. G., 1995, *Design for Excellence*, McGraw-Hill.

Bralla, J. G., 1999, *Design for Manufacturability Handbook, 2nd Edition*, McGraw-Hill.

Brown, J., 1992, *Value Engineering: A Blueprint*, Industrial Press.

Fey, V., and E. Rivin, 2005, *Innovation on Demand: New Product Development Using TRIZ*, Cambridge University Press.

Gawer, A., and M. A. Cusumano, 2002, *Platform Leadership*, Harvard Business School Press.

George, M. L., 2002, *Lean Six Sigma: Combining Six Sigma Quality with Lean Speed*, McGraw-Hill.

Huthwaite, B., 2004, *The Lean Design Solution*, Institute for Lean Design.

Liker, J. K., 2004, *The Toyota Way*, McGraw-Hill.

Locher, D. A., 2008, *Value Stream Mapping for Lean Development*, CRC Press.

Mascitelli, R., 2004, *The Lean Design Guidebook*, Technology Perspectives.

Meyer, M. H., and A. P. Lehnerd, 1997, *The Power of Product Platforms*, The Free Press.

Miles, L. D., 1972, *Techniques of Value Analysis and Engineering, 2nd Edition*, McGraw-Hill.

Monden, Y., 1995, *Target Costing and Kaizen Costing*, Productivity Press.

Mudge, A. E., 1989, *Value Engineering: A Systematic Approach*, J. Pohl Associates.

Park, R., 1999, *Value Engineering: A Plan for Invention*, CRC Press.

Pine II, J. B., 1993, *Mass Customization: The New Frontier in Business Competition*, Harvard Business School Press.

Rother, M., and J. Shook, 1999, *Learning to See*, The Lean Enterprise Institute.

Schwaber, K., and M. Beedle, 2002, *Agile Software Development With Scrum*, Prentice Hall.

Suzue, T., 2002, *Cost Half: The Method for Radical Cost Reduction*, Productivity Press.

Womack, J. P., Jones, D. T., and D. Roos, 1990, *The Machine that Changed the World*, Harper Perennial.

Womack, J. P., and D. T. Jones, 1996, *Lean Thinking*, Simon & Schuster.

9

The Design Review and Freeze Event(s)

Background and Overview

When I reflect back on my years in aerospace, there is one thing about the product development process we used that stands out: We really didn't have a process at all. No phases, no gates, no process maps. In fact, for projects ranging from system-level monsters to tiny, one-person studies, there was only one common process element: design reviews. Project management tools were employed to guide the day-to-day work of development teams, and status reports and other contract deliverables were dutifully created and submitted. However the only time we were truly held accountable to our Defense Department customers was during design reviews. These were not your typical dog-and-pony shows; they were interrogation sessions during which the customer was free to cancel your contract on the spot...and they often did. Needless to say, there was considerable emphasis placed on these "events" both within the development team, and far up into the management hierarchy.

After having my attitude honed on the grinding wheel of such aggressive design reviews, I came to consulting with an abiding respect for what these meetings can accomplish. Yet I have found that many firms treat the design review as an annoyance; just another box to check on their gate-review checklist. This is unfortunate, since there is no more powerful tool for ensuring a successful project outcome than a well-crafted design review. In this final chapter, I will share some recommendations that can dramatically increase the effectiveness of these events. In this endeavor, I can (thankfully) be brief, since most individuals involved with new product development are familiar with the general concept. It is even likely that your company already uses some form of design review, perhaps to great effect. Hence, you should consider the ideas that I present as an opportunity to review your reviews, with the goal of continuous improvement to these vital sessions.

Although the history of design reviews is not well-documented, I can be reasonably sure that some unfortunate project manager was run through the ringer by a Pharaoh over an ill-conceived design for a pyramid. In more recent times, it is certainly true that many highly successful Japanese firms employ rigorous design reviews at several stages during product development (for some early insight into the role of design reviews in Japanese industry, see Ichida (1989)). How your reviews are best conducted depends on several factors, the most important of which is whether there will be customers in the room. If you manufacture products that are sold directly through retail channels, for example, then it is unlikely that customers would be involved in these events. However, if you supply products to OEMs (original equipment manufacturers), or perform any other type of contract work, it is likely that you will have the pleasure of your customer's company. Hence, I will make my first strong recommendation. When the customer is present at a design review, your goal is to please them, not to air your dirty laundry for their benefit. This is not to say that you should be deceptive in any way. Instead, I suggest that you should have already held a thorough internal review to identify every possible weakness in your product design, prior to opening your doors (and your kimono, as the old saying goes) to outsiders.

With this caveat in mind, I will assume henceforth that the Design Review and Freeze Event(s) that your firm executes are for internal eyes only. The approach described in this chapter is flexible enough to handle a wide variety of situations. There are, however, some telltale factors that should be considered when tailoring my recommendations to your

278

specific needs. First, you should consider what your goals are for these events. If your primary objective is to protect your customer (or their customers) from quality-related failures, then you should consider using a structured approach such as FMEA (Failure Mode and Effect Analysis, see Stamatis (1995)). These risk-identification reviews are particularly well-suited to products with a high degree of human interaction, such as medical devices, construction equipment, appliances, and so on. For the majority of products, however, a more generic form of design review will be more appropriate. Another factor to consider is complexity. If your products are best described as systems, then your design review process should be tiered and hierarchical, based on the most logical decomposition of the system at hand. A high-level design review would first be held, followed by several subsystem reviews, and even component reviews for vital system elements.

The last factor to consider when adapting my recommendations to your circumstance is timing. As I have previously stated, holding any type of review (such as the various 3P Events covered in Chapter 8) after a design is etched in stone is wasteful, and potentially ineffectual. Ideally, your design reviews (and there may be several during a development project) would be held at about the 80-percent-completion point of a given phase of design. This is important, since there is every likelihood that design changes will be forthcoming from the review which must be incorporated prior to moving on to the next stage of development. If there is no time allotted in your schedule for these changes, your project will slip by several weeks while the project team scrambles to integrate the mandated improvements. Unfortunately, this ideal timing for design reviews is in conflict with a fundamental law of human behavior: No one likes to fail in public. Asking your designers to share their baby with others before it has fully matured is likely to meet with resistance. It is hard enough for them to have their beautiful child exposed to criticism (even though it might actually be a rather unattractive offspring), let alone suffering such exposure before they are ready. This situation is unavoidable, and may require some tough love on the part of managers and mentors to convince developers that they must overcome their insecurities for the good of the project. Keep in mind, however, that all children are beautiful to their parents, even the really ugly ones.

Description of the Design Review and Freeze Event(s)

An overview of the Design Review and Freeze Event is provided in Figure 9.1. Perhaps the first point to be made about this event is that it should be thought of as a series of events, distributed in logical succession throughout the product development process. The number, duration, and intensity of these reviews are highly flexible, but in general there are three versions to consider:

- **Concept Design Review and Freeze Event** – This is typically the first formal review of a newly created conceptual design. The goal of this event is to aggressively compare the proposed design concept to updated product requirements, and verify that all critical success factors can be met. The level of detail is necessarily minimal, but the breadth of the review is substantial. All factors that can impact the new product's business case should be considered, with the goal of determining whether the development project is on track, or should be recast or even canceled due to risks or performance shortfalls. It could rightly be said that this first design review is more of a project review than a product review. An output of this event is an agreed-upon Compliance Matrix (discussed later in this chapter) which will be used throughout the remainder of the project as a quantitative means of assessing the product design's viability.

- **Detailed Design Review and Freeze Event** – A more detail-oriented review of the specifics of a new product design, held at roughly the midpoint in a development project. The objective of this second type of review is to interrogate both the design itself and all available analyses and prototype test data to determine if the product's Compliance Matrix can be successfully completed. The level of detail is (not surprisingly) deep, and focused specifically on design-related issues, rather than project-level concerns. At this point in the development process, all other business-case considerations should be managed by exception (see Chapter 3), so this is really a technical peer review, not a project review.

- **Final Design Review and Freeze Event** – This event offers a last opportunity to validate the new product design, before it is considered to be ready for production. All aspects of production readiness should be considered, along with verification that the design can successfully meet all quantitative criteria identified in the Compliance Matrix. This should be a data-intensive review, focused on the test results from formative prototypes and qualification units. A heavy emphasis should be placed on identifying any issue that might prohibit a smooth and rapid transition to rate production.

The timing of these events should be consistent with the critical path of the development project, and positioned such that they closely follow the appropriate 3P Event (see Chapter 8), as shown in Figure 9.2. Since the format of each type of review is quite similar, I will treat them as a single topic from this point forward, with occasional mention of the differences that might exist among them. The attendance list for a Design Review and Freeze Event should be comprehensive: A successful outcome is heavily dependent on the expertise represented in the room, so virtually all functions that contribute to new product development should be included. Beyond these general considerations, there are several "rules" that I can suggest that will make any design review more robust and effective.

Rule 1: Question all assumptions – no sacred cows

In my description of Quick-Look Value Engineering in Chapter 8, I emphasized the importance of questioning your assumptions about a given product design. This continues to hold true for every Design Review and Freeze Event that takes place. One of the reasons why set-based design is so powerful (see Chapter 7), is that it forces a design team to make their decision process explicit, rather than it being hidden away in the heads

---

The Design Review and Freeze Event(s)

Objective: To provide feedback from technical peers on the completeness and correctness of a product design, and to identify changes or improvements that would enable elements of the design to be "frozen."

Inputs:
- Market Requirements Brief (updated)
- Engineering requirements (updated)
- Completed knowledge briefs
- Prototypes, test results, analyses, and other supporting data
- Past history: quality issues, customer satisfaction issues, etc.

Outputs:
- Prioritized list of corrections to the design
- Prioritized list of improvements to the design
- Proposed date for "freezing" specific elements of the design
- Action list to enable the design freeze

Attendees (typical):
- Team leader
- Team members (cross-functional development team)
- Gurus, specialists, and other subject-matter experts
- Others (strategic suppliers, technical consultants, customers)

Agenda (typical):

Time	Activity
8:00 – 9:00	Overview of requirements and current design approach
9:00 – 11:00	Review of test data / analyses and Compliance Matrix
11:00 – 3:00	Brainstorming / discussion of design weaknesses, errors, and opportunities for improvement (multiple "lenses")
3:00 – 4:00	Prioritization of errors / improvements for implementation
4:00 – 4:30	Discussion and agreement on requirements to be "frozen"
4:30 – 5:00	Assignment of action items to close out the event

FIGURE 9.1: An overview of the Design Review and Freeze Event(s). These are actually a series of events that are performed at critical junctures in the new product's design and development.

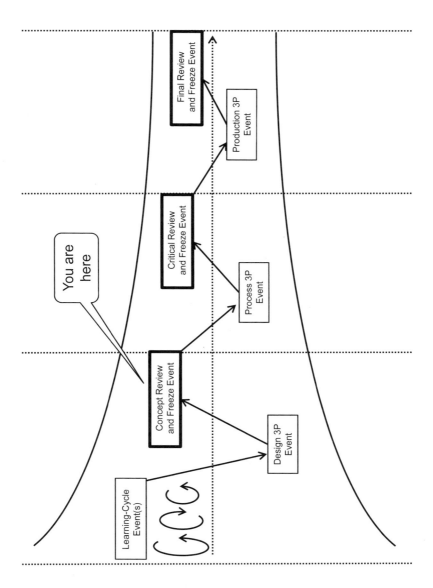

FIGURE 9.2: The Design Review and Freeze Events should be timed to closely follow the appropriate 3P Event. The number and duration of each type of event will be determined to a great extent by the complexity of the product under development, with system products potentially requiring several levels of review at each stage of the design's evolution.

of developers. Every designer worth their salt performs tradeoffs and considers multiple options before arriving at a final choice. Unfortunately, these tradeoffs are often done far too quickly (i.e., in a heartbeat or two), and are not documented or validated by other team members. Instead, the designer presents his or her concept as though it came to them through divine intervention, without sharing the logic that drove their decisions. It is essential that a designer's thinking be exposed to the scrutiny of a design review team, so that any errors in judgment or missed opportunities can be uncovered at that time. If the fundamental logic of a design is flawed, then the product that ensues can never meet its full potential.

Rule 2: Invite the gurus

If a development team has been working together for some time on a product design, they begin to think alike. Much like a couple that has been married for many years, they will finish each other's sentences and see things in an annoyingly similar way. This "group-think" effect can severely limit a team's ability to self-examine their work and be objective about risks, errors, or missed opportunities. It is therefore essential that outside eyes be brought to bear on the product design during a Design Review and Freeze Event. I often refer to these individuals as the "gurus," since ideally they are the most senior subject-matter experts in your firm. Any external and unbiased viewpoint is valuable, but inviting those who are the keepers of the knowledge flame in your firm will elevate your reviews to an entirely new level.

In my aerospace days, these gurus were called "chief scientists." Their sole job in life was to immerse themselves in the literature on their subject, participate in conferences, write papers, and attend design reviews. Many of them were old, crotchety, and had hygiene problems, but all were considered to be the greatest minds in their fields. Passing through the gauntlet of chief scientists at a design review was a victory worth savoring, and the knowledge passed on to teams through these meetings was invaluable, albeit painful. Whether it be internal experts or external consultants, make sure that your invitee list includes the best minds available to review your product design.

Rule 3: Engage all participants

One of the unfortunate lessons that I have learned over the years is that the loudest voices in the room are often not the most intelligent ones. For your Design Review and Freeze Event to be successful, you must hear all points of view, and mine the depths of knowledge of all participants. This is a challenge, since these types of meetings tend to be dominated by strong personalities. A shy individual may be intimidated by the chatterboxes, and as a result, may demure from contributing their opinions. To avoid this situation, I've developed a simple facilitation trick that can be quite effective. It begins by assigning a piece of pre-work to every event attendee: They must come to the event with at least one recommendation for improvement to the product design. This mandate has the benefit of forcing individuals to read through their design-review packages in advance, at least at a cursory level. Moreover, it provides the means to engage all participants during the event's brainstorming activity. Instead of immediately opening up the discussion to the room for comments and inputs, I begin the brainstorming by asking each individual for their pre-prepared recommendations. Attendees should be allowed ample time to share their ideas regarding the product design, and other voices should be kept at bay until each person has completed their thoughts. Once all have had a chance to contribute, the brainstorming can be expanded to the entire room for further discussion. If your agenda includes consideration of the design through several "lenses" (see Rule 6), then you should use this facilitation trick for each lens, thereby allowing the quiet ones in the room a chance to get a word in edgewise on multiple occasions during the meeting.

Rule 4: Look for both errors and opportunities

A few years back, it was in vogue to put a positive spin on all aspects of the business environment. People didn't make mistakes; they had accuracy challenges. Poor-performing employees became mentoring candidates. Those with personality defects were really just "different" or "unique." If management was dissatisfied with the performance of their workforce, it wasn't the workers' fault; management had "trust issues." Well, there is a bit of truth in all of the above, despite the banality of the language. One of these platitudes that really aggravates me, however, is the idea that there is no such thing as an error, just an opportunity that was missed. Forgive me for being blunt, but an error is an error, and an opportunity is an opportunity. There is no need to beat people for making errors, but the errors must be acknowledged at an impersonal level for teams to avoid them in the future. Opportunities, on the other hand, go beyond the scope of the project to achieve something more than was originally in the plan. It is not necessarily a failure of the team that they missed an opportunity, it is simply a new idea that should be considered and potentially incorporated as the development process moves forward. The discussions during your Design Review and Freeze Event should be broad enough to harvest both errors and opportunities.

Rule 5: Make it empirical whenever possible

I will delve more deeply into this topic in the next section of this chapter, so for now, I will just highlight the key point. There is nothing more powerful than data when interrogating a design concept. I believe that at every stage of development, from initial rapid learning cycles (see Chapter 7) to the final review of a design prior to launch, having empirical evidence of a design's compliance with requirements is vital. A fact-based approach to design reviews will attenuate arguments, allow for more objective assessments, and anchor the meeting's results in reality rather than opinion.

Rule 6: Always consider the design through multiple "lenses"

The key to an effective Design Review and Freeze Event is in considering all aspects of a design that contribute to a product's success. Hence, I recommend using multiple "lenses" to help focus the discussion on potential errors and opportunities. Not all of the lenses that I propose below need be considered at every review, but all of them should be utilized at least once during the product development process.

- **System Interfaces and Partitioning of Requirements** – This lens is most applicable to the Concept Design Review and Freeze Event, and is intended to focus attention on the high-level architecture of the new product design.

- **Performance / Functional Shortfalls** – All Design Review Events should include this lens. More about this lens will be provided in the next section of this chapter.

- **Failure Modes** – If your firm does not utilize FMEA events as a means of identifying the potential failure modes of a new product, then you should consider adding this lens to your Design Review Events on several occasions throughout development.

- **Voice-of-the-Customer Issues** – This lens is most appropriate for the first of your Design Review Events, but could also be included in later reviews to emphasize critical customer-related issues such as ergonomics, maintainability, serviceability, etc.

- **Regulatory Compliance** – Only applicable if your product will be subject to either voluntary or mandatory regulatory-agency approval.

- **Quality / Reliability** – Useful for any Design Review Event, but should be a primary focus of your Final Design Review and Freeze Event. Note that there is some overlap between this lens and the topics discussed in 3P Events, but there is no harm in being redundant when the issues are of such a critical nature.

- **Manufacturability / Cost** – Again, there is redundancy here with several 3P Events, but at no time should manufacturability and cost be excluded from discussions: Design Review Events are not purely about a design but rather about the successful commercialization of a new product.

Rule 7: Prioritize your outputs

In any situation that involves brainstorming or idea generation, it is vital that the raw outputs be prioritized for further action. The specific approach that I recommend for performing this ranking activity is described later in this section.

Rule 8: Prompt follow-up is essential

Last, it is important that immediate action be taken to implement the high-ranking suggestions for design improvement. Action items should be assigned before the event attendees leave the room, and follow-up and close-out of actions should occur within a few short weeks following the review. I try to force the closing of actions within a two-week period after the review to ensure that open issues do not have a negative impact on the project's schedule.

Beyond the rules outlined above, the execution of a Design Review and Freeze Event is both logical and straightforward, as shown graphically in Figure 9.3. As with all events, there is pre-work that is necessary to achieve a successful outcome. A preparation package should be created by the development team and distributed to all design-review attendees at least one week prior to the event. I strongly recommend that the team puts some thought into the format and content of this package; it should not be a disorganized mass of documents and data that would require hours of time to sort through. A well-crafted preparation package will enable you to avoid using the first half of the event as a remedial tutorial, and allow far more productive time for idea generation and detailed discussion.

On the day of the Design Review and Freeze Event, the first topic on the agenda should be a brief overview of the requirements for the product, and the overall design approach that the development team is proposing. Again, this should not be a tutorial. Far too many design reviews turn into "design defenses" in which the developers present their approach as a *fait accompli,* leaving little time for interrogation of the specifics of the design. If adequate pre-work has been performed, this

Design Review and Freeze Event

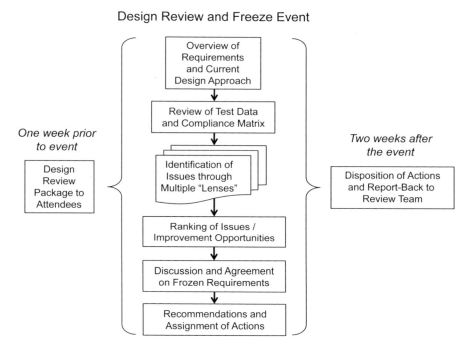

One week prior to event

Design Review Package to Attendees

Two weeks after the event

Disposition of Actions and Report-Back to Review Team

FIGURE 9.3: The general structure of the Design Review and Freeze Event. Note that, as with all Lean Product Development Events, pre-work and follow-up activities are defined as part of the standard work for the meeting.

first activity should require no more than an hour or two for a typical product. The next step in the review process is to present any and all empirical data that is available at the time of the event. These results should be added to the product's Compliance Matrix (discussed in the next section), so that the review team can compare measured performance to quantitative goals. Any shortfalls in performance should be the subject of discussion, and will likely result in one or more issues being identified for future resolution by the design team.

The next agenda item is to consider the design through multiple lenses, as described in Rule 6 above. As this discussion proceeds, the facilitator should be capturing recommendations, issues, errors, and opportunities on a flip chart. Once all applicable lenses have been considered, the resulting list must be prioritized for future action. I suggest using a ranking approach that will be familiar to the reader by now, as shown in Figure 9.4. As you might have guessed, I use two 1-to-5 scoring metrics: ease of improvement, and the impact of a proposed design improvement on the success of the new product. The entire review team should vote on these metrics through a show of fingers, as described in previous chapters, with the product of the two scores representing an Action Priority Number (APN). The meaning of this APN, however, is somewhat different from previous prioritization techniques that I have used in this book. In this case, the "impact" score carries far more weight, as shown in Figure 9.5. If an issue or error is given a 5-score for impact, for example, it simply cannot be ignored, even if the "fix" is very difficult. As a result, the visual representation of possible APN scores shown in the figure is skewed toward including a larger set of mandatory actions. A discussion of where to draw the line on mandatory actions should be held near the end of the event, with inputs from the entire group. Action items should then be assigned on the spot for those issues that are above the line. Ultimately, the team's judgment will guide their actions following the design review, but careful consideration of high-impact issues and errors is certainly worthwhile.

Beyond these basic steps, the execution of the Design Review and Freeze Event includes one additional activity: the discussion and

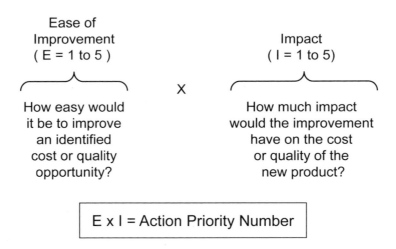

FIGURE 9.4: A suggested, and all too familiar, prioritization approach for issues, errors, and opportunities that are identified during a Design Review and Freeze Event.

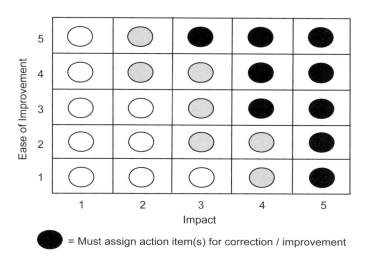

= Must assign action item(s) for correction / improvement

FIGURE 9.5: A visual representation of the two-metric prioritization scheme for issues, problems, and opportunities. Note that the distribution of "mandatory" actions is heavily weighted toward high-impact issues.

selection of design elements that can be "frozen" once all action items are complete. This concept of "staged-freezing" will be described in detail in a later section of this chapter. Since the general flow of the Design Review Event is straightforward, I will eschew the use of a fictional case example in favor of providing more information about some of the key elements of the review format that I recommend. The facilitation of a Design Review and Freeze Event is very similar to that of a Design 3P Event, so you might wish to review Chapter 8 for some pointers. Alas, there will be no more fictional companies to learn from in this book… I hope you can contain your disappointment.

The Compliance Matrix: Adding Rigor to Your Design Reviews

One of the best ways to legitimize the output of your Design Review and Freeze Events is through the use of a Compliance Matrix, such as the one shown in Figure 9.6. This matrix captures all of the critical requirements

Design Requirements	Priority (M / S / C)	Source / Reference	Target Value	Tolerance Band	Verification Method	Prototype Unit(s)	Preproduction Unit(s)

FIGURE 9.6: A sample template for a Compliance Matrix. A matrix of this type should be used throughout the product development process as a quantitative method for verifying that a product design can meet all of the critical requirements necessary to satisfy its target customers.

for a new product, and identifies a specific and quantitative verification method for each. It should be created by the development team shortly after completion of the Market Requirements Event (see Chapter 5), and validated during the Concept Design Review and Freeze Event. Beyond that point, the development team should focus much of their efforts on ensuring the successful completion of their Compliance Matrix. The completed matrix should be carefully considered during the Final Design Review and Freeze Event, and ultimately it represents an essential factor in determining whether a product is ready for production launch.

In addition to a listing of key requirements, the matrix includes columns that capture the priority of each requirement, its source or reference (e.g., the product's design requirements matrix, regulatory agency mandates, industry standards, etc.), and several columns that document the method by which each requirement will be verified. A target value is identified along with the appropriate tolerance band, and an objective and rigorous verification method is described. Finally, the Compliance Matrix should show when during the evolution of the design the verification activity must be performed. For example, a simple and observable attribute of a product (e.g., a red warning light) can be adequately verified on an early, formative prototype. At the other extreme, requirements that involve considerable interaction with the

292

user, and depend heavily on an accurate simulation of the use environment, may only be verifiable by the field testing of preproduction units just prior to launch.

In my opinion, the selection of a verification method is something of an art. The development team must consider several competing factors when making this choice, including the validity of the test or measurement with respect to a given requirement, the number of units that should be tested to provide adequate statistics, and the cost and schedule demands of the method employed. There is a spectrum of possible verification methods that can be used, as shown in Figure 9.7. The methods described in the figure range from the least rigorous and effective (observation), to the most (field testing). Unfortunately, from a practical standpoint the cost and schedule impact of these methods increases in

---

Methods for Verifying Compliance

Observation – Feature can be observed as being present and functional.

Analysis – Feature or requirement can legitimately be verified through analytical means.

Simulation – Feature or requirement can be adequately simulated to verify its performance.

Proof-of-Concept Prototype Test – Requirement can be verified through the testing of a rough or formative prototype.

Functional Prototype Test – Requirement must be verified by testing a fully configured and functional system prototype.

Preproduction Prototype Test – Requirement must be verified through testing of a production-like prototype.

Field Test – Requirement can only be verified through testing in the intended use environment for the new product.

FIGURE 9.7: Some examples of verification methods that can be used in your Compliance Matrix to ensure that the critical requirements for a new product have been met by the proposed design. Note that these methods are listed in order of least rigorous to most rigorous, with the cost and time required to perform the measurements following in the same order.

the same order. An observation can often be performed very early in the development process on initial prototype units at a negligible cost. As the rigor of the verification method increases, however, the timing typically moves to later in the project, and the cost of performing the testing increases considerably. It is far more expensive to perform a statistically-valid final acceptance test on preproduction units than it would be to validate performance through analysis or simulation. Moreover, this verification can only be performed late in the project, resulting in a possible schedule slip if the results are not acceptable.

With this in mind, it is important to note that any form of product testing is nothing more than an approximation of how that product will actually perform in the hands of customers. As the rigor of the verification method increases, the approximation becomes closer to reality, but the only truly valid test method for a product is a field test under representative use conditions. Hence, the development team must make a difficult choice between gathering early information that is inexpensive to acquire, and late information that is expensive, but far more accurate. As an example of the challenge a team may face in selecting the appropriate verification method, I'll provide a real-world example.

One of my clients had developed a machine for the tamping of concrete. They fabricated a testing rig for this new product that utilized a rolling treadmill that the machine would ride on while vibration was applied. Preproduction prototypes of the new product were placed on the testing rig, chained in position, and run for several days of simulated use. After each test cycle was complete, the machines were carefully examined for any form of failure or degradation. Based on this seemingly rigorous testing, all appeared to be well with the design, and the product was launched into production. Shortly after the first units were shipped, however, the firm received several complaints from customers indicating that bolts were loosening and falling off the product during use. Again, the firm subjected samples of the product to stress using the same test rig, and again they all seemed to pass with flying colors. Finally, in desperation, the firm took a sample unit to an open field and ran it over a test course under its own power. Several bolts loosened, just as the customers had observed. Somehow there was a subtle difference between their relatively sophisticated test rig, and the conditions that the machine experienced in real-world operation. Hence, a product development team should carefully consider how well their choice of verification method simulates actual use conditions, and if in doubt, should err on the side of a more rigorous, albeit more expensive and time-consuming, testing approach.

Controlling Scope-Creep through Staged-Freezing

You have no doubt noticed that the title of the Events described in this chapter contain the word "freeze." This reflects the use of a technique known as staged-freezing to control the configuration of a new product design as the development process unfolds (for more on staged-freezing, see Reinertsen (1997)). The idea of staged-freezing is straightforward: At critical junctures during development, the cross-functional design team agrees to freeze a subset of the product's requirements and design elements to ensure that the overall timeline of the project can be met. Staged-freezing provides the project team with a weapon against scope-creep: By clearly identifying those aspects of a design that cannot change without sacrificing either cost or schedule, the team has a means to fight back when invasive changes to the design are proposed.

The driver for the use of staged-freezing is to be able to service critical schedule dependencies. If a given requirement or design element has no critical-path dependencies, then it can continue to change right up to product launch. For example, the color of an injection-molded plastic part can be altered at the last minute by simply ordering a different color of polymer pellet. On the other hand, the actual design of that same part may need to be frozen much earlier, since the lead time for fabricating an injection-molding tool can easily be three to four months. The goal of staged-freezing is not to put unnecessary restrictions on change, but rather to corral those changes that can impact cost and schedule into periods within the project where those decisions are best made. A graphical representation of the staged-freezing process is shown in Figure 9.8.

It is important to recognize that this freezing activity is not permanent. If there are compelling reasons why a frozen aspect of a product design must be changed (i.e., the business case of the product will be positively impacted), then that aspect can be "defrosted," the change made, and then refrozen again. However, the defrosting process comes at a price: Before any frozen requirement or design element can be changed, the team must determine the benefits and disbenefits. Does making the change result in enough improvement to the business case to justify the added cost and / or time required to implement it? An unfrozen requirement can be changed without significant impact on the project plan, whereas changes to a frozen requirement will, by definition, cause some negative impact on schedule or budget. The use of staged-freezing forces both management and the project team to carefully consider such invasive changes, rather than acting without thought.

The diagram shown in Figure 9.8 illustrates a straightforward application of staged-freezing. At each Design Review and Freeze Event,

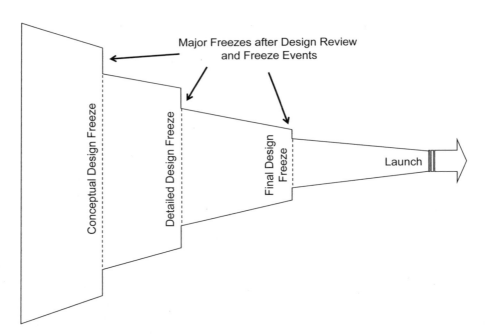

FIGURE 9.8: A diagram of the staged-freezing process. Requirements and design elements that have critical schedule dependencies are frozen at appropriate points during the development cycle to avoid risk to the new product's launch date.

the development team proposes a "freeze list." This list includes those aspects of the design that they feel must be frozen before moving on to the next steps in development. The attendees at the event (including key management stakeholders) will discuss each item on the list, and agree on whether the requirement is ready to be frozen. Once the freeze list has been approved by the group, the identified items will go under informal configuration control. This can be accomplished in many configuration management systems by using an alpha code, with numeric codes being reserved for formal configuration control. However you implement this informal control, there will need to be an efficient method for change management (i.e., the defrosting process). There are two ways in which this can be done, with one being preferable over the other, as shown in Figure 9.9. The first approach involves the establishment of an informal Change Review Board (CRB) for the new product. This board might consist of key managers or executives, technical experts, one or more customers (if appropriate), and the development

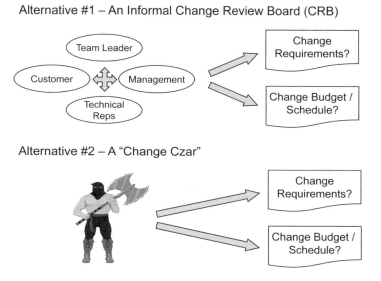

FIGURE 9.9: There are two methods for controlling the "defrosting" of frozen requirements or design elements. The first involves the use of a Change Review Board, while the second and preferred method identifies an individual who serves as a "change czar," with the power to determine whether a change request should be accepted or denied.

team leader. If a change to a frozen requirement is requested, this group would determine the impact on both the business case and the project, and would either approve or deny the request. There should be no need for a formal Engineering Change Notice (ECN) process; just a method for tracking changes when they are made.

A preferred approach to controlling changes to frozen requirements is shown at the bottom of the figure, as represented by the scary fellow with the axe. In this case, a single empowered individual acts as a "change czar," with the power to perform the assessment described above and determine whether a change should be accepted or denied. In my opinion, this centralized authority is far more efficient than the decision-by-committee approach, and will undoubtedly save considerable time during development. However, there is obviously a trust issue involved with this approach: The success of the new product will be heavily dependent on the capabilities of the change czar, implying that this individual must be anointed by executive management, and imbued with their authority. Regardless of which approach you select, the primary benefit of staged-freezing is its ability to corral requested changes into noninvasive periods within the development process. Much of what constitutes scope-creep is really just "window shopping." A marketing manager, sales manager, or executive thinks of a way to improve the product under development, and passes along this whim to the project team as a mandate. Without an objective means to respond to that request, the team is forced to comply. On the other hand, if the requested change will impact a requirement or design element that has been designated as frozen, then the ramifications of this added scope must be carefully considered. In most cases, the need to pass through a change-control process will discourage the window shopping, unless the new idea is truly compelling.

There is one final aspect of staged-freezing that should be considered: At what intervals should the team review the freezing of requirements or design elements? I've tied the staged-freeze methodology to the design review process as a convenience, since these events represent suitable points in a product's development to implement this approach. However, this is not an ideal situation. By waiting until formal Design Review and Freeze Events are held to identify items to be frozen, we have created a time batch that could potentially distort the critical path of a project due to the discontinuities that it causes. A far better way of thinking about staged-freezing is to imagine an almost continuous series of "minor freezes" that occur throughout the development process whenever they are deemed to be necessary, as shown in Figure 9.10. In this way, the team can systematically converge on a design solution, and protect that emerging solution from invasive change at every step of the way. This more sophisticated approach also allows the team to delay the freezing of requirements or design elements to as late as possible in development, thereby providing them with more time to gain knowledge and consider their design decisions (see Ward, et al (1995)). Unfortunately, this ideal implementation requires a high level of organizational discipline and team under-standing. You should consider this vision as a desirable future state, and use the Design Review and Freeze Event as a first step in evolving toward this goal.

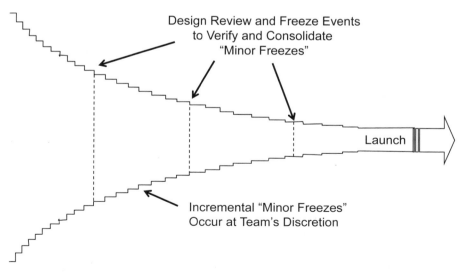

FIGURE 9.10: A more continuous implementation of staged-freezing, in which "minor freezes" are allowed at any point in the development process that the project team believes is appropriate.

Advanced Topic: Sustainable Design and the Bottom Line

The case example that I provided in Chapter 8 (i.e., Bimford Tools) illustrated the potential for incorporating environmental sustainability into the business case for a new product. Although I have a personal commitment to environmental issues, I will not attempt to appeal to your altruism, primarily because I don't need to. The impact that a new product has on the environment is becoming a critical consideration in many markets, and may provide an excellent business opportunity for your firm, both from the standpoint of enhancing price and reducing cost. On the price side of the profit equation (and using the parlance of Chapter 5), the increasing demand for "green" products represents an emerging "market gap" that offers significant differentiation opportunities. From a cost perspective, there have been major advances in sustainable raw materials, low-energy manufacturing processes, recycling of production waste, and the efficient disposal or repurposing of products at the end of their use-life. Any and all of these opportunities may provide a cost savings for your firm, along with enhancing your brand's image in the marketplace. I believe that virtually any product design would benefit from the consideration of environmental sustainability, and I encourage you to add this new "lens" to your agenda for each Design Review and Freeze Event.

The specific path that you should follow with respect to environmental sustainability is highly industry-specific. Some sectors, such as construction materials, furnishings, appliances, and healthcare products, have become hotbeds of green activity, while other industries have yet to embrace this new market opportunity. Your first step should be to become knowledgeable regarding the perceptions of your customers, voluntary certifications and mandatory standards, and your competitors' positions with respect to environmental considerations. In general, the opportunities for both differentiation and cost savings span the entire product lifecycle, from the earliest stages of conceptual design to the end of a product's life, as shown in Figure 9.11. This "cradle-to-cradle" model (see Hawken, et al (1999), McDonough, et al (2002), and Senge, et al (2008)) has become the standard for assessing the environmental impact of a product, and provides insight into the business opportunities that

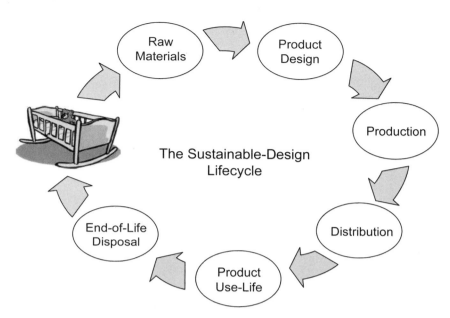

FIGURE 9.11: There are many opportunities to reduce the negative environmental impact of a product throughout its lifecycle. The "cradle-to-cradle" model shown above has become widely accepted as a standard for evaluating the environmental sustainability of a new product.

sustainability can offer. From the standpoint of differentiation, there are numerous ways in which you can establish legitimate green credentials for your new product. The use of post-consumer recycled materials as an input to your production process, for example, is widely recognized as a preeminent way to reduce environmental impact. At the other end of the product lifecycle, offering your customers a convenient take-back program, with the promise of recycling or reconditioning the discarded product, can represent both a practical differentiator and a green opportunity.

Even if your market sector has not yet demonstrated a pull for environmentally-friendly products, the potential for cost savings may still motivate you to consider the incorporation of sustainable attributes into your next new product. Firms that have initiated programs to reduce the energy consumption and waste output of their factories have almost universally found that these measures deliver a rapid and substantial payback. One trend that is showing great promise is the repurposing of the waste output of one firm to become the raw material for another. If your firm's production processes yield an unwanted byproduct, it may be possible to sell that "waste" to another enterprise that can use it for the manufacture of their products. In fact, a growing number of internet-based exchanges are being established to help connect firms in this highly synergistic way. For example, one of my clients specializes in developing equipment for environmental remediation. These products are designed to clean and filter sand that has been dredged from waterways which have been polluted by industrial waste. The output of this process is a sand that is clean enough to be used for concrete production. Firms that have installed this equipment can sell their waste at a profit, while avoiding the significant expense of disposing of it safely, giving them a double kick to their bottom line.

Unfortunately, a detailed description of the business opportunities for environmental sustainability is beyond the scope of this book. I can, however, offer a simple green-design trade-off tool that can help you determine the potential for both price enhancement and cost savings on your next new product. The matrix shown in Figure 9.12 allows you to compare several alternative conceptual designs for a new product from a sustainability perspective. I've listed twenty-one attributes of an environmentally-sustainable product, grouped into seven categories that represent the major phases in a product's lifecycle. A weighting-factor column is provided, along with several columns which can be used to evaluate design alternatives. The "baseline" column represents your current product offering, and the rest are used to compare other design options to that baseline. I use a scoring range of +5 to -5, with positive scores indicating reinforcement of a given sustainable attribute, and minus scores implying a negative impact on that factor. Once the matrix is complete, the total scores can be calculated, with a positive total score indicating that a design alternative might achieve a higher level of sustainability than the baseline. Naturally, this is a very high-level tool,

FIGURE 9.12: A trade-off and discussion tool that can help identify design alternatives that might increase the environmental sustainability of your new product.

Twenty-One Sustainability Factors	Weighting Factor	Baseline Design	Alternative #1	Alternative #2	Alternative #3
I. Raw Materials					
Reduced total material content by weight / dollars		0			
Use of recycled materials		0			
Use of sustainably produced / renewable resources		0			
II. Supply Chain					
Use of local / regional suppliers		0			
Consolidation / simplification of supply chain (fewer suppliers, less distance traveled, etc.)		0			
Use of certified suppliers (ISO 14001, EPEATS, Energy Star, etc.)		0			
III. Design Attributes					
Able to meet applicable mandatory / voluntary environmental standards and certifications		0			
Simplified design - reduced parts count, reduced assembly labor, modular / scalable design, etc.		0			
Reduced use of hazardous materials, non-recyclable materials, high-energy-content materials		0			
IV. Production					
Reduced overall energy consumption during production (size of footprint)		0			
Reduced scrap, wastage, spoilage		0			
Reduced use of non-recyclable consumables (e.g., abrasives, lubricants, finishes, etc.)		0			
V. Distribution					
Use of low carbon footprint transportation (e.g., trains as opposed to trucks, regional distribution, etc.)		0			
Use of recycled materials for packaging / use of recyclable materials for packaging / less packaging		0			
Use of reusable shipping containers (retailer *kanbans*, reusable pallets, ship-to-shelf packaging, etc.)		0			
VI. Use-Life					
Reduced overall energy / resource consumption during use-life (reduced carbon footprint)		0			
Increased reliability, reduced recurring maintenance, reduced consumables during use		0			
Improved quality of life, ergonomics, ease of use, safety, etc. for end users		0			
VII. End-of-Life					
Product is easy to disassemble / separate into recyclable elements upon disposal		0			
Product will be part of a take-back program for refurbishing, manufacturer recycling, repurposing, etc.		0			
Reduced environmental impact after final disposal (reduced landfill volume, haz-mat, etc.)		0			
Total Scores -		0	0	0	0

and should be used to open minds and generate discussion within your firm, rather than as a rigorous decision tool.

■ ■ ■

It is my sincere hope that you share my concerns for the protection of the natural world. However, even if your interest in "green" is limited to the acquisition of U.S. currency, there are still compelling reasons for you to include consideration of environmental sustainability in your next Design Review and Freeze Event.

Chapter References

Hawken, P., Lovins, A., and L. Lovins, 1999, *Natural Capitalism*, Little Brown and Company.

Ichida, T., 1989, *Product Design Review*, Productivity Press.

McDonough, W., and M. Braungart, 2002, *Cradle to Cradle*, North Point Press.

Reinertsen, D. G., 1997, *Managing the Design Factory: A Product Developer's Toolkit*, The Free Press.

Schuyler, J. R., 1996, *Decision Analysis in Projects*, Project Management Institute.

Senge, P., Smith, B., Kruschwitz, N., Laur, J., and S. Schley, 2008, *The Necessary Revolution: Working Together to Create a Sustainable World*, Broadway Books.

Stamatis, D. H., 1995, *Failure Mode and Effect Analysis*, ASQC Quality Press.

Ward, A. C., Liker, J. K., Cristiano, J. J., and D. K. Sobek II, 1995, "The second Toyota paradox: how delaying decisions can make better cars faster," *Sloan Management Review*, Vol. 36, No. 3, pgs. 43-61.

Conclusion: A Practical Approach to Implementation

Congratulations! You have made it through lo these many pages, and can take pride in having eaten the entire elephant (although by this time you might well believe it was actually a woolly mammoth). Before I release you to your enthusiastic pursuit of product development improvement, we must consider one last essential topic: how to best implement the methods described in this book. We all know that change is hard, and there are a multitude of excellent books to help you better understand this ethereal subject (see, for example, the works by Kotter listed in the Bibliography). I cannot, however, allow you to leave my care without offering some suggestions as to how you should proceed once the cover of this book is closed. To accomplish this, I will again resort to some "rules" that should guide your lean product development initiative.

Rule 1: Pick a leader who can lead

The success of your improvement efforts will depend on selecting the right leader, plain and simple. An internal resource should be carefully selected who combines wisdom, strength of personality, a sharp and open mind, management support, and the respect of coworkers. If these attributes cannot be found in a single individual, then you can, at some risk, merge the talents of several people into an improvement team that covers all of these bases. However it is accomplished, the leader of an improvement initiative must become the subject-matter expert within the firm – a thought leader as well as a motivational force. I can offer one last imperative on this subject: Do not delegate the leadership of your change program to an external consultant. Your firm must absorb new ideas and methods intrinsically, and this learning process begins with knowledgeable internal leadership.

Rule 2: Establish a beat that is *allegro non troppo* (fast, but not too fast)

It is often tempting to establish irrational expectations for an improvement program in the hope of moving the organization forward at lightning speed. This is not only a recipe for disappointment, but it will not achieve your goal. The pace with which you implement lean product development will depend in part on avoiding cognitive overload. I've found that developers can only absorb a few new tools or methods at a time. Therefore, the phased approach that I describe in Rule 6 is virtually a mandate. Carefully prioritize your improvement opportunities, and then parse them into manageable sets. Allow the organization enough time to utilize these new methods, and go through several learning cycles to adjust and improve them, before introducing the next set of improvements.

Rule 3: Always begin with a pilot project

One of the most common failures that I've observed regarding the deployment of lean product development methods is the "follow-blindly" mentality of many management teams. None of the tools and techniques described in this book will work perfectly for your firm exactly as I've presented them. The descriptions that I've provided are generic, and are intended to provide you with a thoroughly tested starting point. You must, however, adapt and customize these lean product development methods if your designers are to fully embrace them. I strongly recommend that you select a pilot project to serve as a pathfinder for the implementation of any tool or event. Only after you have gained feedback from that piloting effort, and those improvements have been integrated into your training materials and standard work, should you broaden deployment to encompass all development projects. A second, and perhaps even more important advantage of beginning with a pilot project is that you can control the outcome to a much greater extent. If a lean technique is successful on the pilot project, you can use that positive outcome as a selling tool for organization-wide deployment. On the other hand, if there is a glitch in the pilot implementation, you can limit the damage, and hopefully adjust your approach to ensure future success.

Rule 4: Employ persistence, not insistence

One of the myths of change management is that by force-feeding people new ideas you will achieve greater results. Unfortunately, most individuals who have worked in industry for a while have learned how to weather the "improvement program *de jour*" without having to change their way of thinking one iota. These hard-sell programs typically begin with great fanfare; banners on the wall, plastic-laminated cards, tee shirts, and packs of consultants stalking the halls and disrupting work-flow. However, management's attention span is short, and soon the furor ebbs, and the entire effort dies of its own weight. Rather than taking a confrontational and polarizing approach to change, you should relent-lessly apply pressure over an extended period of time (i.e., years rather than months). Think of it this way: You can fix a person's overbite either by punching them in the mouth or by putting braces on their teeth. Persistent pressure for change is far more effective than adamant insis-tence, followed by the inevitable waning of management interest.

Rule 5: Slip change in under the radar

This rule is closely related to the previous one. Note to reader: The following story is definitely *not* derived from personal experience. Once upon a time, a chef decided that he would serve frog's legs for dinner. However, each time he tried to place the poor critter into boiling water, it would immediately jump out of the pot. He ultimately solved the problem by placing the unfortunate amphibian into a pot of cool water and gradually increasing the temperature. Before the frog realized that things were changing, he was boiled and ready for eating. There is no need, and in fact no benefit, to announcing that your organization will undergo some monumental change. Instead, just select a few high-value tools or methods and start using them. Why directly confront the status quo when you can successfully chip away at it through continuous, incremental improvement?

Rule 6: Spread change systematically and deliberately

Although I doubt that there is any perfect way to implement new tools and methods, I've found that a phased approach, such as the one shown in Figure C1, has a high probability of success. As mentioned above, you should parse the ideas contained in this book into prioritized and manageable sets, based on the unique needs of your organization. The first deployment phase begins with a pilot project that will be used as a testbed for the highest-priority set of tools or events. Feedback from the pilot project team is then evaluated and their learnings are incorporated into your training materials and standard-work documentation. Once the first set of improvements has been well-proven under this controlled environment, they should be introduced to a second layer of projects, and then a third, until all projects within your firm are employing these Phase 1 techniques. The second phase of deployment can overlap the first: As soon as the piloting process for Phase 1 is complete, you can begin the testing and refinement of another wave of improvements on a new pilot project. The duration of your phases will depend on the pace of learning within your organization, but I've found that a six-month period between introductions of new sets of tools is reasonable. One final note: In some organizations, I've seen the deployment of high-value tools go viral, meaning that people who are not involved in the piloting effort hear about early successes and try to use the tools immediately, without proper training and mentoring. While this may seem like a happy circumstance, it can actually backfire. If a lean product development method is implemented incorrectly, without a clear understanding of the human factors that underlie its use, then it can fail to deliver the expected benefits. These failures can poison the waters for future phases of deployment, so it is important to control the spread of improvements to ensure that their integrity is maintained.

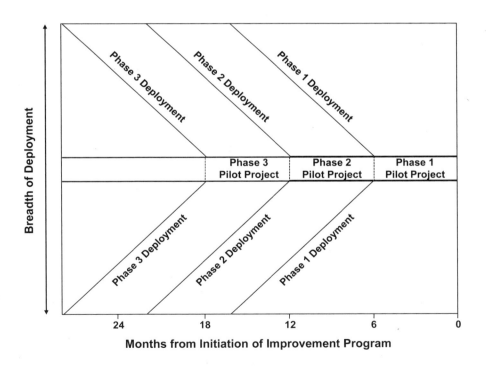

FIGURE C1: Graphical representation of a phased deployment strategy for lean product development tools and methods.

309

Rule 7: Never forget entropy

Entropy is the tendency for anything in the physical world to revert to its lowest and most random energy state. It is unlikely, for example, that the paint job on your house looks better today than it did last year. Even the pyramids will eventually decay into a pile of dust. Hence, you should expect that the crisp and disciplined implementation of new tools that you've achieved in each deployment phase will begin to degrade almost immediately. The only way to fight against entropy is to continuously inject organizing energy into the system. It takes work to maintain a disciplined structure, so you should plan to refresh and revitalize the tools of a previous phase, even as you are rolling out the next wave of improvements. Consider this to be a sustaining-support effort, which will hopefully require consistantly less energy input as each wave of change becomes "the new normal."

Rule 8: Work to change the culture, it will make your job much easier

Finally, remember that Event-Driven Lean Product Development is fundamentally about rapid learning, systematic problem-solving, and knowledge transformation. If you attempt to paste new tools onto an organizational culture that has not embraced these principles, you will have a fight on your hands at every step of the way. Fortunately, I firmly believe that the proper choice of tools can actually change a firm's culture in a positive way. If your firm lacks a sense of urgency with respect to new product development, for example, the implementation of frequent stand-up meetings and visual project boards (see Chapter 4) will ultimately change your culture to one of rapid decision-making, accountability to schedule, and immediate resolution of issues or problems. Likewise, if your firm is highly risk-averse, then an explicit and robust process for risk identification (see Chapter 6) and root-cause problem-solving (see Chapter 7) can give both developers and management the confidence to attack higher-risk new product opportunities. You should always look beyond the tactical benefits of lean product development methods, to the underlying effects they will have on your firm's culture. By creating a culture of learning and problem-solving, you will equip your development teams to more readily absorb each new wave of product development improvements.

■ ■ ■

Well, at last I have run out of words. All that is left is for me to issue you a challenge: Do not be satisfied with what you have learned from this book. You have a wealth of personal experience and creativity that you can bring to bear on the unique product development challenges that your firm faces. Learn to solve your own problems, invent your own tools, devise new events, and improve on the ones that I've described. You have the power to take lean product development to a whole new level. It is my sincere hope that the foundation that I've provided in these pages will give you the confidence to do just that.

Bibliography

(Merged Chapter References)

Akao, Y. (Editor), 1991, *Hoshin Kanri: Policy Deployment for Successful TQM*, Productivity Press.

Allen, D., 2001, *Getting Things Done*, Penguin Books.

Anderson, D. M., 1997, *Agile Product Development for Mass Customization*, Irwin Professional Publishing.

Anderson, D. M., 2003, *Design for Manufacturability and Concurrent Engineering*, CIM Press.

Beck, K., 2000, *Extreme Programming Explained*, Addison-Wesley.

Beck, K., and J. Fowler, 2001, *Planning Extreme Programming*, Addison-Wesley.

Belliveau, P., et al, 2002, *The PDMA Toolbox for New Product Development (Vols. 1 & 2)*, John Wiley & Sons.

Betz, F., 1993, *Strategic Technology Management*, McGraw-Hill.

Bicheno, J., 2004, *The New Lean Toolbox: Towards Fast, Flexible Flow*, PICSIE Books.

Bicheno, J., and M. Holweg, 2009, *The Lean Toolbox, 4th Edition*, PICSIE Books.

Boothroyd, G., Dewhurst, P., and W. Knight, 2002, *Product Design for Manufacture and Assembly, 2nd Edition*, Marcel Dekker.

Bralla, J. G., 1995, *Design for Excellence*, McGraw-Hill.

Bralla, J. G., 1999, *Design for Manufacturability Handbook, 2nd Edition*, McGraw-Hill.

Brown, J., 1992, *Value Engineering: A Blueprint*, Industrial Press.

Brown, T., 2009, *Change by Design*, HarperCollins.

Christensen, C. M., 1997, *The Innovator's Dilemma*, Harvard Business School Press.

Christensen, C. M., and M. E. Raynor, 2003, *The Innovator's Solution*, Harvard Business School Press.

Clark, K. B., and S. C. Wheelwright, 1993, *Managing New Product and Process Development*, The Free Press.

Cohen, L., 1995, *Quality Function Deployment: How to Make QFD Work for You*, Addison-Wesley.

Cooper, R. G., 1993, *Winning at New Products, 2nd Edition*, Addison-Wesley.

Cooper, R. G., Edgett, S. J., and E. J. Kleinschmidt, 1998, *Portfolio Management of New Products*, Perseus Books.

Cowley, M., and E. Domb, 1997, *Beyond Strategic Vision: Effective Corporate Action with Hoshin Planning*, Butterworth-Heinemann.

Davenport, T. H., and L. Prusak, 1998, *Working Knowledge*, Harvard Business School Press.

Esslinger, H., 2009, *A Fine Line: How Design Strategies are Shaping the Future of Business*, John Wiley & Sons.

Fey, V., and E. Rivin, 2005, *Innovation on Demand: New Product Development Using TRIZ*, Cambridge University Press.

Fiore, C., 2005, *Accelerated Product Development*, Productivity Press.

Fleming, Q. W., and J. M. Koppelman, 2000, *Earned Value Project Management, 2nd Edition*, The Project Management Institute.

Galsworth, G. D., 1997, *Visual Systems: Harnessing the Power of a Visual Workplace*, American Management Association.

Gawer, A., and M. A. Cusumano, 2002, *Platform Leadership*, Harvard Business School Press.

George, M. L., 2002, *Lean Six Sigma: Combining Six Sigma Quality with Lean Speed*, McGraw-Hill.

Goldratt, E. M., 1990, *Theory of Constraints*, The North River Press.

Goldratt, E. M., and J. Cox, 1992, *The Goal: 2nd Revised Edition*, The North River Press.

Goldratt, E. M., 1997, *Critical Chain*, The North River Press.

Grief, M., 1991, *The Visual Factory: Building Participation through Shared Information*, Productivity Press.

Groppelli, A. A., and E. Nikbakht, 1995, *Finance, 3rd Edition*, Barron's Business Review Series.

Harvard Business Review, 1998, *Harvard Business Review on Knowledge Management*, Harvard Business School Press.

Hawken, P., Lovins, A., and L. Lovins, 1999, *Natural Capitalism*, Little Brown and Company.

Huthwaite, B., 2004, *The Lean Design Solution*, Institute for Lean Design.

Ichida, T., 1989, *Product Design Review*, Productivity Press.

Imai, M., 1997, *Gemba Kaizen*, McGraw-Hill.

Jackson, T. L., 1996, *Implementing a Lean Management System*, Productivity Press.

Kennedy, M. N., 2003, *Product Development for the Lean Enterprise*, Oaklea Press.

Kennedy, M. N., Harmon, K., and E. Minnock, 2008, *Ready, Set, Dominate*, Oaklea Press.

Kerzner, H., 2000, *Applied Project Management*, John Wiley & Sons.

Kim, W. C., and R. Mauborgne, 2005, *Blue Ocean Strategy*, Harvard Business School Press.

Kotter, J. P., 1996, *Leading Change*, Harvard Business Press.

Kotter, J. P., and D. S. Cohen, 2002, *The Heart of Change*, Harvard Business Press.

Kotter, J. P., and H. Rathgeber, 2006, *Our Iceberg is Melting*, Macmillan.

Leach, L. P., 2000, *Critical Chain Project Management*, Argent House.

Leonard-Barton, D., 1995, *Wellsprings of Knowledge*, Harvard Business School Press.

Lewis, J. P., 1999, *Mastering Project Management*, McGraw-Hill.

Lientz, B. P., and K. P. Rea, 1999, *Breakthrough Technology Project Management*, Academic Press.

Liker, J. K., 2004, *The Toyota Way*, McGraw-Hill.

Locher, D. A., 2008, *Value Stream Mapping for Lean Development*, CRC Press.

Mascitelli, R., 2002, *Building a Project-Driven Enterprise*, Technology Perspectives.

Mascitelli, R., 2004, *The Lean Design Guidebook*, Technology Perspectives.

Mascitelli, R., 2007, *The Lean Product Development Guidebook*, Technology Perspectives.

May, M. E., 2007, *The Elegant Solution: Toyota's Formula for Mastering Innovation*, The Free Press.

McDonough, W., and M. Braungart, 2002, *Cradle to Cradle*, North Point Press.

McGrath, M. E., 1995, *Product Strategy for High-Technology Companies*, Irwin Professional Publishing.

McGrath, M. E., 1996, *Setting the PACE in Product Development*, Butterworth-Heinemann.

McGrath, M. E., 2004, *Next Generation Product Development*, McGraw-Hill.

Mello, S., 2002, *Customer-Centric Product Definition*, PDC Professional Publishing.

Meyer, M. H., and A. P. Lehnerd, 1997. *The Power of Product Platforms*, The Free Press.

Miles, L. D., 1972, *Techniques of Value Analysis and Engineering, 2nd Edition*, McGraw-Hill.

Monden, Y., 1995, *Target Costing and Kaizen Costing*, Productivity Press.

Moore, G. A., 1991, *Crossing the Chasm*, HarperBusiness.

Morgan, J. M., and J. K. Liker, 2006, *The Toyota Product Development System*, Productivity Press.

Mudge, A. E., 1989, *Value Engineering: A Systematic Approach*, J. Pohl Associates.

315

Nadler, D. A., and M. L. Tushman, 1997, *Competing by Design*, Oxford University Press.

Nonaka, I., and H. Takeuchi, 1995, *The Knowledge Creating Company*, Oxford University Press.

Park, R., 1999, *Value Engineering: A Plan for Invention*, CRC Press.

Phillips, P. L., 2004, *Creating the Perfect Design Brief*, Allworth Press.

Pichler, R., 2010, *Agile Product Management with Scrum*, Addison-Wesley.

Pilloton, E., 2009, *Design Revolution: 100 Products that Empower People*, Metropolis Books.

Pine, J. B. II, 1993, *Mass Customization: The New Frontier in Business Competition*, Harvard Business School Press.

Poppendieck, M., and T. Poppendieck, 2003, *Lean Software Development: An Agile Toolkit*, Addison-Wesley.

Project Management Institute, 2008, *A Guide to the Project Management Body of Knowledge*.

Pugh, S., 1991, *Total Design*, Addison-Wesley.

Reinertsen, D. G., 1997, *Managing the Design Factory: A Product Developer's Toolkit*, The Free Press.

Reinertsen, D. G., 2009, *The Principles of Product Development Flow: Second Generation Lean Product Development*, Celeritas Publishing.

Robinson, A. G., and D. M. Schroeder, 2004, *Ideas are Free*, Berrett-Koehler Publishers.

Rother, M. and J. Shook, 1999, *Learning to See*, The Lean Enterprise Institute.

Schab, L., 2008, *Faster, Better & Cheaper: Linking Practice to Successful Product Development Project Execution*, Doctorial Dissertation, Jesus College, Cambridge.

Schipper, T., and M. Swets, 2010, *Innovative Lean Development*, CRC Press.

Schuyler, J. R., 1996, *Decision Analysis in Projects*, Project Management Institute.

Schwaber, K., and M. Beedle, 2002, *Agile Software Development with Scrum*, Prentice Hall.

Sekine, K., and K. Arai, 1994, *Design Team Revolution*, Productivity Press.

Senge, P. M., 1990, *The Fifth Discipline*, Currency Doubleday.

Senge, P. M., et al, 1994, *The Fifth Discipline Fieldbook*, Currency Doubleday.

Senge, P., Smith, B., Kruschwitz, N., Laur, J., and S. Schley, 2008, *The Necessary Revolution: Working Together to Create a Sustainable World*, Broadway Books.

Shimbun, N. K., 1995, *Visual Control Systems*, Productivity Press.

Shingo, S., and A. Dillon, 1985, *A Revolution in Manufacturing: The SMED System*, Productivity Press.

Shook, J., 2008, *Managing to Learn*, Lean Enterprise Institute.

Smith, P. G., and D. G. Reinertsen, 1998, *Developing Products in Half the Time: New Rules, New Tools, 2nd Edition*, John Wiley & Sons.

Smith, P. G., 2007, *Flexible Product Development: Building Agility for Changing Markets*, John Wiley & Sons.

Sobek, D. K. II, et al, 1998, "Another look at how Toyota integrates product development," *Harvard Business Review*, July-August Issue.

Sobek, D. K. II, et al, 1999, "Toyota's principles of set-based concurrent engineering," *Sloan Management Review*, Vol. 40, No. 2.

Sobek, D. K. II, and A. Smalley, 2008, *Understanding A3 Thinking*, CRC Press.

Spear, S. J., 2009, *Chasing the Rabbit*, McGraw-Hill.

Stamatis, D. H., 1995, *Failure Mode and Effect Analysis*, ASQC Quality Press.

Suri, R., 1998, *Quick Response Manufacturing*, Productivity Press.

Suzue, T., 2002, *Cost Half: The Method for Radical Cost Reduction*, Productivity Press.

Terninko, J., 1997, *Step-by-Step QFD: Customer-Driven Product Design*, St. Lucie Press.

Tufte, E. R., 1983, *The Visual Display of Quantitative Information*, Graphics Press.

Tufte, E. R., 1990, *Envisioning Information*, Graphics Press.

Verganti, R., 2009, *Design-Driven Innovation*, Harvard Business School Press.

Ward, A. C., Liker, J. K., Cristiano, J. J., and D. K. Sobek II, 1995, "The second Toyota paradox: how delaying decisions can make better cars faster," *Sloan Management Review*, Vol. 36, No. 3, pgs. 43-61.

Ward, A., 2007, *Lean Product and Process Development*, Lean Enterprise Institute.

Wideman, R. M., 1992, *Project & Program Risk Management*, The Project Management Institute.

Womack, J. P., Jones, D. T., and D. Roos, 1990, *The Machine that Changed the World*, Harper Perennial.

Womack, J. P., and D. T. Jones, 1996, *Lean Thinking*, Simon & Schuster.

Womack, J. P., and D. T. Jones, 2005, *Lean Solutions*, The Free Press.

Index

3P Process, (see Lean 3P process)

A

A3 knowledge brief, 3, 70, 96, 204-228, 251, 266
A / B / C priority projects, 34-37, 51-54
accountability, 97-112, 148
Action Priority Number, 243-244, 290-291
agile programming, 82
Agile Software Development, 145, 272-276
Apple Corporation, 3, 116
arbitration rules, 44-46

B

basic requirements, 139-144
bill of material (BOM), 248
Bimford Tools, 245-259, 300
brainstorming, 149, 240, 252-259, 285-290
burn rate, 164
business case, 78, 118-143
business-case brief, 6-7

C

capacity bottleneck, (see resource conflicts)
capacity management, 11-13, 17-54, 60, 108, 148
capital investment, 240, 260-266
categories of value, 115-118
chaotic work environment, 41-44
change, organizational, 68
change czar, 297-298
Change Review Board (CRB), 297-298
Cicero, 97
collaboration, 60-78, 85
commercialization, 59
commoditization, 114, 116
commonality of parts, 240
communication among teams, 85-114
competitive landscape, 119-121
Compliance Matrix, 280, 289-295
Concept Review and Freeze Event, 235, 246, 260, 280-299
concurrent engineering, 229
confidence level, 162-163
configuration control, 269-272, 295-299

continuous flow, 74-78
coolness factor, 118
cost knobs, 233-234
cost of ownership, 115-118
cost optimization, 229-276
could-haves, 138-144
countermeasures, 218-225
cradle-to-cradle, 300-304
critical path, 21, 30-32, 44-46, 93, 147, 274-276
critical-to-cost (CTC), 241-259
critical-to-quality (CTQ), 241-259
cross-training of resources, 33
culture, changing of, 310-311
current state, 61
customer perception, 114-116
customer satisfaction, 121-123, 246-259

D

daily workflow, 97-112
death threats, 9-10, 70, 174, 180-186, 198-200
decision tool, 131
dedicated teams, 26-27
defrosting of requirements, 144-145, 296-299
delaying decisions, 144-145
deliverables, 148, 155-157
deliverables roadmap, 160-167
dependencies, 162-173
deployment, 66-68, 305-311
description of opportunity, 6
design,
    alternatives, 144-145, 215-228, 232, 253-259
    assumptions, 229
    efficiency analysis, 244
    overshoot, 120-121
    requirements, 116-145, 291-295
    reviews, 68, 277-304
    to test, 193-202
    trade-offs, 224-228
Design 3P Event, 72-74, 234-259
Design for Excellence (DfX), 232
Design for Manufacture and Assembly (DFMA), 74, 230-232, 244

Design for Six Sigma (DFSS), 230-231, 244, 266
Design of Experiment (DOE), 244
Design Review and Freeze Event, 66, 235, 277-304
Detailed Design Review and Freeze Event, 280-299
differentiation, 116-145
discussion tool, 131
disruptive technologies, 228
D-score, 130-144
duration, of project schedule, 166-173

E

economic impact, 44-46, 116
Eisenhower, Dwight D., 147
e-mail communication, 41
enablers, 60
Engineering Change Notice (ECN), 269, 298
engineering requirements matrix, 142-144
Enterprise Resource Planning (ERP), 269
entropy, 224-228, 310-311
environmentally-friendly design, 246-259, 300-304
error-proof assembly, 230
esteem value, 116-118
Event-Driven Lean Product Development, 55-78, 122-123, 199, 218, 236
event-driven process, 60
events,
        close-out of, 63
        general description, 58-78
        inputs to, 62
exception management, 75-78, 93-95
execution, 58
external milestones, 158-167

F

facilitation, of events, 122-142
Failure Mode and Effect Analysis (FMEA), 236, 244, 266, 279, 287
feasibility, 176-180, 203
feedback and control system, 86
Final Design Review and Freeze Event, 268, 281-299
finite development capacity, 11-13, 17-54
fishbone diagram, 208-209
functions, of product, 230, 251-259
future state, 61
fuzzy front-end, 113

G

gate reviews, 76
gauntlet for product ideas, 4-6
General Electric, 250
geographically-dispersed team, 108-112
global priority list, 2, 13-15, 44-45, 51-54
GoToMeeting.com., 110
governance, 58, 75-78
green design of products, 245-259, 300-304
group-think, 284
gurus, 284

H

high-mix production, 38
hoshin-like capacity management system, 20, 27, 50-54
hoshin planning, 51
House of Quality, 134
HW / SW interface, 273-276

I

impact score, 182-186
implementation, 305-311
innovation, 57-62, 120-145, 238-259
integration events, 197
interaction effect, 136-140
interactivity, 88-90
interruptions, 40-44

J

just-in-time communication, 49-50, 82

K

kaizen events, 61-62, 74, 188, 235
kanban, 262
key differentiators, 8, 113, 120-145
key differentiator tool, 128-142
key performance indicator (KPI), 51
knowledge,
        briefs, 182, 204-228, 251
        commercialization, 59
        gaps, 69, 147, 195-228, 232
        gates, 78
        reuse, 205-228
        transformation, 59, 62-64, 192
knowledge-based development, 69, 174-186, 191-228
knowledge-creating process, 59, 191-209

L

language of customers, 134-140
layered development, 128, 142-144
Lazy Rider Corp., 153-186
leadership, of change, 305-307
Lean 3P process, 229-276
lean manufacturing, 168
lean product development process, 56-78, 81, 121
Lean Project Management, 148
Lean QFD, 134-144
Lean Six Sigma, 232-233
lean software development, (see Agile Software Development)
lean thinking, 21
Learning-Cycle Event, 69-70, 186, 191-228
learning cycles, (see rapid learning cycles)
learning organization, 191-228
lenses, 285-288
lessons learned, 180-186
level-loading of resources, 29, 49
line *kaizen*, 235, 268-272

M

management status report, 93-95
manufacturability, 65, 234-276, 287
manufacturing cost, (see cost optimization)
Manufacturing Extension Partnership (MEP), 211
manufacturing planning, 246-276
market,
    gap, 114
    research, 2, 66, 130
    satisfaction, 128-142
    segment, 120-121
    share, 114
Market Requirements Brief, 126-128, 158, 240
Market Requirements Event, 66, 113-146, 150, 154, 246, 292
master schedule, 92-95
meetings, 41
Method of Five Whys, 208-209
minor freezes, 298-299
multi-project environment, 26-28, 84, 88
multi-project wall-Gantt, 102-112
multitasking, 18, 30-32, 38-39
must-haves, 138-144, 217-219, 255
must / should / could prioritization, 138-144, 154, 273

N

NASA feasibility model, 177
net present value, 1, 8
    risk-adjusted, 10-15
non-value-added tasks, 28
obeya, 83
organizational discipline, 42-43
organizational learning, 62, 189
overall project-rating score, 11-15
Overload Inc., 20-29
Panasonic, 251
parity, 130-144
parking lot, 96-97
parsing of work, 32, 168-171
performance curves, 224-228
persistent knowledge, 226-228
phased implementation, 308-311
phase / gate process, 25, 56-57, 74-78, 147
pilot project, 306-311
Plan / Do / Check / Act (PDCA) cycle, (see Shewart cycle)
planned work, 90-95
portfolio planning, 1-15
positioning, 118-120
preparation, for events, 121-123
pricing power, 8, 116-118
prioritization
    capacity based, 11-15
    of key differentiators, 130-144
    of projects, 2-15, 30-37
    of work through queue, 29-33
probability of occurrence, 182-186
problem-solving, 96, 192-228
Process 3P Event, 73-74, 235-237, 260-266
process capability, 230
product and process co-development, 72-74, 232-276
Product Data Management (PDM), 224-225
product development process, 55-78
production, 62
Production 3P Event, 74, 235-237, 267-272
Production Preparation Process, (see Lean 3P process)
production readiness, 267-272
Production Readiness Checklist, 268-272
productivity, 11, 32, 47, 82
product-line steering committee, 10
product vision, 127-128
profitability, 10-15, 114
project,
    assignment overhead, 24, 28-29
    cadence tool, 103-107
    efficiency metric, 12

management, 56, 147-186
planning, 147-173
scheduling, 147-173
Project Management Professional (PMP),
149
Project Planning / Risk-Mitigation Event, 51,
66, 70, 142, 147-186, 196, 246, 268
project / process duality, 55-57, 147, 187-190
project time, 40-44
P-score, 130-144
Pugh matrix, 217-223, 253-259, 264-266

Q

quality, 75
Quality Function Deployment (QFD), 134
quality optimization, of product, 231-276
queuing theory, 19-20, 29-32, 38-39, 46-47
Quick-Look Value Engineering, 238-259,
281
quick-response team, 48-49

R

R&D, 174-186
rapid learning cycles, 69-70, 174-186,
204-228
RCA, 250
recycled materials, use of, 247-259, 301-304
red / yellow / green statusing, 93-95,
108-109
regulatory requirements, 160, 287
relevance to buying decision, 128-142
repeatability of results, 178-180
requirements, (see design requirements)
resource,
conflicts, 14, 18, 23-24, 28, 32,
44-46, 108, 164-167
loading, 33, 36-37, 94, 148, 160
management template, 34-37
plan, 155-173
pool, 107
retained value, 115-118
risk,
analysis, 8-10, 69, 172-186
and rapid learning cycles, 196-228
aversion, 118, 124
buffers, 19
cost / quality, 180-184
identification, 60, 138-144, 172-186,
279-299
market, 180-186
mitigation, 57, 69-70
proactive avoidance, 174-178
ranking, 182-186

taking, 124
technical, 180-182, 279-299
to schedule, 9, 36-37, 172-186
risk-adjusted NPV, 10-13
Risk Priority Number (RPN), 184-186
rolling-window scheduling, 92-95
root-cause analysis, 196-228
rules for capacity management, 25-50

S

sales forecast, 8
scalability, 58, 65
scarcity, 116-118
schedule,
predictability, 36-37
sensitivity, 45-46
slips, 22-24, 154-173
variance, 75, 94-96
schedule-critical tasks, 99
scope-creep, 19, 154-157, 295-299
scope of work, 96, 113, 154-157
scrum, 82, 273-276
set-based concurrent engineering,
(see set-based design)
set-based design, 194-228, 281
setup and changeover waste, 30, 38
Seven Alternatives method, 262-266
SharePoint, 112
Sharp Corporation, 251
Shewart cycle, 207-208
shift-change meeting, 82
should-haves, 138-144
single-minute exchange of die (SMED), 168
single-project wall-Gantt, 96-102
six-sigma methods, (see Design for Six Sigma)
snake diagram, 94-96
software, integration of, 272-276
SpeedFreaks Watercraft, Inc., 124-142
staged-freezing, 144, 277-304
standardized schedule templates, 187-190
standard work, 56, 60, 62, 149, 187-190
standard-work events, 62
stand-up meetings, 52, 81-107
Statistical Process Control (SPC), 75
strategic importance, 10-15
strategic product, 10
subject-matter experts, 29-32, 44-46, 199-200
supermarket of feasible technologies, 176-180
supply-chain optimization, 74, 256-272
sustainable design of products, 245-259,
300-304

sustaining factory support, 24, 33, 90-95, 108
swim lanes, 158-173
synchronization, 37-39, 82
system decomposition diagram, 156-159
system products, 150, 156-158, 236, 287
systems thinking, 156-158

T

takt time, 74, 241, 267-272
target manufacturing cost, 76
team leader, 150
team metrics, 107-109
test planning, 262-266
test-to-design, 193-202
Theory of Constraints, 18-19
time batches, 30-31, 40, 49-50, 57, 76, 85-87
time estimates, 156-173
time-slicing, 37-44
time study, 23
time-to-market, 50, 69, 122, 157
Total Quality Management (TQM), 51, 134, 231
Toyota, 69, 72-74, 168, 192-194, 232
Toyota Product Development System, 144, 204-207, 233-234, 262
Toyota Production System, 83
transient knowledge, 226-228
triage, 47-48
tribal knowledge, 198
trigger lists, 181-186, 241-259
TRIZ, 255
turbulence in workflow, 47-48
Twenty Cost Levers, 245
two-week plan, 98-112
type 1 waste, 60

U

unarticulated needs, 114-115
uncontested space, 118-119
Underwriters Laboratory, 160
unintended consequences, 203
unplanned work, 24, 90-95
use-life cost, 115-118
user stories, 126-135

V

value, definition of, 58-60
value engineering, 74, 229, 238-259
value-stream mapping, 74, 149, 187-190, 262-266
value streams, 261-266
variability in project duration, 27, 30
verb / noun naming of functions, 253-259
verification methods, 207-208, 292-299
virtual project board, 90, 110-112
virtual team, 110-112
vision, of new product, 62
visual planning process, 157-173
visual project boards, 52, 75, 83-112, 172, 273
Visual Workflow Management, 39, 50, 66-68, 81-112, 149, 204
voice-of-the-customer, 126-145, 287

W

wall-Gantt, 97-112, 172
Wal-Mart, 119
waste, 60
Wookchuck Custom Closets, 210-225
work rules, 26